New Urban Worlds

For these inhabitants of new worlds:
Manu, Na'ilah and Rafael

NEW URBAN WORLDS
Inhabiting Dissonant Times

AbdouMaliq Simone
and Edgar Pieterse

polity

First published in 2017 by Polity Press

Polity Press
65 Bridge Street
Cambridge CB2 1UR, UK

Polity Press
101 Station Landing
Suite 300
Medford, MA 02155
USA

ISBN-13: 978-0-7456-9155-8
ISBN-13: 978-0-7456-9156-5 (pb)

A catalogue record for this book is available from the British Library.

Typeset in 10.5 on 12 pt Sabon by Toppan Best-set Premedia Limited
Printed and bound in the UK by CPI Group (UK) Ltd, Croydon.

The publisher has used its best endeavours to ensure that the URLs for external websites referred to in this book are correct and active at the time of going to press. However, the publisher has no responsibility for the websites and can make no guarantee that a site will remain live or that the content is or will remain appropriate.

Every effort has been made to trace all copyright holders, but if any have been inadvertently overlooked the publisher will be pleased to include any necessary credits in any subsequent reprint or edition.

For further information on Polity, visit our website: www.politybooks.com

Contents

Detailed Contents

Acknowledgements

For invaluable assistance in work in the field, much gratitude to Rika Febriyani, Dian Tri, Anant Mariganti, Marco Kusumawijaya, Hannah Schilling, Osmane Dembele and Uzair Fauzan. For abiding discussions and support, gratitude to Ash Amin, Gautam Bhan, Talja Blokland, Teresa Caldeira, Anton Cartwright, Filip De Boeck, Graeme Gotz, Kim Gurney, Katherine Hyman, Irmelin Joelsson, Michael Keith, Achille Mbembe, Sue Parnell, Jo Santoso, Mark Swilling, Tau Tavengwa, Mirjam van Donk and our colleagues at the African Centre for Cities, University of Cape Town. The National Research Foundation of South Africa and the Max Planck Institute for the Study of Religious and Ethnic Diversity support our research. Edgar Pieterse acknowledges the support of the Stellenbosch Institute for Advanced Study in order to get the early research for this book done. Lastly, thanks to Duke University Press for permission to republish work by AbdouMaliq Simone that appeared in *Cultural Politics*, 12/2 (2016).

Preface

New Urban Worlds is primarily a polemic, an impassioned argument that stretches across diverse experiences, literatures and professional domains. It is a polemic because it tries to "call for things" even if all of the evidence is not yet in and often hard to come by. We call for the intersection of long-honed everyday practices of African and Asian urban residents with new forms of governing and with a strategic deployment of technological innovations of varying kinds. We desire to restore experimentation as a normative aspect of living in and running cities and want to think about how concretely to create space for such experimentation to be possible.

We are aware that, when you call for things, the immediate question is "How do you know enough about what is going on in order to call for something specific?" And, even then, should you reveal everything you know is going on, especially at a time when we are all being "read" in ways that we cannot control and often do not even know are taking place? But let us consider briefly what we think is going on – something about the fundamental conditions that drive the "calling" of this book.

If you are one of the scores of millions of residents across much of the urban "South" who cannot depend upon one specific job to earn your keep, who lacks sufficient documentation to secure a place to live over the long term, or who can't afford to get sick or into any kind of trouble, what is it that you pay attention to in order to know something about what to do? What happens if the people you rely upon for support or information are no longer available or suddenly turn against you? What happens when the skills you have to apply are also those of an increasing number of residents, and competition becomes increasingly fierce for opportunities? The question here is how can you best know what is going on and try to situate yourself in a position where opportunities might "come your way"? In other words, how can you be at the right place at the right time when there is no clear map available? We are convinced that these kinds of considerations dominate the minds and spiritual practices of most urban dwellers, yet much of what appears in both urban scholarship and policy prescripts seems oblivious.

In a not dissimilar way, researchers of urban life face difficulties when it comes to engaging with the largely makeshift complexion of many cities in Africa and Asia. The enormous transformations of the built environment and the enhanced possibilities of consumption that have marked even some of the most marginal of the world's cities should not detract from acknowledging just how dependent the majority of the urban residents of these regions are upon constantly putting together some workable form of income and inhabitation. The makeshift character of much of what this majority does is quite literally "make+shift," as pointed out by Vasudevan (2015).

Whatever they come up with is rarely institutionalized into a fixed set of practices, locales or organizational forms. This doesn't mean that relationships and economic activities do not endure, that people do not find themselves rooted in the same place and set of affiliations over a long period of time. Rather, these stabilities come from constant efforts on the part of inhabitants to redefine the boundaries and interfaces between work, leisure, home, neighborhood and elsewhere. It entails constantly addressing the questions "What spaces are relevant to me?," "What do I pay attention to and where?," "Who do I talk to and do things with?," "Who can I depend on and show things to?" In neighborhoods across the urban South, whatever is made, in terms of economic activities, buildings and social solidarities, then shifts in terms of its availability to specific uses and users, as well as its exposure to new potentials and vulnerability.

Drawing upon decades of work in poor, working- and lower-middle-class districts in urban regions across Africa and South-East Asia, this book attempts to weave interconnections among different ways of engaging and thinking about the complexity of how different urban actors decide and act within highly circumscribed and often uncertain contexts.

In methodological terms, it means that we locate our research and propositions within a relational epistemological force field that is anchored by two axes. The first axis stretches from surface knowledge to in-depth understandings of highly localized phenomena, including psychological interiors of actors. Surface knowledge references the insights that one can assemble from quantitative data sets that allow the analyst to consider scale, frequency, relationalities and patterns over time. Quantitative trends are crucial to appreciate the specificities of urbanization dynamics in diverse geographical scales in the early twenty-first century, when the very foundations of the economy, political systems and cultural reference points are undergoing profound change. At the same time, due to the "make+shift" character of these cities, it is equally important to expand dramatically in-depth accounts of the social drawing on relational ontologies (Pieterse 2015a). It is only by triangulating both depth and surface dimensions of contemporary urbanism that can we hope to get a purchase on what is actually going on.

The second axis of our epistemological force field stretches between applied theoretical concerns that we define, in contradistinction to philosophy, aesthetics and the poetic, as "grounded pragmatism." These denote theoretical rest-stops that store conceptual resources to support sense-making of different kinds of data, but also to instigate propositional concepts and experiments. This book draws on an eclectic mix of theoretical resources to anchor our sense-making of highly fluid contexts, but we have deliberately resisted getting into the nitty-gritty of competing theoretical frames or performing a review of the literature. The references offer the reader a comprehensive insight into materials we find most compelling. Moreover, we are not particularly interested in the academic game of theoretical one-upmanship that seems to dominate so much of urban scholarship these days.

In a nutshell, this epistemological force field allows us to adopt a research approach that seeks to articulate the gener-

ous engagement with the details of urban life with the power
of re-description in order to understand what might be going
on while keeping an eye on clarifying resonant propositions.
Thus, the work we have done includes ethnographic and
applied research, forging research, advocacy and policy-making
networks, advising municipal governments and development
agencies, and starting and running urban institutions dedicated
to enhancing broad-based participation in making rules and
plans. The language of the book then reflects these different
viewpoints and engagements with different actors, sectors
and cities. It is a language that covers different "musical
scales" – i.e., styles and rhythms. It looks for different ways
into cityscapes that always seem to be switching, pulsating
and reshaping. Thus the analysis applied and the proposals
suggested are experimental and provisional and invariably
ask for patience to see the conceptual journey to the end.
Our account reflects a need to be able to do things differently
now. While massive and long-term transformations are of
course necessary, this book attempts to make use of what
exists now but is sometimes not seen, not read, and thus does
not become a resource for deciding and acting. While we
offer strategic visions for how to face the enormous challenges
of impoverishment, urban growth during climate change, and
the exigency of justice, we concentrate on mapping out the
potentials of the immediate – the lived realms of the
"make+shift" city.

Just like the processes through which urban actors decide
and act, this task of reworking the immediate is full of twists
and turns. This is in part because the urban is full of paradoxes. Clear differentiations between urban and rural, local
and global, self and other, time and space, human and non-
human, North and South, public and private – long critical
vehicles of orientation – are simultaneously intensifying and
waning, becoming more sharply drawn as they are also being
folded into each other. In a world where there is so much to
pay attention to, where each decision seems more urgent,
imbued with greater significance, it is harder to make distinctions between what is and what is not important to pay
attention to, what is salient or irrelevant. This means that
decision-making gets simultaneously more complicated and
frustrating. The constitutive nature and generative potential
of paradox is foregrounded throughout the book.

The capacities of the poor to get by with little, and thus to be rendered either targets of development or manipulated pawns in a game of continuous displacement, may ironically suggest a conceivable future for everyone in light of carbonated dystopias that become more apparent every year that CO_2 emission reduction targets are spectacularly missed. How is it possible to live through these seeming paradoxes? How is it possible to maintain the productive boundaries among places, between spatial exteriors and interiors, and among distinctive ways of life without being disabled by their paradoxical encounters? How to think the doubleness of things, of ways in which differences can move toward and draw from each other as a movement of justice and equanimity?

In *New Urban Worlds* we try to follow and understand some of the dimensions of the "make+shift," but we do so with the proviso that this pursuit does not end with a systemic conclusion or the pretence that we think we have got our hands on what is really taking place. Much of our uncertainty here has to do with a politics of urban knowledge where, in many instances, the "majority" has been ordered to "shut up" and not make waves. Equally significant is the tendency on the part of government and the apparatuses of the corporate and political elite to unleash violence and exert control over the uses of space and materials. They often either marshal or steal outright the capacities, ideas and resourcefulness of the majority in order to manoeuvre through situations where they otherwise would lack legitimacy and know-how.

At the same time, in order for any "make+shift" to work in a grounded pragmatic sense, it has to embody generosity, reciprocity, a sense of openness and experimentation in order to keep affective ties, information and cooperation flowing. So, in order to create space for such exchanges, residents have often had to make it look like nothing much was ever going on, or to amplify the problematic aspects of their everyday lives so as to appear so depleted or self-occupied that it would seem impossible for there to be any room for experiments, sharing, or give and take.

This does not mean that residents don't have a rough time or that they do not spend a lot of time and effort just to put food on household tables. It doesn't mean that the manipulations and everyday brutalities are simply a deception. They are present, and urban life for many is a constant process of being worn down and wasted. But, at the same time, to circumvent a life of dispossession often means taking the risk of losing everything or of playing with practices and ways of making money that embed individuals in relationships that are both volatile and trusted – that build trust, obligations and reciprocities from the sheer fact that they are not recorded, institutionalized. This can be seen in operations such as gambling, smuggling, pooling, diverting, and bundling time, money, people and things into seemingly weird schemes or hustles.

As such, much of research that depends on getting people to say what it is that they are doing and what it means cannot readily apply, even if there is no choice but to talk to as many people as possible as the primary means through which to try to come to grips with what is going on in a particular place or situation. All of this is to say that, in this book, we are up against a complicated politics of knowledge, of how inhabitants decide and act. This has led us over the years to try out many different ways of engaging different residents and aspects of the cities in Africa and South-East Asia where we have done most of our work.

The research business is full of many tricks, particularly the ethnographic variety, and we have employed many of these throughout the years. Perhaps the most crucial aspect of our engagement with urban processes is that most of the research we have conducted over the past decades has been done at the behest of some local institution or movement that itself is trying to extend its work into new areas of a city or to equip its members with new tools to mobilize residents more effectively around issues that are important to them. This task has meant having to come up with ways that help "sneak" inhabitants – who have been ignored and marginalized – into parts of the city that don't want them there, so that they could find out for themselves more about what is going on. It is a method that combines performance, invention and, at times, just a little bit of deception.

We have worked across many different popular participation exercises implemented by municipal governments and NGOs to try and broaden the constituencies involved in planning, service delivery and program development. We have worked with local markets, political campaigns and municipal restructuring programs. We have worked as retailers in local markets, as journeymen in long-distance trade networks, and as teachers in local schools. We have sometimes been asked by associations of residents themselves to help them look differently at their own dynamics, to become researchers of their own living and economic spaces. All of this work has produced a great deal of stories, glimmers here and there of well-oiled machines at work. But, mostly, these engagements have shown that there is an inordinate amount of complexities at work, even in situations of clear deprivation where the story would seem to be a simple one of dispossession and little else.

We emphasize the point about the politics of knowledge because it is crucial to an overarching point that we attempt to make here. That is, nothing really can be done to make urban life more sustainable, just and economically viable without going through the "make+shift" complexion of the city and urban regions. Whether the processes of urban transformation entail incremental development, militant social activism, smart city management, entrepreneurialism or state-based redistribution, they all have to be effectively linked to the everyday makeshift practices through which the majority of residents in Africa and Asia come to grips with urban life. These links will have to be predicated on a broader, more open and experimental engagement with practices which are often not unambiguous in terms of their ethical composition and efficacy, which are often of limited duration, and which, like the "make+shift," change their looks and ways of operating.

Instead of being quick to rectify apparent problematic situations, what residents are up to needs to be engaged with in its own terms, even when terms, words and concepts may not actually be available. Often, all we have to work with is a vague sense of things or an unyielding determination on the part of residents. Too often activists and policy-makers expect that residents should do more to fight for their rights and for justice. Too often they are criticized for being enamored of consuming the latest products. Too often they are condemned for their fundamentalism, aggressiveness, lack of initiative or dogged pursuit of money. It is important both to step back from those assumptions and to find more ways of stepping into the fray as a means of thinking through what else might be taking place. This is why we insist on the importance of a multiplication of slow research work that falls on the "depth" end of the methodological axis.

Furthermore, we should not assume that residents are interminably resilient and thus capable of finding their ways out of jams and dead-end projects. To engage difficult places on their own terms does not mean simply leaving them alone or relinquishing the responsibility to speak critically. But it does mean, as entailed in the sense of the "make+shift," that researchers, advocates, politicians, administrators and service providers should make their "move." They also must be willing to shift what they do and think in face of the wide range of responses those moves will inevitably elicit, and not seek some overarching, standard set of development procedures.

That said, as we argue later on, there are at least four aspects at the core of an anticipatory politics and research ethic for the city:

1 a rigorous and unromantic engagement with technological change as digital platforms become increasingly pervasive, enabling and predatory;
2 a commitment to walking the street and finding compelling ways to re-describe the affective dynamics of everyday urbanism and the kinds of horizon lines to which they may be pointing;
3 coming to grips with the changing and creaking institutional formats of the state (hierarchy and market), market and civil society organizations (network and hierarchy) with an eye toward figuring alternative formats to curate organizational designs that are fit for purpose;
4 instilling a passion for experimentation in order to forge new concepts and imaginaries that can anchor and accelerate new practices, at diverse scales and in numerous institutional settings. Practically, this points to a sensibility to advance learning through experimentation.

The skills and sensibilities at work in all of the various home-grown, city-specific varieties of the "make+shift" have to be the basis for a pluri-scalar approach to climate adaptation strategies and a more just city. New employment opportunities must be coupled to the deployment of green technologies and implemented through various pilot experiments. City-wide social movements must be engaged in policy debates, planning commissions and sectoral reforms. Grassroots coalition building has to be more creative in terms of coordinating different forms of organization.

Again, a spirit of openness and generosity must persist across these efforts. This entails a willingness to work with the *details* of how everyday life, institutions and technologies actually operate without necessarily rushing to envelop the details in ready-made ideological or interpretive frameworks. In this book we have tried to stay close to these details and to work with the knotty ambiguities of everyday urban life, knowing full well that the epistemological ground is shifting beneath our feet all of the time.

1

Paradoxes of the Urban

Inhabiting the paradox

This is a book about stories, or, rather, about particular ways of telling them, or, in another sense, how to discover and unearth them. It is about story *lines* – lines that connect stories urban inhabitants tell about themselves, other inhabitants and cities near and far. It is about stories that cities seem to tell about themselves, about what needs to be done. What kinds of lines navigate through all of these different stories? How is it possible to draw new lines, lines that make unusual connections, but which allow us to see urban phenomena in different ways, and thus make different kinds of decisions? Such story lines are not straight and narrow. They often end up in such a way that they don't get their stories straight. But perhaps this is the only way to deal with a story of cities that is full of paradoxes.

Cities across Africa and Asia move toward and away from each other in significant ways. No longer, if ever, coherent actors in themselves, cities as social and administrative entities, nevertheless, attempt to posit themselves as dynamic engines of economic growth and social transformation. Urbanization, as a process once embodied by the city form, now takes on varying shapes and sizes, expanding cities into megalopolises, shrinking them into shadows of former selves, or articulating a vast range of places and resources in tight relationships of interdependency.

Cities become the venues for all kinds of countervailing tendencies: where narrowing and expansion, ambiguity and precision, dissipation and consolidation, embodiment and digitalization, movement and stasis are all intensified – and sometimes become indistinguishable from each other. Urbanization is something that seems increasingly to make itself, something independent from its once familiar function as an arena where different things were made, articulated and prompted into new synergies. Associations with density, social diversity, churn, and the circulation of disparate experiences through each other no longer seem to hold as key criteria for designating something as "urban." Differentiations between local and global, public and private, exterior and interior, intensive and extensive appear to fold into and, sometimes, collapse upon each other. The very organization of meaning, with its boundaries of here and there, self and other, citizen and stranger, becomes both more pronounced and more subject to erasure. More and more the urban seems to be a confounding story (Amin 2013a, 2013b; Easterling 2014).

What does it mean to think politically within an urban environment of such seeming paradox? This is the question we attempt to address in this book, particularly by considering how urban politics and programmatic interventions might operate simultaneously through inventions at the level of municipal and metropolitan systems *and* through acupunctural interventions at the level of neighborhoods or districts. This *double* approach assumes that the conventional rules of the game – home and property ownership, formal taxation systems, standardized outlays of infrastructure – are inadequate to the realities in which urban life is actually lived. This is life not layered through orderly scales and sectors but, rather, assuming multiple spatial forms. As such, interventions, policies and mobilizations must be capable of resonating across disparate terrains and vectors of impact.

Some of the key theorists of urbanization – Robert Wirth, Lewis Mumford, Manuel Castells, Henri Lefebvre, David Harvey, Saskia Sassen, Neil Brenner and Christian Schmid – all point, albeit in different formulations, to urbanization as both a process of intensive differentiation of people and things and the subsuming of singular human experiences, technical instruments and spaces of sociality to a continuous remaking of abstract worlds. In other words, urbanization makes things more specific and, at the same time, turns specific things into components of "machines" that appear to have no "real" body, no concrete being, but yet act as a powerful entity. Jennifer Robinson has gone beyond these formulations to develop modes of knowledge creation that, through creative acts of comparison, continually reconstitute a wide range of possibilities for what the urban is and can be.

As such, the city is always something to be remade according to new models, new possibilities of generating value (Sevilla-Buitrago 2015). Cities across Africa and Asia then share the problems of producing more spectacular built environments, accommodating large numbers of recent and usually poor residents, and managing vast and easily bubbled property markets (Watson 2009). Yet, composing these similarities can entail very different procedures and elements. They involve many different stories. When we say that we are going to deal with urbanization in Africa and Asia in this book, we know that these designations are shorthand. We know that we can never cover the intricacies of urbanization in these intensely differentiated regions with anything approaching comprehensiveness. Both Asia and Africa are not countries or stable territorial configurations. Rather, we use them here as signs of an evolving process of urbanization that both corresponds to and diverges from previous epicenters and conventional narratives. They are the backdrop for our stories, a way of narrowing down the lens of our considerations, and a way of pointing to a form of urbanization largely still in the making and thus potentially open to new forms of development and governance.

While cities and urban regions often act like unstoppable juggernauts in their pursuit of spectacular and easy profits, the messy details of how the particular spaces within African and Asian cities get to have the kinds of populations and characteristics they have draw on divergent histories and day-to-day encounters. Cities are arenas of action, and they vary as to how actions are considered, controlled and valued, and for whom certain actions are safe and legitimate. While cities may no longer embody the critical dimensions of urbanization, they remain powerful objects of imagination, sociality and governance (Derickson 2015; Hall and Savage 2016).

In some cities, sex is one of the few vehicles of free expression; in other cities it is full of routinized drudgery (Sheller

2012). In some cities, the household is the bastion of security
and nurturance; in others, it may be a dangerous minefield.
In some cities, vast populations are warehoused with little
to do but are equipped with a basic, subsidized existence; in
yet others, existence is an unrelenting scramble for advantage
(Zeiderman 2016). In some cities, most residents have reasonable recourse to officials designated to manage problems; in
others, problems are addressed simply by temporarily substituting alternative problems for the original ones.[1]

Of course cities differ within themselves concerning the
practices of everyday behavior – actions about friendship and
enmity, care and sexual desire, the circulation and hoarding
of knowledge, the camaraderie or isolation of work, or the
togetherness or apartness of where and how people spend
their days. The veneers of official description – the ways in
which cities seem controlled, the rules and habits, the possibilities and restrictions – also tend to cover up many public
secrets (Taussig 1999). They occlude ways of living that are
not supposed to be taking place, but do so anyway. Of course,
almost everyone knows that these transgressions are taking
place, but they also know that it is more dangerous to acknowledge this reality. The dimensions of this duality are explored
in greater detail in later chapters.

In this book we will often refer to cities *and* urban regions
as a way to point both to how urbanization does not necessarily equate to the city and to the various formats of urbanization that seem either to exceed the familiar scale of the
city or to take on hybrid forms (Painter 2012; Addie and
Keil 2015). These hybrids might include various amalgama-
tions of cores, peripheries, corridors, greenfields and extraction
zones. The notion of regions has been used in many different
ways. Regions point to macro-level articulations or points of
orientation around particular physical terrains or modes of
production, occurring within and among national states (Sassen
2010). Regions might refer to spatial distributions of similar-
ity and covariance in terms of demographics, histories and
politics that cut across clearly delineated scales (Crescenzi et
al. 2012; Zhang 2014). Notions of "new regionalism" refer
to administrative and political constructions of specific transnational or transurban regulatory frameworks of economic
operation. They point to intensifications of particularity and

clustering at sub-national levels (Agnew 2013; Jones 2002; Parr 2008), which seem to have become more salient to the logistics of globally articulated economic value chains. This discourse has also become more prolific with the policy focus on agglomeration economics as the key to prosperity (Glaeser 2012).

Each of these instances of the regional raises questions about the logics of coherence. To what degree are regions administrative artifacts, platforms of affective solidarities, basins of attraction, analytical or vernacular clusters of flows and linkages, or concretizations of specific political, economic or cultural relationships? How are they materialized through watersheds and other geomorphic features (Booth and Bledsoe 2009)? Whether they "actually" exist or are simply ways of materializing particular ideas about critical differences of various kinds is a seemingly moot concern. More importantly, what are the performative dimensions of what regions do in various circumstances and times? For the power of regions as constellations of emplacement lies in the way they both mediate between the stabilities of specific populations and ways of doing things *and* create more open-ended exchanges with larger surrounds (Brighenti 2016; Coward 2012).

The relationships between the forces of global capital and the locally expressed forces of intermeshed and messy encounters are not assignable to clearly distinct scales. It is not that global capital sits above a world of cities orchestrating its circuits below, apportioning things here and there in some kind of command-and-control fashion (Amin and Thrift 2002; Brenner and Schmid 2014; Harrison and Hoyler 2015; Lawhon and Patel 2013). Neither are the intermixtures of inclinations, styles and practices that make up a local vernacular simply confined within the administrative or cultural boundaries of a specific urban region. The articulations are marked by infidelity of scale and thoroughly indeterminate. The prolific dispersal of highly localized African popular urban music is but one visceral example.

We know well just how wage relations, the extraction of surplus, or the hoarding of capacity work their way into the blood, into what may be experienced as the DNA of contemporary urban individuals. We also know the peculiarities of how cities spill over their boundaries. In part, residents embody this spilling by moving across the world, making their performances visible through all kinds of media. It is also reflected in the human inclination to imitate, to coalesce on the basis of people taking things from each other. So what connects or divides cities is a moving target, something shifting all the time across and within geographical scales and times (Lingis 2000).

One thing that seems certain, however, is that substantial demographic changes will constitute proliferating axes of urbanization across African and Asia as a powerful epicenter of global urbanization. While the youth bulge may have peaked across most of the world, the youth population will continue to grow substantially in Africa and South Asia for the coming two decades, which means a key challenge is the provision of work, particularly in cities largely centered on both informal and industrial labor markets, now increasingly overcrowded (ILO 2013; Nayar et al. 2012; Thurow 2014). We explore this imperative in greater detail in chapter 2.

Catch-22

So much of urban Asia and Africa seems caught in a catch-22. The very spatial products and policies undoing long-honed practices of inhabitation are offered as the cure for their loss. Customary land arrangements, public guarantees, forms of tenancy and land- and building-use give way to condominiums, shop–house complexes, and all-in-one sub-cities, almost always fully sold in advance of completion, at least in the Asian context. The actual mechanisms of "full occupancy" often entail complex and shady financial manoeuvres. But there clearly is a market for investments, especially on the part of a younger generation of urban residents who often are able to mobilize significant portions of the sale price up front. In Asia, the peripheries of major urban regions are being filled in with both new town developments and masses of cheaply and uniformly built small housing units, as poorer residents are often evicted from both the urban core and suburban areas.[2] We expect many African countries to mimic this trend as similar stylized investors are likely to set up shop and operational modalities in fast-growing African cities.

The stories behind such financial mobilization are often varied. So, from Lagos to Jakarta to Recife to Kolkata, how such money is actually placed on the table derives from vast mixtures of the licit and the illicit, from savings to borrowing on future earnings, from the proliferation of the marketing of goods and services on and off the books – in other words, from an "urban economy" that does not necessarily become less diverse as the destinations of its proceeds may become more standardized.[3] But even in cities where transitions are happening quick and dirty, where real estate restages piracy on the high seas and speculation becomes a national pastime, conditions now on the ground are more tremulous, uneven and volatile than the consolidation story would seem to make them. This is not so much a matter of the persistence of particular places and practices; it is not the obduracy of specific populations to change or a growing resistance of the marginalized, whether the long-term poor, a fallen middle class, or youth with no employment prospects.[4]

Rather, the intersections of cut-throat competition over the rapid acquisition and development of land, the sense of exigency shared by all kinds of inhabitants to do something quickly to improve their prospects, and the often murky ways in which land can become embedded in a thicket of bureaucratic statuses produce different kinds of voids, leftovers and transition spaces (Benjamin 2015). Perhaps these voids and transition spaces will be eventually folded into the prevailing standardized formats of commercial and residential development. But for now it is not completely clear where they are headed. Current trajectories of urban change take apart interwoven relations of proximity, economic livelihood, local collaboration, mutual witnessing, give and take, and a spirit of opportunism that were based on *both* sharing and theft. They also take apart the articulations of contiguity, where spaces physically next to each other had some kind of linkage no matter the character of the boundaries that divided them, even if transgressing the divides was the only available option.[5]

As such, the rush to parcel, to sort, to convert space to property, to maximize ground rent and to claim turf may generate spatial products that sweep across cities and their growing extensions (MacLeod and McFarlane 2014). But they also, as disentangling machines, produce all kinds of interstices, vague and sometimes troubling vacancies, and wastelands. Sometimes these spaces are situated in conditions that make them costly or impossible to do anything with; other times, they are remnants of contestations that are seemingly interminable, products of uncertain legal status or individual recalcitrance.[6] Sometimes they are small pockets seized upon and held in order to extort compensation or benefit, not now, but in some undetermined future. At other times, they exist simply as the concrete manifestations of the difficulties entailed in drawing lines among all of the disparate sales, remaking and developments taking place, as well the fights among investors, politicians and bureaucrats over the "cuts", the rules, the uses or the jurisdictions involved.[7]

The restructuring involved in today's *consolidation* of urban space, as the maximization of land rent, is not seamless. It is replete with scams, short-cuts, cost-cutting measures, broken agreements, messed-up contracts, plans gone wrong, and fights within and between municipal and state ministries, architecture firms, consultancies, contractors, property developers, construction firms, infrastructure regimes, planners, and local and prospective residents. The power of money, imaginaries of efficient cities and middle-class norms may often trump all of the concrete difficulties entailed, but the process of consolidation remains messy and fraught with unanticipated twists and turns.[8] Confronting these dense and fluid dynamics matters because they are central to the "functioning" and morphing of African and Asian cities in particular.

There is a pervasive paradox, then, in the extent to which social solidarity and purportedly informal urban practices, places and economies conventionally framed as plagued with excessive transaction costs, labor intensity, corruption and deleterious environmental effects continue to provide productive and affordable residential and commercial settings, while, on the other hand, the purported scale efficiencies and regulatory proficiencies of big integrated development end up being replete with fiscal manipulations, pieced-together compensations, and a lot of wasted time. This is a problem that goes beyond the long-term situation where community-built and -managed urban infrastructures and informal economies are implicitly folded into the formal development and regulatory frameworks of states at all scales. This folding-in has acted as a means for states to circumvent their responsibilities to ensure an equitable distribution of resources. Instead, states spend large proportions of their capital budgets to capture inward investment for various "showcase" projects. Most importantly, these community-built and -managed infrastructures and economies become vehicles through which the state can operate when its own legal and policy mandates seem to constrain its ability to manoeuvre (Roy 2009). The paradox here is that much of contemporary urban development actively undermines the very kinds of experiences, histories and relationships from which to substantialize the livelihoods of expanding urban populations.

It is a paradox where the exigencies to fix things, to deal with the massive remaking of urban infrastructure necessary to attenuate the damaging ecological footprints of contemporary modalities of urban development and to survive the rapidly changing ecological conditions of cities themselves, propel states and their array of corporate and multilateral partners into highly formatted procedures of trying to do sustainable development, where what is more relevant is paying attention to experimenting with the singularities of each city. In other words, what is important is to steer how different ways of life, histories, economic capacities and cultural memories interact. Such experiments are necessary in order to address just how climate change, resource consumption and urban expansion, and all the viable efforts to do something effective about these intersections, will inevitably transform everyday life, providing cities are able to come up with the money to fund infrastructure change and maintenance.

So the question is how to inhabit these paradoxes – how to open up space for new political imaginations of urban work. In this book we will attempt to address this through the deployment of several concepts. We are not interested so much in the use of these concepts as a way of summing things up or providing anything close to definitive answers. Rather, these concepts inform the political practice of sustaining a *double view* that affirms the importance of simultaneous experiments at the levels of everyday life *and* in the worlds of policy and official governance. These concepts are intended both to provoke imagination of alternative dispositions of urban change *and* to inform the "grunt" work of tinkering with cumbersome institutional bureaucracies. These are concepts that point to topological resonances among diverse scalar interventions rather than specifying specific principles of urban development subject to consensus across communities and institutions. In other words, how can specific interventions ramify across different spaces and populations? How can a series of events be triggered that open up the possibility of new linkages among things usually kept apart, rather than trying to come up with overarching frameworks about how to tie all of the relevant factors and places together?

As such, the book is organized around a series of conceptual and strategic interventions, and in what follows we lay out a rough sketch of them that will be taken up more substantially in the ensuing chapters. It is important, however, to emphasize at the outset that these conceptual interventions are geared toward developing a concrete politics of experimentation. This experimentation entails concrete interventions into formal government institutions, insurgent social movements, local networks of livelihood formation, and popular culture at different scales as a means of triggering a multiplicity of *topological resonances* capable of putting different places, materials, services, discourses and institutions in different contact with each other. The present rules of the game for urban governance and development do not work in most of the geographies we are concerned with. What we are after is a way of thinking that might come up with workable plans and practices that transpire through experimentation, pedagogy, failure, exchange and persistence.

Conceptual interventions

Re-description

One important concept we invoke is the notion of *re-description*. How can particular spaces, built environments or ways of living be re-described, not as elements or evidence of particular principles, macro forces or structural arrangements, but as aspects of what Celia Lury (2012) refers to as n-dimension spaces, states of existence that *might be?* This is not *only* a matter of imagination, fantasy or forward visualization. The task also entails re-describing existent conditions as components of a process that might be taking place *right now*, but which is opaque, occluded or rendered inoperative. It is rendered inoperative simply because we are seeing and engaging the realities examined in a particular way. So there is a *doubleness* here that involves a sense of aspiration, of making things different, but also of seeing in what exists something other than what we think we are seeing.

This is an "inventive method" in that it attempts to compose urban knowledge of *what can be as well as of what is*. This is not a use of method to establish or confirm knowledge of what the city or urban actually is. Rather, it is knowledge of how different urban realities can be enacted or tested in trials, experiments, or even play (Lury and Wakeford 2012). For example, rather than seeing the interface between the formatted residential complexes – either upscale all-in-one superblocks or cheaply built box-houses or the highly textured built environment of so-called popular districts – in exclusively antagonist terms, how might those terms be re-described by exploring the intersections that *must take place* among them, and do so in *multiple* ways? How might such re-description be used as knowledge of how different trajectories of exchange and influence might move across these spaces? While particular forms and practices of livelihood, residing and circulating may have specific histories, and are the results of specific assumptions and power relations, they are situated in constantly changing surrounds, often having to take all kinds of twists and turns in order to remain "the same" (Muniesa 2014).

Granted, whatever exists in the city is a manifestation of something, and that something is usually a convergence of multiple forces and backgrounds. But that something also exists in an immeasurable series of relationships with other things. Here, intensities of mutual impact cannot be pinned down to a matter of physical proximity or any other set of classifications. Thus, the interfaces where all of these "something" intersect can be the site for re-description. Differences, such as those between the slum and the formal settlement, between illicit economies and standardized production, are of course still powerful and salient. But if we look at the boundaries where they "meet," boundaries which each of these differentiations have in common, something extra about the character of each component can be revealed. It is here that we can see the reciprocal complicities, divergences and interdependencies that exist among things we otherwise just see as diverging.

In contradistinction to hyper-commodification, the urban commons is increasingly invoked as a vital political claim and basis for solidarity. In our reading, the commons is not firstly an equilibrating mechanism of redistributed opportunities and resources. Rather, it is a matter of a condition(ing) of boundaries, not as a specific place necessarily, but what Galloway (2012) calls an agitated friction. It is a moment when something transitions into something else, passes from one medium or scale to another. So, for example, when high-end mega-developments are placed alongside historic popular neighborhoods or low-income housing, the interface between these disparate built environments and expressions of power should not necessarily indicate that one supersedes the other, or that the tensions inherent in this proximity will ultimately work themselves out through one subsuming the other or through the hardening of physical or spectral boundaries. Rather, it is a friction to be worked with as a resource, as an occasion for experimentation that attempts provisionally to articulate the disparate social and cultural worlds seemingly signified by these differences in built form and economic capacity. Here the commons is something immanent in the very marked differences themselves no matter how these differences seem to show incompatible logics and aspirations. In other words, the default binaries between the powerful and the exploited, the elite and the excluded, that structure urban thought and practice must be transcended.

Additionally, re-description simply allows us to continue holding in view aspects of urban life that otherwise seem to have disappeared. While much of the urban world has been regenerated, any forays through cities such as Jakarta, Karachi, São Paulo, Mexico City, Kolkata or Bangkok would reveal the obdurate character of local vitalities masked by apparent decline. For behind this decline remain intricate operations of claim-making. In popular urban core districts of Jakarta that appear to be on their "way out," where nothing seems to be happening, making claims becomes an instrument for residents discovering spaces of manoeuvre (Simone 2014). The built environment and economic infrastructure may appear overburdened from too many uses, too many repairs, and a lack of clarity as to who owns what or belongs where. But these appearances are the backdrop for a process where residents continually circulate through different associations and groups. These groups sometimes seem to compete with each other and want different prospective futures for the area. There doesn't seem to be an overall agenda, and different initiatives "pop up" all over the place and then disappear.

These districts are trying, at least implicitly, to detach themselves from the onslaughts of massive redevelopment, or at least slow them down. Here a process of continual re-description seems to keep a large number of local residents "in play" as they participate in different kinds of collective operations. It is not always possible to assign a particular role or value to a particular person because they wear different "hats" at different times. A religious leader also is an entrepreneur and a politician and runs a local recreation club. A housewife who organizes savings groups is also a prominent religious figure and a local government official who in addition runs a number of stalls in the local market. Residents participate in very different kinds of associations and ways of being with each other, taking on different roles, behaviors, aspirations. They make different kinds of claims. These claims are not usually claims for citizenship, although they might be. Rather, claiming becomes a means of configuring different vantage points on what is going on, different kinds of access to resources and opportunities, and a way to open up new kinds of networks (Bayat 2010). These openings keep important information flowing about what is taking place in the larger city. But, importantly, they also make it difficult for "outsiders" and those who would try to appropriate large chunks of the district for mega-developments to read exactly what is going on, slowing down whatever manoeuvres they initiate to bring about wholesale changes.

Secretion

Secretion is another concept important to us. We use this notion as an amalgam of the work of Bataille (1991), for whom excess is the basis of all urban economy and certain strands of anthropology, most particularly that of Taussig (1999) and Jusionyte (2015), that deal with the importance of public secrets as a critical element of exerting rule. Secretion points to a process where whatever is captivated leaks. Whatever energies of laboring bodies that may be progressively railroaded into underpaid dead-end jobs also have a "secret" life of secretion, spreading out indiscernibly into dispensations that cannot be predicted or pinned down.

Urbanization, according to Brenner and Schmid (2015), is in need of constant retheorization as a process and not as a particular form of settlement or practice. Rather, urbanization enables the instantiation of capitalist value across settings replete with different times and ways of doing things. It parasitically enfolds what exists and, in doing so, converts it into polyvalent scales of accumulation, dispossession, and the renewing and exhaustion of "cheap resources" (Moore 2015). But we know little about how that which leaks into the constant remaking of capitalist virtuosity infects it in ways that prompt more totalizing and innovative forms of recovery, which in turn widen its exposures to tipping points and hacks. Given that so much of urban theory and thought is obsessed with the exclusionary powers and effects of capitalist processes, we prefer to foreground contestation and the vulnerabilities of predominant forms of power.

Attempts at "immunization" of course attempt to forestall such secretions. Large numbers of urban populations are secreted away to the most peripheral areas of the city or in various forms of detention to keep them from leaking into the "cleaned-up" city. The management of these disappearances and dislocations become apparatuses concerned primarily with their own replication. For example, as Gottschalk (2014) argues, the carceral system is still on the surface linked to cops, courts, attorneys, lawmakers, regulatory authorities. It continues to discipline and punish particular populations with varying degrees of severity, coupling justice and injustice in inextricable fashion. But, as Gottschalk points out, the carceral system today largely exists simply to reproduce and extend itself as an apparatus in its own right. It is something essentially cut off from any other functions, even though it depends upon those functions in order to cover its tracks.

Power is also secreted through the infrastructures rolled out to convey specific representations of it. It attempts to secure traction on uncertain ground and to establish particular forms of articulation among people, things, institutions and places. But power also leaks through its structures of conveyance in ways that cannot completely control the terrain according to the professed agendas of politicians, professionals, developers and financiers. Excess financial liquidity may require a place to land and for configurations of land, such as cities, to absorb and congeal it. But people, places and things also intersect in the elaboration of strange hybrids. These hybrids are sometimes complicities and sometimes are mutual deceptions among the strong and the weak, the legal and the illegal (Anwar 2014; Sundaram 2009).

Here, power finds itself party to new zones of affect and collective sentiment, as well as the capacity to affect them. In city after city, no matter where, there is the surface veneer of rules and regulations, strategic plans and intersectoral arrangements, and the tightly and often efficiently run systems of providing what the city needs to maintain a semblance of order, compliance and provisional consensus. But almost all cities are also sustained through substrates of improvised repair, compensation, off-the-books deals and tacit understandings (Amin 2014). There are wellsprings of passions, tactics and rapidly generated hypotheses for how to act that always threaten to twist the best-laid plans and policing mechanisms slightly out of shape. It might be conceptually more productive to focus our attention on these dynamics instead of endlessly rediscovering the disciplinary power of neoliberalism.

As Agamben (2014) suggests, there are the possibilities of what he calls "destituent" power. Here, secretion takes the form of detachment, of acting as if something is not operative or connected in the midst of conditions in which persons or things seem clearly defined and accounted for. For there remains something about the urban that "hits you in the face," an aesthetics of appearance where things can be anything whatsoever, detached from any clear meaning. It is a secretion that doesn't so much bleed into the dominant regulatory apparatuses as slip away.[9]

Resonance

Across cities and urban regions there are many populations, provisioning systems and political accommodations that are off or only partially connected to the "grid." In other words, municipalities, regional administrations, service sectors, or systems of interconnection and nested scaling are never fully operational. Of course, many cities manage to enfold inhabitants and the material flows that support them into coordinated infrastructural and institutional frameworks. While these frameworks may suggest or impose the ways in which various dimensions of the city are to interconnect, such interconnections may be barely discernible or functional; they may break down, may fail even to take place.

Particularly in urban Africa and much of Asia, the grids, frameworks and reticulations have varying degrees of concrete presence. But much of what residents do to secure water, power, food, work and health treatment is the result of both localized and trans-local figuring of relationships with what is at hand (Jaglin 2014). Materials and places are put to use for functions for which they were not intended. Residents reach out into a larger world to search for opportunities whose proceeds are remitted back "home" in various forms. Residents with access to particular information, supplies or skills are cobbled together in largely provisional and frequently revised arrangements (Simone 2004, 2010).

Resonance is both the modality and the by-product of people, materials and places "feeling each other out," of attending to each other, of being drawn to or repelled in the midst of so many things to which attention could be drawn. In other words, resonance is the affective process of people and things associating with each other, of having something to do with each other, of acting as components in the enactment of operations larger than themselves and their own particular functions and histories. When things resonate with each other there is a connection that proceeds, not from the impositions of some overarching map or logic, but from a process of things extending themselves to each other. It is a matter of institutions, practices of knowledge production, and different tacit ways of doing things finding concrete opportunities to take each other into consideration. This process of resonance is critical to urban development work. It is critical in that it points to mechanisms of gathering up what already exists and "collaborating" with it in new ways that might open up access to needed resources and concepts. How one does this is obviously not an easy question to answer and certainly cannot be guessed out of context or the flows of meaningful time that shape daily interactions.

If – and it is a big if – cities and urban regions are able to come up with the huge amounts of financing necessary in order to make the required infrastructural adjustments to accommodate growing populations and to adapt to environmental exigencies, most actors in the urban development business will have to work with a lot of uncertainty. There will be uncertainty as to how to roll out such infrastructure, how to relocate populations in areas of intense vulnerability or that need to be moved while new infrastructures are developed and reticulated (Adelekan et al. 2015; Bulkeley et al. 2014). Financing and infrastructure inputs are likely to be incremental in most places over the coming decades – more a matter of targeted adjustments. There will be some selective "big ticket" items assumed to have substantial multiplier impacts. There will be a major emphasis on localized systems of sustainability dependent upon exerting the judicious use of natural resource inputs through carefully tailored consumption practices, recycling, and maximizing the generation and renewal of local ecologies of material flows. This includes local processing of waste materials, the maximizing of locational advantages (such as riverbeds, flood plains, wind chambers), job creation through local environmental management, and the materialization of flexible design prototypes able to make fine-grained adjustments to local specificities and promote multiple uses of buildings and other inputs.

How are disparate tools and ways of doing things put together? How do granular and "acupunctural" interventions "make their way" across places and scales? How do institutional policies find traction in the everyday lives of residents?

This is largely a matter of resonance, of distinct objects, actors and practices getting a "feel" for each other, of inciting, luring and synchronizing in rhythms capable of generating "big effects" through the resonation of "small things." Here, it is important to keep in mind the amount of energy that a city generates. This is energy not limited to the powering of machines, but energy also as a matter of all of the transactions and intersections that take place among the components of city life. When we popularly say that the city is an information-rich environment, we are referring to the subjective form, the recognizable entities through which such energetic forces can be identified, tracked and harnessed, such as specific media and institutions (Szeman 2014).

But information has an effect; it refers to events and conditions information as a resonance, a force of difference, in relationship to realities that are not perfectly, seamlessly aligned. The transmission of information is the transmission of an anticipation to affect a difference in the receiver (Terranova 2004). The effects attained are also always "wearing off" and "fading away," as both transmitter and receiver are not only part of a larger world of information transmissions but are themselves realigned in ways that cannot be precisely predicted by virtue of the information. The receiver may show the anticipations expected in how they respond in the moment, but they are also caught up in numerous other anticipations that continuously shift the playing field and are always resonating elsewhere. Of course there is much about how urban space is organized and built that functions to block resonance, channel it in narrow streams, and limit the way things can be connected to each other. Even in the widespread calls for innovation, updating and urban transformation, there are the constant reminders that change has to be "continuous" and transformations "stable." Innovation is something proffered not as a one-off process but as something continuous, just as stability is now largely perceived not as keeping conditions the same but as a situation of continuous assessment and adjustment.

Part of the seemingly constant redoing of urban life, its inherent restlessness, pushing and shoving people and things around, stems from an ongoing obsession with *redemption*. Here the inheritances of the past now to be remade, preserved or effaced in the present need to be redeemed, almost like a book of "green stamps" avidly collected over weeks and years, placed along grids to the end of the book ("road") and then turned over for cash. Whatever something is now merely conceals its "real" value, which is determinable only later on. There is also a spiritual dimension at work, as if the mistakes of the past, all of the wrong moves, policies, enmities and convictions, can be cleansed of their connotations and then point to a new existence where all is forgiven.

For cities have long been sites of redemption. They signal the possibilities of starting over, of keeping the past in view. The past is kept in view as the justification for what a people have become, which now needs to be changed. It is not about using the past as a source of continuity or ideas about the specifics of transformation. Nor is it a way of making whatever transpired in that past count for something different in the present. The past is not a source of roads not taken that could have been taken. It is not a series of potentials yet to be fulfilled. Nothing, then, stays the same or changes, as the past doesn't so much haunt as posit the prospects of constant ruination. In trying to redeem the waywardness of the past, a horizon must appear whose primary function is to make other possibilities recede (invoking Agamben 1993, 2013).

The footprints of industrial production and mass consumption are the city "walking all over itself." It is as if all of the uprooting, dispossession, disciplining and frenzy that went into making life urban carried with it a pervasive sense of guilt or glee that has to be redeemed by constructing virtuous "splendors" that do little justice to all the costs entailed. Then, there is the redemption increasingly sought for the way in which the expansions of urbanity promise to implode life itself. So the intensification of urban processes reflected in design, engineering, fantasy and speculation becomes the only means to get ourselves out of the mess we are in. Additionally, the city attempts to redeem itself by paying attention to all of the dimensions of life to which it really wasn't paying attention before in the "microphages" of everyday life. All of the affects, street intelligences, relational capacities that cities have been collecting all along are now to be redeemed into the possibility of an ongoing, sustainable life in face of looming disaster. The frenzy of "transformational" discourse that erupted in the run-up to the United Nations Habitat III conference in Quito in 2016 is but one illustration of this.

Invariably, governing has changed and is being adapted all the time. Governing increasingly relies upon on "reading" the desires and behaviors of individuals so well as effectively to intervene in their next moves. What will they buy, decide and want? Algorithmic formulations aggregate an enormous of amount of data as to how individuals or groups acted in the past as a way to attempt to determine what they will do from now on. It is a matter of calculating the probabilities that some particular event or outcome might occur by inter-relating increasing amounts of data about how bodies act, what places look like, what environmental conditions transpire, and what kinds of impacts all of these things have on each other. This entails a process where the parameters that are set up to measure how different built and social environments operate, in terms of volumes, speeds or intensities, come together without any guarantees (Parisi 2013). In other words, bringing all kinds of different data sets together can generate unreadable outcomes no matter how the interactions of these parameters are controlled. At the same time, the actions and characteristics on which these data are based become locked into specific forms of assessment and calculation.

The more that municipal administrations employ various forms of large-scale simulation, scenario planning and big data crunching in hopes of exploring the "deep relations" that exist among various dimensions of the city – transporta-tion, energy supply, municipal finance, economic productivity and demographics, to name a few – the less these dimensions seem to resonate with each other, the less they are able to find various ways of intersecting, gathering up or working together. In part this is because the modes of calculation that attempt to identify their relative impact upon each other tend to strip them of their contextual embedding, extracting them only as probabilistic values and parameters. The intangible receptors and conductors of resonance are not captured or seen.

At the same time, digital and algorithmic governance endeavors to guarantee specific decisions predicated on opera-tions which by their nature themselves have no guaranteed course of action, which offer the possibilities of incomputable data. While algorithmic operations attempt to affect what specific entities will do, they, themselves, need make no reference to how these entities are emplaced in a physical world. Through inter-referencing data derived from various sources and appearing in various formats, they bypass any form of established representation, looking for previously unknown patterns, and potentially discovering eventualities for which we have no map (Amoore and Piotukh 2015; Parisi 2012). While this process may seem to promise a wide-open future with which to work, the act of searching things out, of seeking relations, is taken out of our hands.

On the other hand, despite the very real vulnerabilities under which many urban residents exist, there is not so much resilience as there is a capacity on the part of individuals to play out plural versions of themselves. As pointed out earlier in the example from Jakarta, they can often think from multiple perspectives and switch among a broad repertoire of performances given the occasion at hand. It is this very kind of resource base of multiple resonances that portends the most adept opportunity to make use of the contingent and strange realities that urban computation and algorithmic governance might bring about. This capacity has sometimes been referred to as the general intellect, an expansive commons of interacting ideas and thought, which constantly has to "fight for its life" in the face of various efforts to standardize knowledge, to individuate and thus domesticate its relational character. This is knowledge as a function of people being different things for each other at different times and therefore enlarging the very number of relations to which people have access and through which they can discover different feelings, skills and versions of themselves (Virno 2004). Thus, without falling into a technology-determinist trap, we think there are important informational, infrastructural and relational shifts afoot that are worth paying attention to and articulating within a fine-grained reading of the everyday, not only to discern resonances but also to deploy them.

Governing the urban

The usual assumption is that bad governance in Africa and Asia holds back viable urban development. The usual lament is that, if only governance was more rational and coherent, the incipient resourcefulness of inhabitants would fully express and apply itself. But government is not a cohesive, integrated system, either of mutually reinforcing, recalibrating feedback circuits or functional segmentations of an overarching logic. Rather, government is much more an ad hoc construction of different knowledges, practices and institutions that "has no internal consistency apart from the network that connects its elements" (Braun 2014: 61). Government is always in the process of trying to figure itself out. Its authority is always partial. It depends upon ways of doing things that usually don't fit seamlessly with the ways it professes to be doing things. Its power lies less with its ability to prescribe and specify than it does with its control over particular kinds of knowledge, techniques, practices and facilities. It reserves these for itself; it puts them to work in a limited set of ways and thus removes them from more general, popular uses, where the results entailed could be very different (Aradau et al. 2008; Dillon 2007; Foucault 2009).

While urban residents across Africa and Asia certainly desire some recourse to planning and decision-making processes that make sense to them, that posits an atmosphere of stability through which they can reasonably anticipate what the immediate future holds and then plan accordingly, the ability of government to constitute such stability does not inhere in the apparent solidity of its own sense-making. Rather, it is more a problem of performance. In other words, it concerns the ability of those who govern to take the heterogeneous elements and knowledge they work with to convey a persuasive connection between actions such as taxation, democratic procedure, land regulation and budget allocations and make them indeed seem connected to each other. Such a performance of modern reasonableness would seem to assure that those who share a common residency in particular governmental jurisdictions are somehow then themselves connected to each other beyond the efforts they make, either as individuals or as collectives. Such performance would seem to constitute residents as living "in the same boat."

But there is nothing definitive about urban government that necessitates a clear sense of normative procedure or that requires "effective" government to be in place in order for residents themselves, albeit within limits, to create viable platforms for their existence, using some of the very same knowledge that government usually reserves for itself.[10] After all, the *details* of what residents do with each other belongs to them, not just as a reflection of what takes place when they act but as components for making their own conclusions about what is or is not possible. The comprehensive ways in which residents, developers, brokers, local authorities, religious associations and other local institutions negotiate the organization of space, the provision of services, and the mechanisms through which various forms of asset accumulation take place are also articulated in particular detail with the larger surrounds, including the various scales of state power, which mediate how that power is experienced and what can be done with it.

Government agencies and other large institutions may have the capacity to aggregate these details – provided they are paying attention – into specific overall patterns, which then inform planning and budgetary decisions. Yet, both formal and informal mechanisms of working with these elements within localities themselves are critical aspects of governance. How such details can be made known, visualized and accessed are matters of inventive political practice.

Governance across a wide range of African and Asian urban regions certainly has gotten better according to conventional standards. It is less corrupt, and it is widening tax bases, offering municipal bonds, rationalizing procedures, and developing new infrastructure (UCLG 2016; UN-Habitat 2016). However, the by-products of this improvement also raise uncertain implications. The oscillating consolidations of property and the displacement of large number of poor people, as well as the incessant hunt for affordable land, seem to increase exponentially the physical size of urban regions (Fox 2012; Turok and McGranahan 2013). Addis Ababa, soon to cover 1,200 square kilometers, disrupts delicate ethnic balances as it swallows up a series of peripheral towns (Mota 2015).

The continuing elaborations of stronger government certainly feed into the burgeoning impression – albeit an impression that has been around for a long time – that Africa is finally booming. Never mind the persistence of internecine conflicts, massive unemployment, and the continued growth of religious populisms as the most important object of many people's loyalty and time. Never mind the conversion of thriving highly mixed districts into the targets of conventional forms of urban regeneration. Take the example of Surulele in Lagos. Surulele is a district of working- and middle-class households on the Lagos mainland. It has long housed teachers, police, commerçants, civil servants, tradespeople, artisans, musicians and crooks. Keeping costs low in a locale where most residents were assured some steady but modest income provided opportunities for lateral operations of all kinds. These operations concerned bundling and unbundling pieces of land, constructing an intricate built fabric, linking skills, money and networks into various enterprises and services, and creating a "shadow world" of institutions, schools, service providers and associations "behind" the official ones that did not work so well.

Surulele could get overcrowded and rough, but most residents always had the means to keep the district grounded and dynamic. It was steady enough to build traditions and legacies of the everyday practices that went into making the district a key engine of growth for Lagos. But what happens when the regional government targets a district as a space of "conversion," when it becomes the recipient of a large array of spatial interventions and products? What happens when new land policies encourage fast-tracked resolutions of seemingly ageless land disputes and ambiguities that had functioned as hedges against speculation? What happens when old and slightly dilapidated commercial centers are converted into high-end shopping malls? What happens when multi-family dwellings are converted into condominiums and when road repairs and infrastructure renovation are used to "straighten out" all of the messy lines of reticulation – physical, economic and social? What happens to all of the linked-up stories and people that on the surface would not seem to go together?

Shifting to China, other kinds of conversions have taken place. Peri-urban villagers surrounded by farmland converted by the state for urban uses still possessed prime land in the village. They maximized its value by constructing high-density rental accommodation for migrants or small- and medium-scale manufacturing zones. As village landlords did not pay tax to the municipal government, property management companies provided essential urban services. Villagers were usually able to retain residence inside the village, since local governments sought to reduce monetary costs with in-kind compensation. Land was transferred back to them to be collectively managed, mostly through development corporations in which villagers were shareholders. As local and metropolitan governments attain larger volumes of land under their direct jurisdiction, many existing villages are incorporated into municipal systems, as the pressure to provide low-cost accommodation extends the peripheries of urbanization (Bach 2010; Wu et al. 2013).

In Chongqing, shareholder corporations assembled fragmented agricultural plots which had been contracted to village households. In doing so, they acquired the capital necessary for infrastructure upgrading. They then rented and sold lots to manufacturers. They manipulated a grey area of the existing law, which has subsequently been changed. Economic power, consolidated in the corporation, put pressure on long-standing social support practices and networks, which had been reinforced through continual adaptations of the available built environment. Villagers increasingly had less land and fewer built assets to work with. As municipal governments, under pressure to generate higher returns through the intensification of land use, expropriate larger volumes of land, the social and spatial fabric of villages becomes increasingly fragmented (Smith 2014).

The thing is that, in both Nigeria and China, we do not know where such "conversions" are headed. But it seems likely that, if they are going to build upon the resourcefulness of the residents who made these places viable for redevelopment in the first place, it is important to consider how to incorporate that kind of resourcefulness into new forms of property and daily living. But who or what is leading the way? What kinds of influences or models are Lagos, Chongqing and other rapidly "modernizing" cities of Africa and Asia drawing upon? What kind of project is this game of rapid development? Do there exist other projects taking place in cities and urban regions worth paying attention to? What kinds of impact will these urban conversions have in regions that seem to be heading toward many different places at the same time? These are themes we explore in greater detail in chapters 3 and 4 to substantiate a research agenda that can deepen new knowledge exchanges across the global South.

African and Asian cities can boom and still exhibit large swathes of wretchedness. Whereas good governance is that which would normally be expected to reconcile such an apparent contradiction, it may not in the end matter all that much. More precisely, good government may be an important precondition for mitigating inequality and injustice, but there should not be a presupposition as to just what that government looks like. For governance is not necessarily that of imposed models but is, rather, a case of readapting the many different kinds of "micro-government" that already exist on the ground. There are also many examples of non-formal deliberative bodies that plan, decide and judge in ways that draw upon a wide range of mechanisms to encourage broad participation and strict accounting, that share authority but delegate clear lines of responsibility.[11]

These do not constitute the seamless scaling up of already suitable techniques and frameworks. Some of these governments on the ground are simply ramped-up imitations of official law, with their specifications of correct behavior and excessively punitive responses to any infraction; others are simply implicit understandings about how to "lie low" in response to the conditions of intense vulnerability. The apportionment of land, housing, services and justice may be seized at the ground level by mafias and gangs. But these seizures, more often than not, take place as incitements and collusions of formal government itself, as a dirty shortcut to avoid having to spend the money to exercise its own rule (Chatterjee 2011). Collective deliberations are sometimes difficult when the prevailing atmosphere portends nightmarish futures even more precarious then the present. Turning over actions to community institutions that turn out to be the fronts for powerfully thuggish actors can then become a self-fulfilling prophecy, speeding up the very futures dreaded. It is as important to disabuse ourselves of caricatures of neoliberal governmentality as it is to jettison romanticized accounts of everyday and bottom-up democracy. It is more useful and interesting, rather, to decipher the lived entanglements of rule and desire that animate local polities.

Additionally, when planned and unplanned, regularized and unregularized areas exist in close proximity to each other, not only do tensions arise over discrepant prerogatives and interests but contrasting forms of collective regulation may emerge – i.e., different types of groups that attempt to manage everyday economic transactions, access resources, and enforce political loyalties. Planned areas tend to develop state-like, hierarchical organizations in the absence of strong official state penetration. Unplanned areas often subsist through a plurality of smaller, more network-like collective actions, which largely exist in an equitable distribution of opportunities, but where gangs and mafias can also take hold (Gazdar and Mallah 2013).

At times, relations between residents seem either weakly or excessively mediated in many African and Asian cities, where the enactment of government fails to reach across the diversity of residents, events and activities to provide demonstrable instances of interconnection or uses a heavy hand that constrains what residents can do. When this is the case, residents have to come up with ways to move toward or away from each other. What William Connolly (2014) sees as "cloudy strivings" may be a useful depiction of the ways in which residents generate creative acts to affect each other. These cloudy strivings make up a vast substrate of gestures, inclinations and incipient understandings that may be actualized in collective projects. In cities, full of lots of things happening without clear indications of where they are going, residents will try to read this noise as some kind of signal, setting off on some course of action. In our reading, it is the sound of resonance.

As residents make local efforts to emplace themselves in rapidly changing and vulnerable circumstances, it is these cloudy strivings that often make it difficult to determine where the real powers governing such efforts actually lie. The capacity to acquire land, build a house, and access services for a large numbers of residents often depends on complicated negotiations between landowners, brokers, local customary authorities, bureaucrats working in municipal tax, land registration and infrastructure agencies, political party representatives, religious leaders, unofficial mediators and enforcers. It depends as well both on long periods of waiting *and* on a capacity to act quickly at a moment's notice. But the formats of deliberations, the calculations of costs, the circumvention or creation of rules, and the formulas that dictate specific outcomes are often not clear and therefore not amenable to simplistic procedures of democratic deliberation or participatory governance.

This is not because they are by nature opaque, although the ability of these diverse actors to work together does require large measures of invisibility. Rather, the processes of working things out often take many different twists and turns and generate multiple unanticipated feedback loops. The actors are not simply trying to get their financial cut. They also use their involvement in these processes to open up different spaces of manoeuvre and reach, cultivate dependencies and obligations, and carve out new spaces of autonomous action. In other words, while every actor may be seeking to fill their own pockets, there are also more cloudy strivings at work.

While these cloudy strivings point to a kind of *doubleness*, a "both–and" approach to getting things done, we have a somewhat different notion of doubleness in mind here in terms of dealing with the constitutive inability of formal government institutions and processes to address the enormity of housing backlogs, jobs to be created, and basic services to be provided. Efforts to address these issues require sensitivity, knowledge and interventions on *both* molecular and macro-political scales. It requires a respect for how things get done on their own terms without abandoning an ethical commitment to how things could work differently as well. For interventions at one scale reverberate across others in ways that are difficult to predict but which do exert force.

Urban political interventions must simultaneously keep in view *both* the formal structures of government *and* insurgent mobilizations of resistance, *both* the public sphere *and* the intimate terrains of local practices and inhabitation. Such an approach requires a more *elastic* sense of time capable of tracking the implications of interventions as they weave their ways across various places and sectors, at different speeds and in different formats. As such, a conscious politics of experimentation always entails *imperfect* practices, those that will frequently miss their intended targets but, in this shift away from policy and economic targets, still set into motion cascading ramifications that can be steered and assessed.

Signposts

Across the rest of this book we attempt to elaborate a praxis of doubleness. In the following chapter we seek to outline the present and prospective urban conditions in which such doubleness will be situated and the exigencies at hand that require refreshed analytical and political tools. An essential manoeuvre in configuring tools that precipitate and choreograph multiple trajectories of impact across various networks of urban forces and institutions is to *re-describe* present conditions in ways that make visible the operations and potentials of what might already be taking place. Chapter 3 attempts to do just that through a reframing of what is considered to be habitable or not and also to revisit sites such as markets as contexts to suggest different practices of organizing the relationships between social and material flows. As that which *might be already there* suggests the simultaneous presence of multiple, contradictory tendencies, capacities and potentials that are not acknowledged, or that are actively repressed or occluded, or that simply take on forms of opacity as a means of distributing their influence across disparate terrain, chapter 4 takes up the concept of secretion. In this chapter, secretion itself entails a doubled play between leakage and secrecy, containment and diffusion, visibility and invisibility, relations and detachment.

Looking at the city as an assemblage of five disjointed operating systems – infrastructure, the economy, land, governance and cultural systems – in chapter 5 we chart the ways in which policy and political tools might be used to generate new forms of *resonance* among them. Any political and policy intervention will have resonances in a multiplicity of ways that hold the potential for specific culturally informed mobilization in concrete settings. Figuring out what the most powerful resonances might be is essential to forging a grounded, and therefore more successful, politics that can have reverberations well beyond the local. In chapter 6 we outline the possibilities of a radical praxis of experimentation. It intimates an expansive political repertoire that can accommodate and extend insurgent politics comprised of militant resistance as well as prefigurative development work to attend to urgent livelihood imperatives. At the same time, it is able to take in the dull, reformist, potentially reactionary work of bureaucratic rewiring, enhancement and consolidation as manifest in state institutions and the endless myriad co-producing formations that live somewhere betwixt and between the state, the market, civil society, academia and households. Finally, we draw the book to a close through a meditation on the power of story-telling as an act of city-making and re-description. It is also our story about how to inhabit prospective new urban worlds.

2
Precarious Now

In a music video entitled "Capture" that runs under four minutes, Baloji, the Congolese-Belgian musician-poet, offers a dense tapestry of almost all the constraints and potentials we invoked at the end of the last chapter. These include the coexistence of a colonial, neocolonial and bastardized present, reaching forward to circumscribe the future; the co-presence of abject poverty and cultural lyricism; the boundless capacity for pleasure and bodily enactments no matter the context or tragedy; and the inescapable effects of extractive economies driven along by the technological imperatives of the global mobile technology revolution. All these observations and much more are wrapped in glorious and dreamy musical cinematography as an expression of the track's insistence that "concrete utopias" are indeed imaginable and available. It is not possible to evoke the same affective resonance as Baloji's singular art, but in this chapter we present the contextual armature for the book to give the larger argument some grounding and depth of field.

Filip De Boeck's (2011a, 2011b, 2012; De Boeck and Baloji 2016) thoughtful excavation of Kinshasa's flows and fluxes suggests that precarity and uncertainty represent a material and psychic threat, but they may also provide an opportunity to reimagine and re-enchant the world. In other words, we cannot access an imaginary about alternative urban futures without confronting the violent impossibility of that future.

In this chapter we aim to foreground the scope of emergent change at a macro level by looking at the intersections between demographic, cultural, economic, technological and political shifts set against the imposing shadow of irrevocable environmental change. Invariably we remain on a macro plane because we are trying to situate the broader forces that impact upon and shape the rich emergent processes foregrounded by the rest of the book. We are also trying to capture the macro pressures and opportunities that connect Africa and Asia and in turn point to important comparative considerations.

Urban politics and development agendas seem particularly stuck at the moment. Both the United Nations' sustainable development goals (SDG) agenda, agreed to in September 2015, and the New Urban Agenda, adopted at Habitat III in October 2016, offer significant discursive opportunities to confront the multiple ways in which current urban development models are failing majorities. In formal policy arenas the predominant institutional reflex is to fall back on technocratic certainties wrapped in consensual politics (UNEP 2011).[1] This kind of discourse is particularly stark in the New Urban Agenda, which is meant to provide a reference point for urban policy and politics over the next two decades.

In the preceding chapter we intimated why simplistic top-down manoeuvres are bound to fail in their efforts to erase the constitutive indeterminacy of rapidly changing contexts. Here we underscore those conceptual claims with reference to data and trend analysis. In particular we want to foreground how cities are implicated by the confluences of a youthful labor force in Africa and Asia and a fading prospect of formal and stable employment against a backdrop of dramatic technological disruption. It is impossible to consider the changing nature of work without paying attention to the dramatic repositioning of the global economy through new centralities, intensified financialization and the growing influence of disruptive technologies.

It is impossible not to pay attention to smoldering political dissatisfaction within and beyond political establishments across the South and the North (Mason 2012). We are particularly interested in the territorial implications of these broader processes and how they generate unprecedented environmental and social pressures. These are pressures that can only be addressed through a radical reconsideration of localization and strategic regionalism.

Shifting sands: people, work and aspirations

During 2015, the United Nations provided a number of timeous updates on demographic, economic and environmental trends, undoubtedly to anchor the horse-trading that accompanied the negotiations around the SDGs, the 21st Conference of the Parties (COP) in Paris and the never-ending Doha trade negotiations under the aegis of the World Trade Organization. The *World Population Prospects* report (UN-DESA 2015a) projects that almost all demographic growth will be concentrated in Africa and Asia for the remainder of the twenty-first century. In contradistinction to Asia, Africa will retain an expanding demographic profile until the end of this century, whereas Asia is expected to level out from around 2060 onwards. A simple and stark way to put this is that, at present, 15 percent of the world population is African; by 2050 it will be 25 percent, and by 2100 above forty per cent (see table 2.1) This suggests a staggering socio-cultural transformation that neither the world nor Africa is fully prepared for. To ram this point home, we refer mainly to Africa's

Table 2.1 Population per world region

Major area	Population (millions)			
	2015	2030	2050	2100
World	7,349	8,501	9,725	11,213
Africa	1,186	1,679	2,478	4,387
Asia	4,393	4,923	5,267	4,889
Europe	738	734	707	646
Latin America and the Caribbean	634	721	784	721
Northern America	358	396	433	500
Oceania	39	47	47	71

Source: UN-DESA (2015a).

changing dynamics and place in the world, with cross-referencing to Asia.

One of the central arguments of this chapter is that urban areas will carry the impacts of the dramatic mismatch between a youthful demographic in Africa and Asia and the formal labor market. In light of the overall demographic shift for the remainder of the twenty-first century, it is not surprising that Africa has a much larger share of children (0–15 years) and youth (15–24), compared with other regions of the global South. Europe and much of the OECD are irrelevant in this discussion because their populations will effectively shrink over this time-frame, exacerbating the strains on welfare state provisions, especially pension and health systems. The UN Department of Economic and Social Affairs finds that:

> In Africa, children under age 15 account for 41 per cent of the population in 2015 and young persons aged 15 to 24 account for a further 19 per cent. Latin America and the Caribbean and Asia, which have seen greater declines in fertility, have smaller percentages of children (26 and 24 per cent, respectively) and similar percentages of youth (17 and 16 per cent, respectively). In total, these three regions are home to 1.7 billion children and 1.1 billion young persons in 2015. (UN-DESA 2015a: 7)

Youth unemployment is at a record high in the aftermath of the 2008 economic downturn, and there are very few prospects on the horizon that this condition will improve anytime soon (ILO 2013). However, what is more significant is that, even before the 2008 crash, the vast majority of the labor force in Africa and Asia, and even more so among the youth, was and remains trapped in precarious or what the ILO refers to as "vulnerable employment."[2]

There are two lenses through which to understand the scope and gravity of the current situation. First, the ILO provides a breakdown of the distribution of employment status by country income group. Since almost all low-income countries are in Africa and Asia, figure 2.1 is instructive. Second, the ILO also provides time series data (from 1991 to 2014) which show the percentage of wage and salaried employment as a share of total employment per world region,

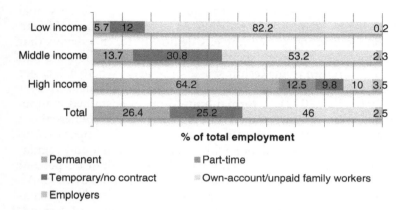

Figure 2.1 Distribution of employment status by country income groups
Source: ILO (2015).

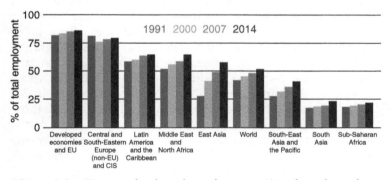

Figure 2.2 Wage and salaried employment (% of total employment), world and regions
Source: ILO (2014).

as reflected in figure 2.2. This data set demonstrates the phenomenal improvement in East Asia (incorporating China and Korea) and the modest if not negligible changes in South Asia (including India, Pakistan and Bangladesh) and Africa. South-East Asia and the Pacific represents a mid-point between these extremes (ILO 2015: 29).

The most important aspect of vulnerable employment is that of low and highly erratic incomes. For a poor household that cannot predict levels or frequency of income, it is essential to live as adaptively as possible. As research on South African public housing policy impacts demonstrate, this means that people could forego such public investment as housing and opt to return to makeshift shack settlements where it is easier to manage limited and irregular income flows (Huchzermeyer 2014; Ley 2012). A formal house implies sustained mainte-nance expenditure and consuming basic services (where those are provided) on a paid basis, apart from the imperative to "behave" in accordance with stipulated norms and regula-tions that apply to formal areas. For more than 60 percent of households in the urban areas of sub-Saharan Africa (SSA), formal living is simply not an option. But living in a perma-nent state of adaptation and makeshift is complex and demand-ing and involves enormous social effort.

But there is a broader, more pernicious implication as well. The large-scale prevalence of vulnerable employment also points to the problem of small tax bases, since government revenue tends to be derived from formal businesses and the income taxes associated with earning salaries above given thresholds. Data reported by Anton Cartwright (2015) graphi-cally demonstrates the minuscule resources available at a local level for public expenditure on a per capita basis in a sample of African cities. To put this in context, table 2.2 includes averages for three key Northern cities, although those figures include both local and national expenditures.[3] It is obvious that it is impossible to address the vast and growing need for essential services in most African cities, with South Africa being the primary exception in this sample.

With these truncated expenditure levels in mind, it is oppor-tune to reiterate data on slum prevalence and the underly-ing scale of infrastructure deficits against the larger story of continued urban expansion in Africa and Asia. With the following data we want to demonstrate that it is simply not useful or productive to approach questions of the right to the city and access to urban essentials as simply a matter of political will or political economy. There are indeed hard resource constraints that limit the institutional possibilities for urban governments in the poorer parts of the global South. Table 2.3 sets the context of projected increases in urban population by world region, and table 2.4 demonstrates the

Table 2.2   Select African cities by population size and local fiscal capacity

	Population (million)	Local fiscal capacity (US$ per person per year)
Dakar	2.8	22.4
Addis Ababa	2.8	91.0
Accra	2.1	12.5
Kampala	1.4	29.2
Kigali	0.8	39.8
Dar es Salaam	2.9	29.4
Johannesburg	3.9	702.0
Cape Town	3.7	727.3
Maputo	1.1	43.8
London		14,799
New York		6,770
Seoul		6,901

Source: Created with data from Cartwright (2015).

Table 2.3   Urban population, total and per world region, 1950–2050

Major area	Urban population (millions)				
	1950	1990	2014	2030	2050
World	746	2,285	3,880	5,058	6,339
Africa	32	197	455	770	1,339
Asia	245	1,036	2,064	2,752	3,313
Europe	283	506	545	567	581
Latin America and the Caribbean	69	314	496	595	674
Northern America	110	213	292	340	390
Oceania	8	19	27	34	42

Source: UN-DESA (2015b: 38).

changes in slum prevalence between 2000 and 2012, with a 2007 mid-point. This reflects that the vast majority of urban dwellers in SSA coexist in makeshift conditions, while a third are classified as such in South-East Asia and South Asia. Given the scale of poverty in South Asia, the trend for SSA is indeed

Table 2.4   Percentage slum prevalence in regions of the global South, 2014 and 2005

Region	Slum prevalence, 2005 (%)	Slum prevalence, 2014 (%)
Africa	53	49
Southern Asia	40	31
South-East Asia	34	27
East Asia	33	25
West Asia	26	25
Latin America & the Caribbean	25	20

Source: Mo Ibrahim Foundation (2015: 46).

profound. Our interest in the (problematic) aggregate data on slum prevalence is not so much the actual percentages; rather, it is to underscore that the norm in terms of urban living and social reproduction consists of a set of conditions that cannot be thought of in neat, ordered modern categories. Nor are they susceptible to systematic modernization efforts to achieve formal human settlements and supporting infrastructures.

Given the scale of urban growth in these geographies over the next thirty to fifty years, it is essential to make our peace with this makeshift reality and horizon line. We think the findings and arguments of Sylvy Jaglin (2014) and Asef Bayat (2010) are particularly helpful for doing so. Jaglin demonstrates that, amid large-scale deficits in formal service delivery in SSA, a rich and multivalent system of compensation pulses to support everyday lives and livelihoods. These systems are hybrids of formal service delivery processes provided by the state, formal private delivery mechanisms for those who can afford them, informal private delivery agents who respond to the day-by-day consumption rhythms of the urban poor, intermediary actors that connect supply and demand, and various categories of place-based collectives that take charge of the institutional requirements to ensure a modicum of service delivery. As formal and informal investments shift and recalibrate, these hybrid systems are continually reconfigured, representing the makeshift, adaptive pulse of the city.

For Bayat (2010), the sociological character of these processes is best understood as the "quiet encroachment of the ordinary" casting its shadow and influence over the formal city. In other words, city-building is predominantly an organic and quasi-state affair, hinting at vast systems of social organization, exchange, oversight, regulation, violence, reciprocity and continual recalibration – aspects of sociality we explore in much greater depth in the following two chapters, given its constitutive importance. Once one accepts that the scale of informality as a mode of urbanization is insurmountable for states in poorer countries, and that urban residents are the primary builders of the city, then our conceptual vocabulary has to shift away from simply accounting for structural drivers of urban inequality to providing an understanding of how things get done amid overlapping and dense social relations.

Moving away from the makeshift dynamics of daily service delivery and exchange, it is equally important to bring the larger question of infrastructure systems into the frame. By recognizing the prevalence and complexity of compensatory systems that structure access to essential services (water, sanitation, waste, transport and energy), it does not mean that broader political claims for universal access to the grid (or micro grids) should be eschewed or ignored. On the contrary, since makeshift service delivery hybrids do connect into and co-constitute the aggregate urban infrastructural architecture, it is essential to understand the political economy of infrastructure availability, provision, expansion and potential access (Jaglin 2014; McFarlane 2011; Swilling 2016).

And, indeed, across the global South, infrastructural investments have become the mainstay of counter-cyclical macro-economic moves in an era of economic slow-down and austerity (Scoones et al. 2015). Typically these programs are conceptualized and planned in muscular nationalist or transnational terms, but increasingly the connection between infrastructure investment and agglomeration dynamics is being recognized and pursued (UN-DESA 2013). In this articulation, there is a strategic political opportunity to make claims that seek to expand access to essential urban services and reorient the metabolic dynamics of urban systems in more efficient directions. We return to this theme in later chapters (5 and 6). So,

	LIC Africa	Other	MIC Africa	Other
Paved road density	34	134	284	461
Total road density	150	29	381	106
Density of fixed-line telephones (subscribers per 1,000 people)	10	78	142	252
Density of mobile telephones (subscribers per 1,000 people)	55	86	277	557
Density of internet connections (subscribers per 100 people)	2	3.2	8	235
Electrical generating capacity (MW per 1 million people)	37	326	293	648
Access to electricity (% of households with access)	16	41	37	88
Water (% of households with access)	60	72	82	91
Sanitation (% of households with access)	34	51	53	82

Figure 2.3 Infrastructure endowments for African LICs/MICs[4] compared to other global regions
Source: Created with data from AfDB (2013) and Yepes et al. (2009).

with these links in mind, let us consider some of the highline data on infrastructure.

A starting point is the scale of infrastructure investment deficits and how this ties in with financing models that regard urban majorities as unbankable, rendering investment packages unaffordable for most urban areas in Africa and Asia (Pieterse and Hyman 2014). Unsurprisingly, the global infrastructure challenge is experienced more severely in the least developed countries of the global South. In aggregate terms, the US$0.8–0.9 trillion annual investment meets only 45 percent of the requirements of low- and middle-income countries that have an estimated US$1 trillion infrastructure financing gap[5] (World Bank 2012). Put differently, this level of investment needs to increase to approximately US$1.8–2.3 trillion per year by 2020 to address the massive backlog and cope with future demand (Bhattacharya et al. 2012).

Table 2.5 Infrastructure investment levels and shortcomings for world regions of the global South

Region	Need ($bn)	Actual spend ($bn)	Spend as % of GDP	Financing gap ($bn)
Latin America[6]	81.2	43.5	1.9	37.7
East Asia	406.7	207.0	7.2	199.7
South Asia	191.1	46.0	4.6	145.1
Middle East & North Africa	78.5	43.8	6.9	22.7
Sub-Saharan Africa	93.3	45.3	7.1	48.0

Source: World Bank (2012).

Table 2.5 reflects the severe underinvestment in infrastructure across the global South, broken down by region. The data demonstrate the scale of the deficits, which are particularly acute in Asia and Africa.

It is crucial to appreciate that the issue is not simply a question of adequate finance but also a matter of affordability. Furthermore, from an effective government perspective, it includes as well the imperative of an institutional platform conducive to extending and operating effective infrastructure systems. Affordability is connected to the policy imperative to achieve cost recovery, which in turn translates into the "user-pays" principle. Noting that approximately half of African households live below the U$1.25 per day poverty level and another 30 percent (246 million) find themselves surviving below the $2.50 a day threshold, it is clear why the World Bank concludes that Africans are simply too poor to justify large-scale investments for rolling out infrastructure networks and basic services:

> Most African households live on very modest budgets and spend more than half of their resources on food. The average African household has a budget of no more than $180 per month; urban households are about $100 per month better off than rural households.... To test the affordability of utility services priced at a level sufficient to allow the utilities to

recover their costs, we calculated the percentage of urban households that would need to spend more than 5 per cent of their income to purchase a subsistence level of any given utility service. The finding is that the countries fall into three groups. In most countries, between one- and two-thirds of the urban population would face difficulties in covering the cost of service. In eight countries, at least 70 per cent of urban households would be unable to afford a monthly expenditure of $10 for water or electricity. Only in the remaining seven countries would most urban households be able to afford a monthly expenditure sufficient to allow the utility to meet its costs. (Banerjee et al. 2009: 4–5)

It would be a misreading simply to present the lack of infrastructure finance as a matter of poverty or low household incomes. Infrastructure investors use complex and expansive criteria to determine the risk profile of countries and regions (Pieterse and Hyman 2014). Because of the limited extent of effective decentralization in SSA, the absence of fully transparent and accountable public accounts, the haphazard regulatory environment, the potential for corruption and rent-seeking, and many other dynamics, African countries are typically considered "high risk," and this makes finance capital even more expensive (AfDB 2013). Also, the expected rate of return, depending on the type of project, is higher.

These dynamics essentially mean that it is impossible in the current operating environment of globalized infrastructure finance systems to raise the requisite capital for investments to achieve city-wide infrastructural networks. This is irrespective of the fact that almost all governments have signed up to the pledges of the SDGs that would require an infrastructural revolution to ensure the level of access to basic services that are set out as targets. It is too soon to determine whether the emergence of new players such as the BRICS Development Bank and other Asia-based investors will change the nature of the game, but, since they operate within the same paradigmatic framework as the World Bank, it is unlikely.

Since the urban majority is largely beyond the financial calculations of the mainstream infrastructure delivery system, it is essential to confront the implications of delivery systems that can cater only to the needs of those who are bankable – i.e., formal businesses, government agencies, the middle classes and the elites. Since formal business sectors are essentially a blend of local and international firms, their infrastructural and building requirements are in line with what is considered most modern, creative, connected and recognizable in the globalized symbolic economy of convenience and interoperability. The consumption preferences of the middle classes are equally in step with global suburban norms for educational, religious, shopping and mobility convenience, which fuels the demand for gated suburbs, anchored by business parks, shopping malls, golf courses, exclusive clubs, elite hotels and extravagant places of worship (Cruz 2004). Crucially, these consumer yearnings also fuel much larger aspirational systems where an excluded urban majority, attempting to do anything to compensate for their marginalization – such as incurring large levels of indebtedness or building in environmentally precarious areas – ends up reinforcing the hegemony of inappropriate and unaffordable urban infrastructural landscapes.

On the back of the decent economic growth rates in Africa and Asia over the past decade and a half, these consumption preferences have clearly been the dominant signature of formal expansion of the built environment as driven by "accepted" real-estate business models. It is these models which, in turn, capture the bulk of the limited resources for infrastructure, public space and social facilities. The material manifestation of a few decades of this kind of investment in the built environment is of course in evidence all over South-East Asia – e.g., Bangkok, Manila, Jakarta, and the emerging Indian cities – in gargantuan shopping malls, exaggerated religious venues, high-rise condominiums, golf courses and polo fields, often encircled by massive ring-road systems to ferry the 4x4-driving middle-classes between leisure spaces, home and work. A variation on this theme is the self-contained gated estates at the edges of these large cities, forging the promise of opting out of the real city (Simone 2014).

If we consider the transformation of skylines across African capital cities over the past decade, Asia is seemingly prefiguring what the tiny African middle classes are aspiring to, even if the official imaginary is the cleansed cityscapes of Dubai and Singapore. A group of retired Singaporean planners are currently working on a masterplan for Kinshasa and are positioning themselves to render their services far and wide across the continent as policy "hit men."[7]

In summary, the bifurcated urban landscapes of Asia and Africa that instantiate parallel worlds (connected with secret passageways) between those who have normalized access to modern infrastructural conveniences and those who have continually to hustle, pilfer and labor to resecure a measure of access to energy, water and information on a daily basis will become even more stark in the near future. Public resources earmarked for network infrastructure systems will increasingly be captured by urban elites and middle classes whose standards for "quality access" are rising in tandem with their disposable incomes but always lagging behind their aspirations. The fiscal effect of this dynamic is that fewer resources are available to address the profound lack of infrastructural backbone that should be inserted into popular neighborhoods and large hunks of the city. Intensifying economic uncertainty and volatility – enduring aftershocks of the 2008 crisis – will simply reinforce these tendencies, because infrastructure capital will become more risk averse and governments will feel compelled to buttress fragile middle classes with even grander schemes to ensure a desirable form of urbanism for these elites. The dramatic uptake in popularity and investment in "new town" models, spearheaded across much of Asia, is the most visceral indicator of these processes (Watson 2013). There are two dimensions of these new town models that we think are worthy of closer attention: the ubiquity of ICT-based smart urban management gadgets and the search for enclave living that is environmentally benign and reflective of the new urbanism mantra: live, play and work in the same space.

Urban scenarios

We concur with much of the eruption in critical infrastructure studies that demonstrates the social implications of these processes of splintering and fragmentation of the urban landscape (Amin 2014; Chattopadhyay 2012; Howe et al. 2015; Larkin 2013). At the same time we think it is important to use the mainstream preferences for the gradual roll-out of modern engineered infrastructure systems (taken-for-granted status quo) as a *device* against which alternative possibilities can be plotted. This can instigate a more incisive critique than simply pointing out the unjust nature of mesmerizing "new town" schemes that seek to aggregate high-tech modern infrastructure solutions for the elite. But, more importantly, it can also make room for a grounded political economy discussion on how different spatial-infrastructural dynamics *coexist* in order to rebalance power and cultural influence over time, as well as instigate active political contestations about competing rates of return on scarce public investment resources (see figure 2.4). We return to these potentialities in greater detail in chapter 5.

Figure 2.4 sets out four potential scenarios in a highly stylized manner to capture the possible investment *directions* of urban landscapes across African and Asian cities. The status quo scenario reflects a mindless continuation of the predominant trends that characterize contemporary urbanization, as laid bare in the previous section. It reflects the stalemate between inept (or competent) but, ultimately, unresponsive urban governments held in place by powerful political machines

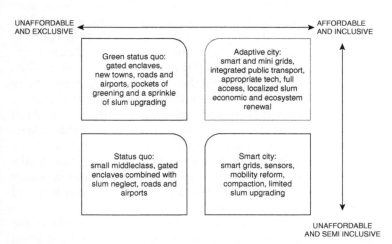

Figure 2.4 Stylized scenarios for competing urban investment approaches
Source: Adapted from Pieterse (2015b).

that seek to guarantee their sources of accumulation, patronage and control. In this scenario, urban politics and management is characterized by nothing but more of the same, underpinned by a lack of responsiveness to exogenous pressures or localized dissent or disdain.

It is obviously easier to perpetuate these patterns in more authoritarian societies, but it might be just as easy in democratic contexts where urban majorities are so used to getting by on their own terms, despite the state, that they cannot really be bothered to embark on sustained political mobilization. What would be the point? In most cases the reality would be a reproduction of the status quo combined with a battery of urban reforms to ensure a degree of slum regularization, land tenure reform, upgrading and infrastructural investment. However, because of small budgets, cited earlier, the number of households and communities that can be reached to advance these policy goals in a given fiscal year is almost negligible, but, even though there is little substantive follow-through, at least the political elites can be seen to be saying all the "right" pro-poor things. It is in such contexts that apolitical and celebratory discourses of informality can be unhelpful and counter-productive.

Most importantly, these cities are stuck with an imaginary whereby, over time, as the economy grows and state coffers swell, modern infrastructure will systematically carpet the city, eliminating the drudgery and chaos of pre-modern survival practices and habits. In this mindset, the real, makeshift, emergent and adaptive city of the urban majority is essentially a cancer that needs to be excised through modern planning, infrastructure standards and standardized regulation. And, as we know, this conceit is a recipe for arbitrary slum clearance, evictions, surveillance and generalized neglect of the most vulnerable households and citizens in the city. Sadly, this remains the norm for far too many communities in countless cities across Asia and Africa (Davis 2006; Mansuri and Rao 2014; Neiva et al. 2012).

Moving on, the next green status quo scenario reflects the recent tendency to create an enabling environment for international investors who wish to bypass the messy, opaque and makeshift city by building new towns and cities on peripheral greenfield sites. Typically, these real-estate propositions offer high-tech and environmentally sensitive (architecture and engineering) environments from which an emerging middle class and the elites can run the city. Of course, more often than not, these enclaves are extraordinary globalized spaces where the staff of multinational corporations, multilateral development agencies and their local counterparts find common cultural ground in which to operate, live and work. Increasingly, globalized norms about green building standards and other sustainable infrastructure systems are in evidence, adding to the global cultural currency of mobile elites.

The advantage of adopting expensive cutting-edge green construction standards for these upper-end real-estate propositions is that they offer political elites an opportunity to present a progressive green face to the world without doing much to address the deeper systems of exclusion and inequality that mark the makeshift city.[8] In the real world, this kind of urbanism can be only a marginal part of the first scenario (status quo), because the share of private real-estate development backed up with mortgage finance is hardly ever more than 5 to 10 percent of the total new stock added to these cities (CAHF 2015), especially in sub-Saharan Africa. Yet, their symbolic and distortionary effects should not be underestimated, for they can be a powerful green foil to allow for the prolongation of the status quo. Since they chime with the policy yearning to start with a green slate, so to speak, these proposals can prove immensely seductive for policy-makers who are impatient with the effort involved in dealing with the makeshift city.

The third scenario – the smart city – reflects the increasingly assertive agendas of private-sector actors such as IBM, Siemens, Cisco and many others in the debate on how best to address the wide-ranging and competing demands placed on contemporary urban management (Greenfield 2013; Swilling 2016). As with all technocratic fantasies, these interests (and their think-tank apologists) operate on the assumption that the problem with the city is a lack of systematic information, resources and human capability to understand what is going on. Corrective measures are therefore methodically implemented. Granted, this is an important part of the general functioning of cities. But the historically produced spatialities of particular path dependencies that manifest in splintered landscapes, deep spatial inequality and environmental abuse are not simply a function of information asymmetries or weak institutions. They are the very stuff of captured urban politics, exclusionary economics and unequal power relations at multiple scales of intensity.

Importantly, almost all variations of the mainstream smart city agenda are aligned with what can be considered the progressive language of mainstream urban development policy as exemplified in the discourse of UN-Habitat and echoed by UNEP, OECD, the World Bank, and so on. A recent assertion by Joan Clos works well as a prop for what this agenda promotes:

> Good cities do not come about by accident. The prerequisites for a good city are broad community consensus, long-standing political determination and sound urban planning which, over the course of time, engender urban environments that can provide wellbeing and security to their inhabitants, guarantee the supply of water, energy and food, and promote a compact and diverse urban structure in which innovation, trade and economic prosperity are encouraged. It definitively protects...urban communal space in which individual rights and opportunities are most respected. *Results like these have never been achieved through spontaneous urbanization, nor by the adoption of wrong-sighted decisions.* (Clos 2014, emphasis added)

There is indeed a very powerful mantra that does the rounds in almost every high-profile urban development conference where the great and the good from business, academia, think tanks, governments and multilateral agencies gather to deliberate on the future of the urban species or cities: a compact, mixed-use urban fabric, interlaced with ample green public space, and a vibrant public life rooted in a growing creative economy is the very stuff of the good city to which everyone should aspire.[9] And, most importantly, it can be designed, planned and regulated into existence. If gotten right, it offers an endless revenue stream because it will spur a diversified and resilient economy driven forward by people and investors who simply cannot get enough of such cool cities, especially if their kids can get into "good" schools and there is a modicum of safety, not just in the gated enclaves but also on the streets in general. The typical reference points are Barcelona, Stockholm and other Nordic cities and a few outliers in the US. Smart city proponents make the seductive promise that ICT-based algorithmic governance can indeed deliver this "switched-on" cosmopolitan urbanism, irrespective of geographic region or the extent of deeply entrenched problems. Within this approach, arguments to promote better mobility and effective public transport, as well as smart slum upgrading, can all find a place. There is no reason to see the needs and wants of the urban middle class as being in competition with the urgent demands of the urban majority. Significantly, a careful read of the New Urban Agenda points one to this kind of vision but, importantly, underpinned with a rights-based conceptualization of democratic reform and achievement.

However, the smart city promise requires massive upfront financial investment to ensure the ICT hardware that is a prerequisite for the application of the myriad smart city innovations. But therein lies the rub, because in most cities in Asia and Africa this literally means having to weigh up the relative cost–benefit analysis of investing in a desperately needed sewage treatment plant versus fibre cabling. This dynamic is particular acute in India, where the president becomes the leading proponent of accelerating the establishment of smart cities. Upper-middle-income cities can probably accommodate most, but for cities with 40 to 60 percent of the population below the poverty line, trapped in precarious occupations, there are hard trade-offs to be made, especially when the ICT backbone will invariably prioritize the enclave estates that offer the investment landing strips for international capital. Later in the book we return to ways in which the potential of ICT-based urban actions can play a vital catalytic role in enabling what we call for: adaptive cities.

The final scenario – the adaptive city – hinges on an opportunistic reading of urban possibility as cities become the theatre in which the contradictions between the declining industrial era clash with the imperatives of the emergent sustainability era, as we explore in the next section. In this scenario, the disruptive potential and power of relatively low-cost ICT investments are treated in relation to an enlarged agenda for how to increase access to essential services driven by localized economic systems, enhance the capacities of the public realm, and provide affordable and safe public transport as well as genuine security. At its core, this scenario envisages a balance of forces that can reshape urban investment agendas so that the lives and livelihoods of urban majorities, not the accumulation imperatives of urban elites, are at the center. This scenario stylizes the political and cultural agenda we are putting forward in this book. We therefore devote chapters 5 and 6 to elaborating on this scenario and now move to the final section of this chapter, which sets out the conceptual underpinning of the adaptive city that is yet to come.

Urban transitions and technological waves

A powerful prejudicial undertow characterizes outside opinions about the inability of most cities in Asia and Africa to deal decisively with slum urbanism and what is perceived as non-existent planning. This perspective shines through most clearly in reportage accounts about the teeming slums in the megacities of the third world, held in place by a blend of corruption and authoritarianism (Iweala 2016). The unspoken question is this: If London and Paris could solve the problems of slums one hundred years ago, why is it so hard for the developing world to get this right, especially in view of accumulated knowledge and much greater economic resources? Of course, this perspective fails to consider long-term historical impacts of colonial plunder and the deliberate underdevelopment of countries and cities that have to be kept in an economically subservient and supplier relationship with former colonies (Davis 2006).

There is also little regard for the fact that the rate of urban growth and the overall numbers of people considered to be urban dwellers are fundamentally different during the second wave of urbanization as compared to the first, as explicated in great detail by Satterthwaite (2007). Most importantly, there is a fundamental disregard for the relationship between urbanization, technological change and modes of economic development. The technology historian Carlota Perez (2009, 2013, 2014a, 2014b) provides a useful schematic account of

the changing patterns of economy, technology and governmental policy from the onset of industrialization in the mid-
eighteenth century up to the contemporary moment, marked
as it is with uncertainty, incalculable risk and promise
(Appadurai 2015). At the core of Perez's exploratory work
on what the current phase of technological disruption might
mean is the following analytical frame:

> Technological advance might appear as a continuous process,
> but in fact the world has gone through five technological
> upheavals since the Industrial Revolution in the late 1770s.
> Each of these shifts (see figure [2.5]) brought with it a whole
> set of powerful new industries and infrastructures – canals,
> railways, electricity, highways, telecoms and the internet –
> which have enabled a quantum leap in productivity and quality
> in all industries.... The Industrial Revolution introduced
> mechanisation, changing the role of skills in production, and
> initiated the era of British power. The following railway age
> led to the rise of the educated and entrepreneurial middle
> classes. The third, from the end of the 19th century, was the
> first globalisation based on empires and saw the emergence
> of Germany and the US as challengers of British hegemony.
> Subsequently, the US led the age of the automobile and mass
> production, bringing the American way of life to the working
> classes and increasing the role of the State in economic stabil-
> ity. The current information and telecommunications technol-
> ogy (ICT) revolution has enabled the second globalisation;
> yet its full transformative impact on society is still to be defined.
> (Perez 2014a: 20)

As figure 2.5 illustrates, each technological era is linked to a
surge in speculative investments that invariably balloon into
a speculative bubble that bursts. Once the crash happens, the
state intervenes and an era of widespread dissemination and
growth follows within which the new technologies become
the new mainstream, embedded in profound cultural and
institutional changes, until the pattern gets disrupted by a
new cycle of innovative entrepreneurs pushing at the gates.
It is relevant to set Perez's argument alongside the demographic transition defined as the first wave of urbanization:
in 1750 the North was 10 percent urban (15 million people),
but two hundred years later, in 1950, this figure had risen to

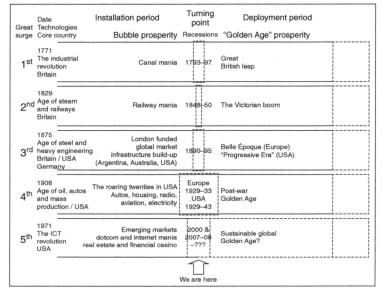

Great surge	Date Technologies Core country	Installation period Bubble prosperity	Turning point Recessions	Deployment period "Golden Age" prosperity
1st	1771 The industrial revolution Britain	Canal mania	1793–97	Great British leap
2nd	1829 Age of steam and railways Britain	Railway mania	1848–50	The Victorian boom
3rd	1875 Age of steel and heavy engineering Britain / USA Germany	London funded global market infrastructure build-up (Argentina, Australia, USA)	1890–95	Belle Époque (Europe) "Progressive Era" (USA)
4th	1908 Age of oil, autos and mass production / USA	The roaring twenties in USA Autos, housing, radio, aviation, electricity	Europe 1929–33 USA 1929–43	Post-war Golden Age
5th	1971 The ICT revolution USA	Emerging markets dotcom and internet mania real estate and financial casino	2000 & 2007–08 –???	Sustainable global Golden Age?

We are here

Figure 2.5   The historical record: bubble prosperities, recessions and golden ages
Source: Perez (2013: 11).

52 percent (423 million people) (Satterthwaite 2007). The harsh impacts of urbanization were unevenly felt, as the pains-taking sociological insights of Friedrich Engels (1845)[10] remind us. But, as political opposition grew, there were considerable resources in these metropolitan economies to undertake the necessary infrastructural investments which, in turn, provided the mainstay of a working-class movement seeking political power in the first half of the twentieth century (Mikkelsen 2005). It was on the back of these mobilizations that the welfare state ideology and investments achieved spectacular material effect in the post-World War II era (Mason 2015), when the majority world started to emerge from the iron fist of colonial rule (Nederveen Pieterse 2010). Of course, the decolonial period hardly translated into economic freedom or autonomy, nor did we see the dilution of Western influence in the routine political and economic governance of these territories – to disastrous effect in most African and a large number of Asian countries (Slater 2004).

As the Cold War dynamics set in with full force through the 1950s to the 1970s, the autonomous capacities of so-called post-colonies were thoroughly undermined. This unloosened over time but took on a much more pernicious form in the 1980s with financial conditionalities premised on fundamentalist neoliberal dogmas. This situation slowly thawed toward the end of the 1990s, when Asian counterpoints started to gain serious political, economic and ideological traction. The collapse of the official communist world provided spectacular impetus to the dilution of Western hegemony and opened up a radically multipolar and conflictual reconfiguration of development agendas and pathways. Materially, however, it has proved much harder to disentangle economic interdependencies and strangleholds, especially as the power of multinational corporations has grown disproportionately since the 1980s (Mitchell 2008).

To put the dynamic of urbanization in Africa and Asia into perspective, it is important to contrast this dynamic with the first wave of urbanization. In 1950, as Europe went beyond the 50 percent urban tipping point to reach 51.5 percent (283 million people), Africa was 14 percent urbanized (32 million), compared with 17.5 percent (245 million) in Asia and 63.9 percent (110 million) in North America (UN-DESA 2015b: 40). It is of course striking that, already at this point, Asia had three times more urban dwellers than North America and only slightly fewer than Europe. Fast forward to 2020, when Asia will reach its 50 percent urbanization mark (2.5 billion people), and 2035, when Africa is projected to be half urbanized (900 million people). Clearly, Africa and Asia have to manage a complex demographic transition from rural to predominantly urban in one-third of the time that it took Europe, and on an unprecedented scale. Furthermore, Africa and Asia have to achieve this without the benefit of blood subsidies that slavery and colonialism afforded the imperial powers to extract value and achieve economic dominance.

The point of these statistical juxtapositions is simply to underscore that it is a historical absurdity to expect African or Asian countries simply to replicate the "knowledge" and institutions of the global North to "solve" pernicious problems associated with slum urbanism. The same structural dynamics that made it possible for Europe then to garner the resources,

knowledge and technology to make public health advance-
ments are still at play in the contemporary world, fuelling a
political ideology that renders universal access to basic services,
welfare and a universal basic income as lunacy. The ideological edifice of this power dynamic is neoliberal capitalism
(Douzinas 2014). This conclusion is obviously a blatant over-
simplification and flattening of vast historical specificities and
conjunctures. However, in a polemical vein, it is crucial to
shine a light on the long-term effects of ideological assumptions that operate on the basis of historical amnesia and
Eurocentrism (Howe et al. 2015). That said, we are interested
in fashioning an approach that is historically alert, spatially
informed and anticipatory of new possibilities on the horizon.

Crisis, disruption and possibility

The most salient point from Perez's work (2013, 2014a) is
that economic and technological change is neither easy nor
conflict-free. On the contrary, it represents profound social
upheavals and, once the state responds to the crisis and presages societal deployment of the new technological era, profound social-cultural and institutional changes have to take
root to embed the "new era." In the analysis of Perez and
others, the full disruptive impacts of the 2008 financial crisis
have been softened by the unprecedented bailouts of finance
capital, resulting in low growth, worsening inequality and a
dramatic increase in the wealth of the top 1 percent (Mason
2015; Perez 2014b). A growing number of analysts (Mason
2015; Rifkin 2014; Srnicek and Williams 2015) are in fact
suggesting that this crisis could spell the end of neoliberal
capitalism and the painful and uneven emergence of a new
post-capitalist era if we are open enough to consider the
possibility of disjunctive change.

Paul Mason's analysis is most consistent with the perspective of Carlota Perez. As a dyed-in-the-wool British Marxist,
he comes to the startling conclusion that ICT displaces the
role of the working class as the driver of transformative change
and suggests that "info-capitalism has created a new agent
of change in history: the educated and connected human
being" (Mason 2015). This human being forms an integral

and dynamic part of a network, echoing the notion of "networked individualism" as theorized by Manuel Castells (2014). This is not surprising, given that Mason is a veteran analyst of the recent social upheavals across Western Europe – Turkey, Spain, Greece, Portugal and further afield, as in Brazil and Tunisia – which were enabled, sustained and adapted through social media and the virtual public sphere (Mason 2012). In Mason's reading, it is not simply about new forms of social protest and political agitating but also about the material possibility of different kinds of economic and social interactions that are consistent with the emerging discourse on the so-called sharing economy.

However, Mason does not think this is where the post-capitalist economy will spring from. Rather, it will be connected with the new technological breakthroughs that will flow from the radical interactions between nano-, bio-, neuro-, green and digital technologies that, in turn, will result in gene-splicing, communication devices embedded in the body, driverless vehicles, and so on (Bratton 2016). As the complementary analysis of Srnicek and Williams (2015) suggests, the future can be anticipated as marked by the need for fewer workers on account of large-scale automation and therefore the possibility of a universal leisure society that is optimized for the higher pursuits of culture, aesthetics, love and justice.[11] In these books, the reason why these prospective futures are not being understood or seized is because the left is pathologically fixated on structural constraints and the impossibility of collective action based on ideological and cultural diversity. Douzinas captures this critique presciently:

> [Left] philosophers cannot respond to the political and social upheaval because the epoch of resistance is still too new for theory to catch up. Or, is this enduring melancholy the result of a certain theoretical and political sclerosis of theoretical radicals? Failure, defeat, persecution and the accompanying paranoia have marked the left. It is true that the left has lost a lot: a unified theory, the working class as political subject, the promised inexorable forward movement of history, planned economy as alternative to capitalism.... In psychoanalytical theory, mourning a love object is necessary and liberating, while melancholy is the result of a failed and incomplete period of grief. (Douzinas 2014: 82)

A number of urban theorists have echoed this sentiment and point to the urgent need to be less obsessed with an endless rediscovery of differentiated processes of neoliberalization but, rather, *also* explore grounded and speculative alternatives that can animate and stitch together a plethora of diverse and divergent molecular experiments (Amin and Thrift 2013; Ferguson 2010; Inam 2014; Mbembe 2015; Tonkiss 2014). It is important to carry the following rumination of Jim Ferguson into the rest of the book: "But what if politics is really not about expressing indignation or denouncing the powerful? What if it is, instead, about getting what you want? Then we progressives must ask: what do we want? This is a quite different question (and a far more difficult question) than: what are we against?" (Ferguson 2010: 167).

In many ways, this book is a partial answer to this question by two old dogs who have been in the game too long – having worked across diverse and conflicting institutional settings of the city but remain unshakably wedded to a politics of freedom, autonomy, pleasure, justice, experimentation and aspiration. However, we do not think it is possible to have a substantive answer without addressing the style of politics and institutional weaving that goes along with figuring out the substantive meat of what we want, or what the city desires. At the outset of this experiment we thought that four aspects are probably at the heart of an anticipatory politics for the city: an engagement with technological change; a belief in walking the street and understanding the affective game of everyday urbanism; confronting the institutional formats of the state, market and civil society organizations; and promoting a passion for experimentation to forge new concepts and imaginaries that can anchor and accelerate new practices. Yet, apart from the idea of learning through experimentation, none of these dimensions of where we could go helps all that much with how to bridge the divide between the precarious now and possible futures.

In this regard, the explorations of different political approaches to effecting purposive green transitions in general (Scoones et al. 2015) and at the urban scale (Allen et al. 2016) are instructive. Scoones and his colleagues differentiate between four narratives of green transformation or diagnosis: technocratic, marketized, state-led and citizen-led. The technocratic approach refers to approaches and perspectives which assume that we can deploy technological innovations to address the environmental limits of the current economic growth model by decarbonizing production and consumption and delinking resource consumption per unit of economic output from growth. More enlightened versions of this frame envisage a commitment to a global public goods or commons agenda as the fundamental political driver of sufficient investment in bringing these technologies to scale.

Unsurprisingly, the marketized story line seeks to use the price mechanism as the primary driver of change. Here, the core argument of environmental economists is heeded and negative environmental and social externalities are appropriately priced to create the necessary momentum for green entrepreneurs and investment funds to come into their own. This is the new generation of venture capitalists that will drive the speculative bubble in green technology as envisaged in the schema of Perez (2013) and as illustrated in figure 2.5. If one considers the dramatic increase in the growth of renewable energy investments over the past five years, it seems as if this approach is gaining traction, at least in the energy domain (Byrd and Matthewman 2014). However, as a mature literature tells us, markets cannot be disembodied from the state and society (Easterling 2014; Gupta and Sivaramakrishnan 2012; Mazzucato 2015) but, rather, demand active state action and, always, cultural embedding.

The most consoling narrative for the old left is of course the state-led perspective. Essentially this approach sees the state as the primary catalyst of a sustained transition toward a green economy. The assumption is that an investment program into sustainable infrastructure (Pollalis et al. 2012), combined with active regulation and taxation instruments, will lead to a more far-reaching shift in the formal economy to invest in new technologies that will see a reduction in resource requirements, substitute non-renewable inputs with renewable ones, as well as non-biodegradable with degradable ones, reduce waste and pollution, and restore biodiversity and ecosystems services (UN-DESA 2013). Furthermore, there is purported scope to introduce suitable social policies to minimize the fallout for labor as these transitions work themselves through the economy over time.

In contradistinction to the three narratives, the final one is skeptical of top-down impositions and sees the only viable approach to a societal transformation as one that comes from below, from citizens and popular aspirations. The stronger versions of this approach are rooted in a sharp analysis of power that sees state business elites as the primary problem, not the harbingers of solutions. In fact, given that these elites are fundamental to the unsustainable and unjust status quo, they have to be exposed, delegitimized and removed through an insistence on fundamentally alternative economic models based on, for example, degrowth and solidarity-based economic and exchange relations. Overlapping with state-led narratives, this perspective is typically rooted in a rights-based political perspective. This is an understanding of rights as something won through tough struggles against the forces that nullify the right to water, or food, or energy, or meaningful work.

It is striking that this neat social science typology immediately feels inadequate to grasp fully how the contemporary times of deep crisis and uncertainty can be deployed to concretize an adaptive urbanism agenda. The sheer scale of technological innovation required to address the dramatic imperatives of resource decoupling, decarbonization and the restoration of biodiversity in the processes of production and consumption points to the role of public–private research and development coalitions. Similarly, the volume of soft regulation and anticipation that will have to be borne by the state is undisputable. And it is equally obvious that, unless popular culture and mediated aspirations find different resonances through a social enactment of new patterns and forms of consumption, there is hardly any impetus for technological innovation or politically charged regulation. So, how can we think in more intertwined and dynamic terms about these imperatives that pay homage to institutional divisions but also reach for a much more enmeshed and unknown conceptualization of urban change?

Theoretically and practically, this will emerge only when we systematically articulate the dense registers and sensibilities of the street with the technocratic utopias of future times, which in turn points back to a series of political choices and possibilities in the precarious now. No matter how dire conditions may appear, forging a new political imagination requires a generous engagement with the molecular *details* of urban life. These details are those not only of the street but of institutions as well, and of the interfaces among them.

This generosity is reflected in a capacity to re-describe conditions in ways that extricate the details from serving as locked-in evidence of particular dispositions and instead treat them as secretions that may mix and congeal in ways that go beyond our available vocabularies. We must always act and intervene. But for too long the urban has been experienced primarily as the exigency for intervention and redemption, without paying attention to all of the resonances among seemingly discordant things and times that have in some ways adapted themselves to each other all along. In the next chapter we attempt to show what such re-description might look like and what kinds of urban engagements they offer both above and under the radar.

3

Re-Description

When it comes to adaptation, one of the most frequent questions asked of people around the world for a very long time is "How can you live like this?" The question may refer to very different conditions and circumstances. Yet it not only asks how a person could tolerate living a particular way, it also implies that the person has or could have a choice to live otherwise. The question usually implies the presence of some deficiency. But it could also be more open-ended and not require an account of all of the things that have gone wrong, or how the person is too messed up to do things right, or doesn't have the opportunity or resources to do them. In addition, it could point to a situation for which there are many contradictory answers.

Many parts of African and Asian urban regions are considered uninhabitable. They are the homes of marginalized black and brown bodies that cannot really be homes because their environments are incompatible with what normally would be required for human sustenance. Because these regions are, in the end, the "responsibility" of those who inhabit them, the fact that they appear as uninhabitable also renders their inhabitants not fully human. That many African and Asian urban regions remain engulfed by an underclass thus becomes an almost unspoken proof of the normality of spatial inequality that either will not be overcome or, alternately, requires an almost unfathomable deployment of effort and resources to undo. This view also suggests that a definitive and unyielding image of urban efficacy and human thriving exists and should be the object of aspiration by those living in supposedly uninhabitable spaces.

The extent to which certain kinds of people are inundated with toxins, pollutants, bacteria, viruses, violence and disaster is well documented (Nixon 2012; Parenti 2011). We know the various ways in which the extension of urbanization as a planetary phenomenon has completely refigured geographies of sustenance. What we are more interested in exploring in this chapter are the oscillations among that which is experienced as habitable or uninhabitable, as a way of extracting untapped potentials from what already exists. We are interested in how particular features of the urban environment – practices of describing it, making economies from it and managing it – might operate in ways very different from how they seem to appear. We are interested in how instruments developed to bring about greater certainty and precision to the operations of governance and infrastructure might actually intensify uncertainty. We are interested in how the roll-out of building projects at different scales sometimes seems to become an instrument, not of immediate profit or discernible use, but of "wild" attempts to make the city into something that it is not (yet) – where the most powerful forays of urban capital attempt to go beyond rationality as if seeking to become some mystical power. We are interested in how domains that otherwise might be seen as the exemplars of cut-throat competition might also be important spaces for rehearsing collective thought and action. All of these are instances of re-description – ones that challenge clear distinctions between what is habitable and uninhabitable.

Life appears in different forms, sometimes making it difficult to know exactly what is "alive" and what is not (Lorimer 2012; Parikka 2010). Not dissimilarly, then, we want to explore some of the ways in which the habitable and the uninhabitable in the time of a precarious now are *re-described* in terms of each other. How can what is predominantly described as useless, normative, entrepreneurial, dissipated or standardized become something else? How do we pay attention to the proliferating interfaces in both the extension of urban processes to a broader range of places and their intensification in existing urban centers? For what happens when increasingly disparate spatial products, urban development agendas, and land uses and values find themselves right next to each other but without any overarching governance or planning framework to connect them functionally? How do we find ways that work with the frictions, the incompatibilities, the fissures, and the supposedly seamless confluences in these interfaces to generate new potentials of urban thought and action? We certainly do not assume to know the answers to these questions but insist on foregrounding them in the renovation of urban studies.

Additionally, as cities and urban regions are more intensively and extensively linked to each other – where individual city futures are tied heavily to global commodity and financial markets, where economies are linked more and more to servicing local instantiations of globalized circuits of exchange – it is the character of the articulations among cities that is increasingly critical.[1] As Read et al. (2013: 390) indicate, "we inhabit layered constructions of technological spaces and worlds that articulate with each other, and it is these located articulations and interfaces rather than the spaces themselves which underpin the places of open creativity and vitality of the city."

In an era where the normality of any standardized version of humanity is continually upended in the constantly mutating assemblages of biological, technological and digital materials,[2] these standardized versions are nevertheless obdurate in their application to the ways in which the value and efficacy of African and Asian urbanities are judged. A supposedly countervailing move, whereby the resilience and resourcefulness of those who have almost nothing is emphasized, ends up reiterating these same modernist versions of the human (MacKinnon and Derickson 2012; Prashad 2013; Watts 2015). This is because such a countervailing move is usually couched in a form of patronizing surprise, a kind of "oh, yes, even the poor have a way of proving their humanity."

Surviving the uninhabitable then becomes testament to human will and capacity, echoed through the in-vogue parlance of social resilience. It minimizes the impact of injustices of past and present and also fuels sentiments which would claim that, if only the inhabitants of these cities would do what humans are truly capable of doing, of deploying those inordinate skills of survival to the exigencies of urban remaking, then new cities would be truly possible. More importantly, perhaps, such an orientation does not pay sufficient attention to the *details* of what actually takes place in many urban domains. This is particularly the case with many government institutions, which see such details as interference, preferring to remain at the level of broad policy survey, pronouncement and one-size-fits-all regulation.[3]

Given how hard it is to barely govern many cities, it is understandable how many details remain out of view, how many judgments about the efficacy of districts and economies are based simply on the way things look (Ghertner 2010), or where details are valorized as specific data sets subject to complicated algorithmic calculations. But details are not simply proof of some overarching abstractions or instantiations of macro-structural dynamics. They are also evidence in their own right. The task is how to re-describe them, not in terms of best practices, but in vernaculars that can convey their singularities and also their possible relevance in relation to other settings. For details constitute a medium through which links among supposedly disparate places, people, histories and materials within specific regions can be interwoven and reworked. They lure curiosity; they can exist without excessive ideological baggage; they don't necessarily belong to anyone in particular; they are like wildcards that can bring out or complete something unfinished and point everyday experience in other directions beyond the repetition of routines. To be sure, re-discription implies a capacity to cope with enormous variation and texture, which is hard to hold on to when the urgencies of inequality and deprivation are overwhelming.

In the massive demographic urban growth still underway across much of Africa and Asia, as well as in the wholesale conversion of public goods into private assets in these regions and elsewhere, there is little denying that a continuous and incremental recasting of urban landscape and livelihoods takes place. It progresses through a substantial plurality of practices: saving, borrowing, stealing, sharing, manipulating, pooling, threatening, luring, building, repairing and dissimulating. All of these practices fold in various histories, resources and connections. They work largely by generating evidence simply of their endurance – the fact that they continue to exist, even if the city's predominant institutions and discourses that decide what kinds of practices really count largely ignore them.[4]

But all of this comes at an enormous price. Even if particular urban neighborhoods are not plagued by constant criminality or threats of violence, more silent, even more insidious forms of wounding and undermining often take place, whether inside the house, on the street, or in daily transactions with authorities of various stripes. Experiences of schooling, religious worship, civic association and public deliberation may be stultifying, boring and badly managed (Auyero 2012; Gupta 2012; Hull 2012). There will usually not be enough jobs to go around, adding burdens to already stretched incomes. So many neighborhoods experience a "big picture" where there is dynamism, resourcefulness, indolence and waste, where the good and ugly are so intertwined that the value of anything that does seem to be unequivocally effective and worth investing in appears compromised or doubted.

The intended and unintended experiments of everyday urban life

The details of how many, perhaps most, residents in urban Africa and Asia attempt to live reveal messy, unwieldy and often violent natures that push and pull people and materials in all kinds of directions, keeping them off balance and thus roped into a lifetime of half-baked compensations.[5] When I, Simone, step out of my house on a small lane in a very heterogeneous district in Jakarta and turn the corner into a busy street, I step into the midst of a seemingly interminable argument between two storekeepers over whose responsibility it is to make sure that the trash container doesn't overflow, two young men who voluntarily sweep the streets for several hours every morning in order to strike up quick conversations with people waiting for transportation to go to work, the beginning and endings of furtive couplings in the cheap by-the-hour hotels, and the same convocation of customers at the small eating places where they "compare notes" and plot both sensible and outrageous conspiracies to elevate their incomes.

I step into the lining up of devotees in front of the shabby office of a major local politician who moonlights as a spiritual adviser, the constant loading and unloading of trucks that, in the frenzy, always deliver goods to "wrong" destinations, the constant milling about of people of all ages seeming to wait for real responsibilities but nevertheless feed the street with eyes and rumours, the daily appearance of some new construction or alteration, of something going wrong and being left unfixed for only seconds or decades, battered or bored lives going about pursuing the same routines and routes, as well as those who approach this street where they have spent every day of their lives as if it were this first time.

These multiple encounters and parallel, separated enactments, neither "good" nor "bad," are the substrate that "inhabit" this popular district. They are its real politics, even as hierarchies of authority and institutions are also obviously in place. Varying distributions of capacities to affect and be affected, to bring things into relationship, and to navigate actual or potential relations are political matters. Particularly in ostensibly under-regulated cities, where infrastructures have been overly partial or fragmented and thus limit the effectiveness of available ordering devices, kinaesthetic and affective performances provide critical measures for how people and things arrange themselves, make use of and circle each other (Anderson 2012; Clough 2012). From overcrowded public transport, rambunctious markets and chaotic streets, residents seemingly know what to do. They know both how to defer being overwhelmed and to use what was overwhelming strategically in order to propel different configurations of bodies, sense and livelihood.[6] Matters could be literally overwhelming, debilitating and joyous. It was often hard to tell exactly what could hurt or help you. These are matters about who gets to acquire particular emotional patterns, thresholds and triggers, and they are connected to a complex virtual field of differentiating practices – what Protevi (2009) calls *bodies politic*.

What Protevi means by "body politic" is the unfolding of a history of bodily experience, of *specific* modulations in ongoing processes of people and things encountering each other. It is an assemblage of bodies intersecting the somatic and the social that, in turn, "feels out" specific capacities in relationship to other assemblages. Given common genetic heritages emplaced in specific environments governed through specific policies and institutional forms, an array of triggers is distributed across specific individual and social bodies. These triggers incite particular forms of paying attention to and acting on the world. Political categories, such as race, class and gender, at times can embody particular registers of affective engagement. But these are broad markers in a much more textured landscape of feelings, perceptions and behavioral styles. As Connolly (2014) suggests, the question is what kinds of interweaving of historically cultivated registers of interpretation, neurophysiological response systems, cognitive styles and policy environments shape how variously aggregated bodies engage the conditions in which they are situated. How do these, in turn, try to reinforce or change the composition and emotional atmosphere of collective life?

All of the encounters a person has inside and outside the house, at work, in the streets and in institutions inform what a body is able to do at any particular time, where they do it, and what it is possible to perceive and pay attention to in a given environment, as each body acts on and moves through other bodies (Massumi 2015).

This notion of *bodies politic* is important because it shows how the functioning of districts full of different kinds of people, backgrounds and activities does not work by residents forging some sense of community. Collaborations among residents are not honed primarily through a consensus of interests, division of labor or proficient organizing techniques. Rather, things work out through an intensely politicized intermixing of different forces, capabilities, inclinations, styles and opportunities that stretch and constrain what it is possible for residents of any given background or status to do. That no matter what formal structures, stories, powers or institutions come to bear on what takes place, no matter how they leave their mark, there is potentially a constant process of encountering, pushing and pulling, wheeling and dealing, caring for and undermining that opens up the *possibility* of residents to manoeuvre "outside the box."

When and how such manoeuvrability "shows" itself is not always clear. We know that the histories of urban modernity in much of the global South at times entailed images of normative inhabitation that were brutally imposed and enforced. But the elaboration of urbanization also depended largely upon stitching together very different times and ways of living, of a plurality of initiatives, all of the messy details of the Jakarta neighborhood cited earlier.[7]

Urbanization involves complex relay systems, including the relationships of people to specific places and functions, the relations among specific production activities and sectors, and the distribution of commodities, services and information across variously composed spaces. Coming to terms with emergent patterns of urbanism requires of us to ask: How are these relationships stitched together? How loosely are various dimensions of urban life coupled together? To what extent can different populations and activities respond to each other? How flexible is the stitching in terms of facilitating or impeding different things taking place both within and across the domains, materials and populations? As modernization entailed the outpouring of enormous volumes of concrete, or at least the determined intention to do so, it also acted to cement these stitches according to rules, calculations and values that fixed the relays between place, people and things into one-way streets of top-down commands and discipline and clearly delineated grids of interchange (Larkin 2013; Marshall 2003; Monstadt 2009).

Writers such as Jean-Paul Sartre, Guy Debord, Mamadou Diouf, Michel de Certeau and Henri Lefebvre, to name a few, have long pointed out the ways in which broad disseminations of everyday economic experiments and caring practices, as well as the intensive shifting arrangements of collective effort, constituted the real underpinning of urban life. These dynamisms were increasingly corralled into sedimentary routines and disciplines. Acting as concretely etched definitions and constrictions in space, bodies and actions, with sufficient mobilization of popular effort, they could sometimes be circumvented or resisted. Depending upon the kinds of residents targeted, particular apparatuses for domesticating or constraining them could also be converted into platforms for consolidating new forms of claim-making and provisioning. Here it is important to note the history of the Black Power movement in the US (Joseph 2009; Williams 2005).

In response to these fights and autonomist actions, the stitching of the relationships among the governed was altered, and the interfaces between them were complicated by more fuzzy governance arrangements that attempted to include the resistant, the poor and dwellers in "popular" self-constructed districts in promises of enhanced accumulation and security.[8] This inclusion tended to come, however, with increased levels and forms of debt, and it could even broaden the ways in which dominant powers excluded and repressed those unwilling or unable to concur with such promises (Yiftachel 2015). Additionally, one-way streets of hierarchical rule were supplemented with the dispersal of scrutiny and control. Environments were saturated with devices that make more aspects of life measurable and visible so that the apparatuses of rule could better govern in advance by anticipating probable outcomes (Amoore 2013).

Particular stitching was actively undermined to enforce individual self-reliance and self-improvement as the primary means of being able to make things happen. Urban inhabitation has been subject to a more uniform and transparent series of rules and norms, while at the same time encouraging more individualistic forms of accountability and livelihood. This is increasingly or potentially substantiated with the overlay of a vast infrastructure of sensors, monitoring and tracking systems (Crandall 2010). Bernard Stiegler (2013) is right to say that the digital is above all a process of generalized formalization. What he means is that the locus of decision-making and governance increasingly relies upon anticipating the likely behaviors of the various human and non-human components of the city as they are enacted in relationship to each other. Such surveillance hardware continually builds upon continually updated categorizations of bodies and behavioral patterns, as well as constantly referring to and altering past ways of scrutinizing the "social." The implication is that memory is not so much the recall of past conditions or events as something projected forward as a means of detecting potential trouble.

So, various practices of making life, of feeling and thought, have been subsumed within post-industrial capitalism's seeming aspiration to go beyond the concrete details of material life. The stitching has been largely loosened, if not let go, and, while urban areas are more textured and varied in terms of what makes them urban – i.e., in terms of their multiplicity of articulations to larger surrounds – the material and social formats of inhabitation become increasingly narrowed and segregated from each other.[9]

Far from being ancillary to the production of value, the affective and cognitive spheres of life so central to urban residents making their way "through each other" are constantly appropriated as factors and objects of production (McQuade 2015; Walker and Cooper 2011). Distinctions between work and leisure are virtually erased. Capital intervenes in the entirety of a person's lifespan as a means of maximizing their capacity not only to perform normative standards of optimality but also to live continuously with a sense of dissatisfaction compensated only through self-improvement and niche consumption (Marazzi 2010). Far from urban modernity taking shape through concrete materials and any endeavor to sum things up once and for all, the seeming dissociation of finance capital from the production of "real" things for "real" lives in actuality becomes the critical operating mode for the capacity of life to become increasingly singular and resilient. Lives are constantly reassociated and redistributed in shifting networks of affiliations and experiences (Lazzarato 2014).

In other words, the capacity resiliently to become many different things has become standard operating procedure. Of course, the relative absence of anchoring cultures, discourses and norms does not open up complete freedom and instead ushers in a flood of guidelines, instructions, pointers, expectations, to-do's and indicators whose applicability is for the moment and then quickly altered (Virno 2009). Invariably, residents have constantly to pay attention. The acts of paying attention – residents to each other, to all that took place in surrounds that inhabitants felt they could know and map in their heads and with others – created spaces of inhabitation. However, the incessant paying attention to signals, messages, tweets and floods of images tends to produce deficits of attentiveness, as well as shrinking the horizons of what a viewer can actually do with the things he or she pays attention to. This is a profound paradox of emergent digital sociality.

Where residents may once have borne witness to each other as a means of creating multiple forms of collective effort, from place-based affiliations to kinship to occupational clusters to shared school attendance, urban life today entails an incessant cursory "reading" of an increasing volume of events as data, geared toward rapid assessments of their usefulness in seizing opportunity and visibility across shortened time-spans.

The fragile threads of collective action

Some have argued that collective effort draws upon long histories of fleeting and fugitive sociality, ethics on the run, and an appropriation of what is available to turn the tables on propriety, so as to produce undomesticated residents nevertheless capable of forging loyal bonds with each other (Harney and Moten 2013). Deeply ingrained experimentations of established and emerging power may set out architectures that would seem to detract from substantive collective interchange and provoke only vague urban social movements based on negative reactions to the present. Still, the task for redescription is more than simply finding ways of translating critical elements of a mourned-for past into the Google paradigm or appropriating it for more progressive objectives. Rather, it is to find the possibilities within the interfaces between what endures outside the Google world and that world itself as an incitement to hack out insurgent spaces of operation. This is what Harney and Moten (2013) call the act of being a fugitive, always on the run even if you are basically staying in place.

As such, particular positions and forms of living are created as spawning grounds for the production of particular kinds of value – positions that are valuable in the very fact that they seem to have no intrinsic meaning or future on their own. Here, the abstraction of life intersects with the wasting of actual individual lives to generate value in particular aggregates of living, which on the surface appear to be uninhabitable. We discover possibilities for how human life can be reshaped out of its very vulnerability – out of the lengths that individuals go in order to piece together a barely viable urban existence out of fragments, and the kinds of associations they stitch together among characters of all kinds. Thus, migration and temporary and flexible labor come into existence as abstract entities suggesting new ways of being in the world but which, simultaneously, act to devalue the real lives of individual migrants and workers (Mezzadra and Neilson 2012). This intersection of the abstract and the concrete is brokered through a growing apparatus of security, monitoring and policing, which in turn fosters intermediary levels of mediation and brokerage. Those that would seemingly enact these new ways of being in the world are not to be the ones who derive value from them.

This brokerage extracts exorbitant payments and indebtedness from devalued individuals. They accrue such debt as a means of trying to guarantee the future savings of lifetimes. For example, taxi drivers in New York, food sellers in Jakarta, or bar workers in Manila will work decades in fourteen-hour shifts every day to pay back debts accrued simply to put one child through school or pay off loans on a house that may fall apart long before the debt is paid (Tadiar 2012).

The sheer desire to live, to go beyond the status of waste, compels enormous sacrifices and indebtedness, generating vast profits. The ability to generate new potentialities from life thus operates in tandem with expansions in the capacity to waste life (Cheah 2007). Those whose lives persist under the constant prospect of being wasted are increasingly caught in a seemingly endless cycle of debt in their efforts to earn a livelihood that will take them beyond the immediate future. Work hours are extended, shifts are doubled, and risky ventures are undertaken in order to create a horizon where waiting to earn money that is not already owed somewhere – to brokers, contractors, owners or family members – is not the norm. This is the world of New York City taxi drivers, construction workers in Qatar, domestic workers in Singapore, dishwashers in Hong Kong. In a certain sense they reflect downward spiralling story lines.

To circumvent a life of dispossession often means taking the risk of losing everything or playing with practices and ways of making money that embed individuals in relationships that are both volatile and trusted. Trust, obligations and reciprocities are built from the sheer fact that they are not recorded or institutionalized. This can be seen in operations such as gambling, smuggling, pooling, diverting and bundling time, money, people and things. As Tadiar points out, there are remainders of life, neither strictly virtuous nor toxic, that cannot be subsumed within the totalizing logic of capital. Tadiar (2012: 799) explains that this is "a lifeworld replete with propitious meaning and ambient power or potential, the capture, accumulation, preservation and privation of which both determine and are reflected in social relations of obligation and patronage that are never completely fixed or static, but rather are always dynamic and relative."

Much of Asia acted as fodder for the proof of developmental dreams. It was proof that backward economies, with determined and sometimes coercive governmental action and inward financial flows, could produce well-planned, thriving metropolises. That Africa now seems poised to follow in these footsteps points to this sense of endlessly renewable habitation. But something else may also be going on, for some cities seem to expand without clear economic logic. In this chapter we endeavor to substantiate why it is so important to keep an ear to the ground to understand the complex and paradoxical rhythms of popular neighborhoods. The format of making this case is also meant to incite a conceptual and methodological openness not always to try and squeeze everything into singular theoretical and political registers. However, it is not just the intimacies of highly localized spaces that call out for more effective accounting; sometimes cities as a whole can be equally confounding because they refuse to be bound by economistic dynamics. We now turn to Kinshasa and Jakarta to explore this.

Kinshasa

Kinshasa is the world's poorest city of its size. Although its historic core fronts a semi-circle of the Congo River, which acts as a national boundary – limiting the trajectories in which its physical growth can take place – the real boundaries of the city expand exponentially each year in other directions, so that one can still claim to be inside Kinshasa some 90 kilometers from that historic core. It is hard to determine precisely the demographics of the city. Depending on whom

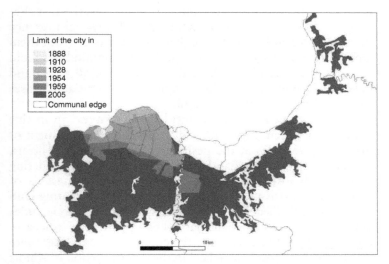

Figure 3.1   Urban growth in Kinshasa from 1888 to 2005
Source: Kayembe wa Kayembe et al. (2012).

you talk to, its population ranges from 9 to 15 million, which involves a lot of uncertainty, and even GIS analyses are hard-pressed to come up with reasonably accurate figures. Allowing for even the vast tracts of land near the center that are tied up as military encampments or the remnants of colonially demarcated buffer zones, much of Kinshasa hovers across tightly packed nodes dispersed across long distances.

So, while many opportunities for systematic infilling may exist, the near universal perception in Kinshasa is that the city is increasingly moving elsewhere. As a result, many inhabitants hurry to stake their claims at ever-shifting peripheries, which still seem to be in the middle of nowhere. In order to maintain a staked claim, a household has to implant someone on site in order to protect it, as the relative newness and vacancy of such areas mean that households stay where they are for the moment. As this sense of expansion is being materialized in all directions away from the river, households are also concerned about missing the "real action." So they will stake additional claims at completely different parts of the city's periphery. The actual acquisition of land at these sites may not consume large amounts of money. But the fact that households have to support some kind of physical presence in these different locations, run back and forth between them along intensely congested roads, and still maintain household economies in the place where they have been all along and have been barely making it as it is, means substantial increases in expenditures of time and money.

As increasing numbers of residents are swept up in this anticipation, their efforts indeed concretize a complement of urbanizing features at the periphery, with markets, schools, churches and outposts of administrative offices. The rendering of the bush into concretized extensions of Kinshasa is of course in part driven by the "old standard" of escalating land values through speculation. In Kinshasa's case, it also includes nebulous external finance that hikes up property prices in older residential districts near the commercial core. Yet there is something almost evangelical in the determination of Kinois to stretch the city, as if these efforts offer some redemptive compensation for all of the difficulties most of them face just putting bread on the table.

As Filip De Boeck (2011a, 2011b, 2012, 2015) in his magisterial writings on the city points out, Kinshasa is a city of micro infrastructures and minimal gestures that take on substantial power. The exigency is to make as much as possible out of articulating imagination and small things, to act as if one is in the midst of intensive urban life by inserting oneself into every conceivable interstice, using whatever is available as a support for commercial activity. It entails efforts to captivate the ability or inclination of someone to buy something from you at a moment's notice, to perform everyday life as if it was replete with abundance when in actuality most of the population is living on less than $1 a day.

As De Boeck indicates, Kinshasa is a city of the "now," in that it emphasizes the need for individuals to be prepared to act in many different places and in many different ways without warning, without preparation. This orientation reinforces the tentativeness of social life, because the recognition of a social body requires a sense of delay, of memory, of rehearsing ways in which different backgrounds and capacities work together. I talk to you, you talk to me, we talk to others, and in the process we acquire memory and develop understanding based on the delays involved in this process, the circuits of call and response and call again. But in Kinshasa the imperatives to act without reference, the immediacy of the all or nothing, make the consolidation of social life difficult. It is also precisely in these fundamentally different bases of existence and sociality that many cities of the global South stand apart from the predictable rhythms of modern Western urbanism during the twentieth century. One is tempted to conclude that Kinshasa is a city that both frightens and surprises itself with its endurance. So, expressions of confidence take shape through these investments in the city's extension. It makes habitable that which lies fallow, a bush in waiting.

It does not seem to matter that these sentiments make daily life all the more difficult. Running around to manage an extended presence in the urban region leaves little time to tend to more localized relationships. In a city where many youth are deeply suspicious of the adults closest to them, where early death is usually explained as the malicious actions of immediate family, where the management of critical cultural conventions, usually the purview of elders, are seized upon by youth as expressions of the vacuum of any real authority, households would seem to make their current living spaces more uninhabitable as the impulse for new habitation intensifies. So the relationship between the habitable and the uninhabitable oscillates, diverges and reconnects in ways that provide for unanticipated opportunities but may also entail substantial costs – something which extends and builds upon the solidity of the existent city but at the same time also seems to waste it.

Jakarta

If you walk through the central city districts of Serdang, Utan Panjang, Sumar Batu, Cempeka Baru and Harapan Mulya in central Jakarta, you will see an enormous diversity of residential situations, none of which could be considered as either a slum or a suburb. As is the case with residents of any city, there may be many complaints and irritations. But these largely self-constructed areas provide both enough differences from each other to allow the congealing of particular lifestyles and affordances and enough commonality to mitigate any sense that residents of different walks of life constitute some kind of threat to each other.

Such districts may be at a disadvantage in terms of the complexity involved in managing how important maintenance activities are reticulated to each other – in other words, the ways in which energy, water, sanitation, waste removal, material inputs and commodities are connected to each other in reliable fashion. Yet, the diversity of skills and experiences residents acquire in developing and repairing various local infrastructures help keep these different sectors attuned to each other. Districts may be crowded not simply with people but also with aspirations, tactical manoeuvres and conflicts. These push their way out into the city and require significant expenditures of tolerance, local ingenuity and mediation.

For the strict delegation of responsibilities to specific individuals, groups or institutions cannot always address the adaptations necessary in a timely fashion. Because districts of such intensities may have to reproduce similar functions with a changing cast of characters, knowledge about how to run things is spread around. But at times it also leaves gaps in terms of deciding who has the authority to intervene in particular problems. In other words, advantages come with disadvantages; it is not a univocally clear story of win–win benefits. Nevertheless, there is much that can be worked with in terms of what already exists.

The question then becomes why such districts, embodying many of the characteristics that most urban policy-makers and planners would want from sustainable development, aren't viewed and engaged as the resources they indeed may be. While the majority of edifices may be small, rather cramped pavilions, there are no structural or prohibitive financial considerations within the existent legal allowance that still prevails across much of Jakarta that would prevent vertical development of four to five stories. Could the infrastructure bear such a potential increase in population load? Here, again, Jakarta, through a past World Bank-coordinated neighborhood improvement project, demonstrated that significant increases in carrying capacity can be affected *in situ* as long as conjunctions between primary and subsidiary water and waste systems are adjusted (Cowherd 2002). High-density, effectively serviced, well-maintained and green neighborhoods – all the trappings of sustainability – seem simply not to warrant any policy-maker's attention.

Undoubtedly the location of such districts near the heart of the city exerts all kinds of pressures. Medium-scale enterprises, such as banks, automobile dealerships, restaurant chains and supermarkets extend outward, increasing land prices and drawing commercial-based revenues into municipal coffers. Still, many districts roll with these punches, as local entrepreneurial networks coalesce and upscale their own operations or where residents themselves add on rooms to rent to cover increases in property taxes. The crux of these considerations seems to imply less the technical or fiscal impediments to the local productions of centrally located districts and more a very truncated image of exactly what exists across these districts and a limited view of just what can be viable (Kusno 2013).

The persistent repetition, even hounding, of urban residents, with the supposedly proper images of middle-class attainment and overall wellbeing, chips away at the convictions residents may yet retain about their abilities to construct viable living spaces for themselves. Time becomes an increasingly precious commodity, particularly as maximizing consumption and skill sets remains a critical indicator of self-worth. A younger generation of urban residents is more eager to escape the obligations of tending to parents and kin, let alone neighborhoods where the "rules" for belonging may become more stringent and politicized. A widening dispersal of interests and commitments is harder to piece together into complementary relationships and collaborations. The efforts at repair and development that could be matters of volitional association in the past now require more formalized and contractual deployments of labor.

Inhabiting extensive parametric space

What makes up inhabitable space and distinguishes it from uninhabitable space is something that seems always to be changing. Just as spaces of public life, sociality, self-construction and certain kinds of industrial production seem to be shrinking, other spaces are created and extended, whether in various media formats, communication and imaging networks, or even in the very ways in which spatial products, such as buildings and other infrastructures, are built and managed. This is not to underplay the enormous impacts and costs on working-class households and various kinds of entrepreneurs as these transitions unfold but, rather, to draw attention to a fluid time of change entangled with all manner of costs, opportunities and uncertainties. Thus, it is important to consider how these other emergent spaces are inhabited.

This question brings us back to the ways in which things, people and information are connected to each other, and what kinds of operations and orders ensue from these connections. If urban management increasingly relies on calculating the relationships between different conditions and aspects of the urban environment through programmed and interoperable data, what is the space between the 0's and the 1's of digital operations? How does the creation of an abstract space end up as urban domains disjointed from so-called real life, particularly when that space is, at times, incomputable, given that histories of data are being constantly moved around in different formats of assessment and use? How do seemingly advanced strategies deployed to make urban living as inhabitable as possible end up creating new uncertainties as to just exactly in what kind of space inhabitation takes place?

The design of buildings, projects, budgets, capital investment plans, strategic visions, coordinated infrastructures of material flow – water, energy, waste, information, transport, food – increasingly takes place through constantly updated recalibrations of the relationships among increased volumes and types of data. This process creates a space of deep and extensive relationships that impact upon the "real city" but which is something else "besides" it, even as it is a "part" of it. Here, the interfaces between the "real city" and the "data city" are uncertain even as the pragmatics of these calculations emphasize the sense of stability and order brought to bear on the "real city."

The design and management of urban operations is increasingly centered on parameters. Parameters track how particular things act. They attempt to specify a range of probable actions, as well as the ways in which different circulations of materials and behaviors affect each other. This is not just about the operations of "smart buildings," where power generation, atmosphere controls, lighting, wired and wireless infrastructure speeds and capacities are automatically adjusted to the oscillating uses or "statuses" of the building at any particular time. The range of modulated impacts to be registered can also be built into large-scale tracking systems at the level of the city itself (Parisi 2012). In this way, for example, patterns of rainfall, traffic flow, water usage, power generation, capital budget allocations, density levels and service consumption – to name select parameters – can all be brought into some kind of relationship with each other. The impact of these parameters on one another can be subject to measurement and the production of quantitative values (Batty 2013).

Take a typical construction of an office complex. The actualization of the project entails calculations of the interrelationships among different types of components. These components might include the soil composition of ground coverage, morphology, water levels, rates of subsidence, the state of ecosystem services, the legal and regulatory systems that mandate particular bidding processes and construction procedures, the corporate organization of sectoral contributions to the construction process (relationships between designers, engineers, financiers, construction workers), the sourcing and provisioning of material inputs, land statutes, strategies of marketing, revenue streams, composition of investors, and so forth.

Each component "lives in its own world." In other words, it is actualized through processes and dynamics that reach far beyond the scope of any project, which has its own internal logic and operating procedures, typically encased in deep professional knowledge systems and norms. So the bringing together of components entails, for example, where water comes from and how it is used; it entails how particular professions are trained to read certain events and possibilities; it entails how financing is generated from many different sources according to its own logics. Everything that is required to compose a project is itself being composed by a wide range of external forces and spaces. The project may attempt to stabilize how each component behaves through establishing a series of relationships – for example, accessing water through certain physical and institutional conduits, channelling it in particular ways, attempting to control the costs through regulating the volume and the ways it will be distributed. These factors hold true not only for water but also for every other material that goes into the project, as well as for organizing the necessary labor, skills and marketing. In addition, projects attempt to sequence the interrelationships of these components across varying temporalities. Particular densities of components impact upon each other with different intensities during the various stages of putting up a new residential or commercial complex. The intricacies extend even further.

The procedures of land acquisition, for example, might be managed largely without much direct connection to the procurement of design firms. The mobilization of low-skilled labor may have little to do with structural adaptations to the building. Not every relevant component, then, has equivalent access or weighting in relationship to each other. Yet, what we emphasize here is that all the characteristics and potentials of the components that go into these projects need not be what they are when they are incorporated into these calculations. All need not be what they are, whether it be the interest rates at which finance is borrowed, the bodily capacities of the labor force, the prevailing climatic conditions, the political atmosphere surrounding the construction, the calculations of required profitability, the configuration of investors – one could go on and on. Components are "captured" at a particular moment in time, according to the particular status of their internal functioning and connections to a larger world. The project can use all of the engineering, contractual and project management tools it can muster to maintain components according to the stability desired, but this is always a kind of gamble, and slight alterations across the board – with the costing and availability of materials and labor or government policies regulating interest rates or import duties, or rumors about hidden investors, to name a few – can have substantial impact on how any project proceeds. It is for this reason that it is more productive to read cities as much more unstable and vulnerable than is typically assumed or projected in most scholarly accounts of either so-called smart cities or entrepreneurial governance (Harvey 1989).[10]

Another way of looking at this is that the actualization of the project may assume a particular degree of stabilization as to what each component is, what each component is capable of doing and most likely to do. After all, this sense of definitiveness is a critical assumption when it comes to assessing the viability and prospects for completing the project. At the same time, no component is a definitively fixed entity, in that its inclusion in the project, its ability to be drawn in as a part of a larger assemblage, requires an ability for each part to feel out, anticipate, open itself up onto the other parts in a way that introduces contingency. Hansen (2012) observes astutely that this contingency is not the intrusion of unanticipated external conditions but a condition of the "inside" of the project itself.

The planning and construction of most projects is largely a matter of multiple negotiations and consensus around normative measures and contracts that establish the parameters through which the participation of each component is made possible, regulated and assessed. Increasingly, however, simulation, modelling and other probability devices are used in order to make the process more precise and adaptable to contingency. These tools also introduce new materials, money, designs, relationships and values that were not previously possible. The information generated from these devices, however, covers more ground, often folding in the complicated securitization of mortgages, financing deals with prospective tenants, and ambiguous layers of ownership, as well as new technical compositions and specifications for construction. All of which, as Parisi (2013) indicates, generate increasing volumes of data that cannot be compressed, and thus readily systematized. She goes on to emphasize that data are mobile. They are always being recombined and retrieved, moved around, stored and restored in different settings, which are also mobile. So while these "histories" of data cannot always be computed, they can still affect any algorithmic operation that attempts to interrelate the variables at work in the production of an "actual project." Ironically, the actuality of any project then has to consider its own incomputability.

Why is this extended discussion on the dimensions of parametric management important? Because it seems to account for what has been a rush to build that is taking place across many cities in the South, especially in Asia. It is a rush that seems to recognize all the things that could go wrong, all of the contingencies that need to be taken into consideration, and thus the need to act fast because assembling all of the components needed to complete any project may be affected by changing external circumstances. No matter how well planned out projects may be, no matter how advanced the tools of calculation that attempt to lessen the risks involved, this rush to build seems to instigate futures for which there is no clear measure of effectiveness or profitability. Put differently, the more computing power promises the possibility of control, the more is known about the extent of interrelationships that, by their sheer density, defer the possibility of control.

The development of spatial products and infrastructure projects offered up as "package deals" to urban governments by private-sector players not only constitutes a guess on where the city is "going"; it also seems to instigate a temporality "set loose" from calculation – a process of associating place, people, institutions, finance and politics that ramifies in unanticipated ways. This instigation can be materialized as the disentangling of landscapes, ecologies and territories; it can be materialized as the regeneration of places otherwise considered dissolute or beyond repair; it can be materialized as the redemption of past efforts and histories, the realization of long-held aspirations, or the concretization of the possibility of another way of living.

Beyond speculation

This instigation is something that encompasses and exceeds speculation. It operates as the financialization of risk, as a means of hedging a multiplicity of probable futures for how a specific infrastructure will operate and the value it will have. And this instigation also aims to posit infrastructure as *detached from reason* within a scenario that cannot be fully calculated now, and which imbues it with an adaptability to futures where, no matter what happens, there is the possibility of recouping something which itself cannot be specified. To be clear, we are talking not about explicit deliberative conclusions or planning parameters but, rather, about a set of dynamics that are put in motion through the sheer belief that programmed computing power can be deployed to neutralize risk, assemble profitable partnerships, and offer a discernible roadmap to a "better" future – the very essence of the marketing tropes of the smart-city industry.

In our reading, even if contracts, policies, projects, technical instruments and brute force hold in place the constitutive components of roads, rails, housing developments, flood mitigation conduits, water reticulation, or sanitation treatment systems, each of these components is also enmeshed in a plurality of other relationships and statuses. In Jakarta, and in many other cities of the so-called South, the rush to build tries to outpace escalating land prices, labor shortages, changing policy frameworks, cost overruns and widening disparities in interest rates incurred by borrowing in different currencies. It tries to outpace a creeping diversification of options in the housing market as both available and anticipated stock remain unaffordable to 70 percent of the population looking for accommodation.

In the commercial property market, developers try to outpace the intense competition waged at the level of occupancy rates, a by-product of which is for owners to offer attractive long-term leasing arrangements or leases with flexible escape clauses, but which are paid for in US dollars. As many new commercial buildings are being constructed on the sites of a first generation of office towers, the rush to build also tries to maximize the locational advantage of half-empty commercial stock that is no longer appealing. But, in order to do so, developers face the prospect of waiting out long leases to existing tenants or compensating for early termination. The rush to build is also rooted in the fact that almost all developers have to offer their own so-called cheap payment plans because of prohibitive bank mortgage rates. These payment plans require a nominal down payment and anywhere from twelve to forty-eight subsequent monthly payments prior to the completion of the project – money that is immediately reinvested in new construction projects. As the value of an apartment appreciates on average 30 to 35 percent between the time of sale and its completion, many sources of financing are applied to the acquisition of such property in order to attain eventual rental income or simply to play the game of capital appreciation. While real demand seems to be sustained, developers still rush to outpace possible bubbles and oversupply.

The rush to build is also shaped by the recent opening up in numerous Asian cities of perpetual leaseholds to foreign investors at the high end of the housing market, which has the effect of extending the territory of the luxury property market into solidly entrenched working-class districts. It is also related to the fact that only a minority of new apartment owners actually occupy the premises, instead renting them out in all kinds of tenancy arrangements. The initial round of providing so-called affordable vertical living has demonstrated the complex everyday politics that can ensue as a large base of heterogeneous residents with no prior history with each other try to consolidate particular spaces and styles of operation. It is not clear what kind of contested or accommodating atmospheres this is going to produce in the long run, so developers rush to build before particular negative impressions take hold.

All of this, in aggregate, creates the very conditions that developers seek to outpace. In their very efforts to stabilize, they introduce intensive instabilities in the system, which has to be continually reformatted. At a broader level, there is the widespread conversion of residential into commercial property, but largely under the radar, so there are efforts to stabilize this trend without prompting rezoning or commercial licensing that would increase costs, and these efforts entail maintaining the trappings of a residential façade. Older, largely vacant commercial buildings are surreptitiously refurbished as large-scale rooming houses in order to maintain some viable income flow.

Variegated and rapidly shifting land-use patterns, speeded-up circulation of residents across different housing locations, the marking of growth boundaries in the form of massive industrial land estates at the urban periphery, the youth demographic that floods the market with new workers every year, the accelerated roll-out of flyovers, bypasses and rail systems, the uncertain morphological and ecological implications of massive concentrations of new developments in particular parts of the city – all impact upon each other in ways that amplify the sense of exigency to deploy infrastructure as a marker of stabilization. But this deployment requires its own twists and turns. It entails complicated negotiations as to the extension of road widths, the resettlement of hundreds of thousands of workers who use roads, sidewalks, verges, riverbanks, rail lines and underpasses as places of residence and employment. It entails the consolidation of land replete with various histories, ownership structures, entitlements and functions. It entails negotiations with different kinds of authorities who derive their power from the mobilization of different interests and constituencies frequently living and operating side by side, but often in very different worlds.

It means responding to the demands of a more politically involved middle class that wants a better quality of life and the realization of particular imaginaries about what a functional city looks like. It means staying under the threshold of potential antagonisms that might slow down the progress of projects, producing the prospect of substantial financial loss. It entails trying quickly to establish particular facts on the ground, which even if deemed to be violations later on are too sizeable to be removed or substantially altered. So infrastructure here is a politics of modulation, of bringing volatility to a workable slow motion so that particular projects can materialize. But their materialization largely instigates a new round of uncertainty, raising again questions about what really is inhabitable or not.

This is why the production of contemporary urban space attempts to have it "both ways." On the one hand, it attempts to account and control for all of the variables – the promise of algorithmic urban management. On the other hand, it wants to throw accountability to the wind, where the objective is not so much to plan for and bring out a specific imagined future as to consolidate the capacity to deal with the eventuality of any future. Here the concern is not whether a project is viable or profitable in the present but, rather, to use it as a way of "colonizing" and generating some kind of financial value from that which cannot be computed or assessed now. This is, once again, reflected in investments in new technologies of calculation. For example, in the eventual operation of today's buildings, devices are usually added which establish various parameters of functioning. These parameters keep track of energy use, changes in the population of the building at different times of day, weather and other atmospheric conditions, and measures that concern the material and behavioral effects of particular uses and designs. In many instances these parameters are designed to "speak to each other" and reciprocally modulate their operations. This is clearly at the core of the promise of green building design, embedded in smart urban infrastructures and associated financial packages.

As the design of urban operations shifts ever more toward increased quantitative calculations that intercalibrate not only the inside operations of buildings but larger swathes of the overall urban environment, incomputable, random and contingent realities are produced as a very function of such parametric computations themselves. Despite calculations and the creation of mathematical languages that enable distinct parameters to become interoperable, when each of these parameters interacts with the others, the interaction of so many different realities tends to stretch the individual reality of the parameter – i.e., how the parameter behaves. So, even when we have attempted to specify a particular range of functioning for every parameter in advance, calculations about the interrelationships of multiple parameters produce gaps and juxtapositions which become realities in their own right, but for which there is no available language to analyse them definitively.

In other words, if we attempt to interrelate how fast traffic moves through the city at 3:00 p.m. on Friday afternoons with the structure of the transport budget for the metropolitan region with the history of road construction during the past decade with the available loan financing for new public transportation with the average increase in number of vehicles owned by households, we need to compress a lot of different messy realities into a series of coherent, stable formats. But as soon as we start running programs that interrelate these formats according to various combinations, they become infused with new non-denumerable quantitative dimensions (Parisi 2013). In other words, the sheer attempt to consider and quantify all of the variables produces particular outcomes that the interaction of all these variables can't really account for. The output of the processing does not necessarily correspond to the inputted instructions. This is the case because the interrelated parameters start to "bring with them" data of the past. They bring with them histories of being facets of other relationships and thus point to incalculable potentialities, which cannot be incorporated into an overarching computer program that tries to take account of continuous variation.

In the elaboration of rapid response systems, various streams of data, such as crime and truancy rates, infrastructural breakdowns, and contagious disease outbreaks, for example, are usually channelled to control rooms, such as the famous ones in Rio de Janeiro and Hong Kong (figure 3.2), where representatives of different municipal departments are gathered to assess the implications of actual or prospective events ensuing from these actualities. Here, data streams either come in visual forms through various surveillance technologies or are visualized in various formats, and the two combine to support an overview of situations as they unfold.

But as these control systems are distributed across the urban fabric and are extended to assess the impacts of an

Figure 3.2   Rio de Janeiro Control Center
Source: Julia Ruvolo and Cityscapes.

increasing number of intersecting facets, materials, volumes, intensities, social differentiations and flows, the notion of a centralized control room and overarching perspectives dissipates in decision-making systems that rely more on algorithmic relationships among parametric quantities (Kitchin et al. 2015). This is a process that opens up new spatialities of operation, as multiple dimensions of urban life, formerly incommensurable in terms of common measures and translatability, can be accorded quantitative and probabilistic values in terms of their impact on each other. But, in the process of such quantitative extensions, new forms of incomputable data, not compressible in terms of definable categories, also ensue. The more that sophisticated systems of control are applied to calculate precisely the urban future, the more uncertain that future seems to become (Luque-Ayala and Marvin 2016).

In a recent gathering of developers, city politicians and civil society activists in Jakarta, there was constant discussion about what it was important to pay attention to in terms of trying to get a hold on what was actually taking place in the city. Everyone complained about growing uncertainties and about the need to have more and better data. But the question we raise here is whether better data and more sophisticated tools of tracking the relationships among an increased number of variables will make things any more certain.

Urban politics and markets

In some sense, these new emergent forms of algorithmic urban decision-making act as a kind of "mop up" operation, promising to get rid of all the messy wheeling and dealing that still takes place in any attempt to manage complicated urban dynamics. No matter how proficient the calculations, it may be that the game of urban business hasn't changed all that much, and possibly cannot change that much. Neighborhoods seemingly full of shakedowns, skewed deals, moneylending, compounding interest, favors, sorcery, over-invoicing, resale, gambling, extortion, loaded gifts, kickbacks, pay-to-play and hoarding *morph* into statistical tendencies, branding, big data sets, probabilities, risk profiles, stochastic modelling, preemptive intervention, analytics-as-service, interoperable standards, clouds and ubiquitous positioning, all of whose ethical implications and efficacy are not necessarily more advanced or clearer.

Urban politics basically has to find ways of working with what exists. Despite all of the innovations that digital media bring to participation in municipal affairs, people continually invent, monitor and transform social relations. Markets are one important site for such work. Thus, we consider markets – some, not all – as examples of collective self-management, as ways in which residents in many cities have attempted to address the complex, interacting dimensions of their everyday lives. Transformations of knowledge politics through the use of social and spatial media emphasize the importance of immediate contact with and direct observation of events underway. Markets have long provided contexts for witnessing how economic and social realities get "done." In other words, markets become methods of assembling different, non-coherent practices into the "economic" reality that markets appear to service and embody.[11]

Today, markets are often seen either as invisible exchanges transacting enormous volumes of financial entities broken down into infinitesimal units at enormous speeds or as quaint outposts of meticulously sourced niche products – free-range organic foods, and so forth. Across much of Africa and Asia, while many markets have been supplanted by mega-outlets of various kinds, the so-called traditional or popular markets persist. We want to talk briefly about how these markets operate because we believe that markets constitute a possible venue of re-description, a means of thinking about the possibilities of urban politics now and in the future. As the basis for these observations, we thus draw upon many years of studying and working in "popular markets," in Kinshasa, Johannesburg, Jakarta, Phnom Penh, Abidjan, Khartoum and Lagos. Even though these markets are replete with many differences, we will speak in general terms here, trying to sum up our various experiences across the sensorial nuances of physical market places.

It is conceivable that the technologies of calculation that we have just discussed draw many of their logics of operation from those of markets; that the basis of interoperability and the instigation of incalculable futures initially draws their impetus and shape from how markets have functioned. And now these urban management technologies have become "markets" of relationality – trying to crunch out relations among entities that do not exist but from which it is anticipated that new entities will emerge as part of capital's very remaking of life itself. It is also conceivable, since these technologies of computation produce increasingly abstract urban spaces, that, where the relationships among people, places and things is less a process of negotiation than a matter of probabilistic computation, markets might be re-described as a venue for reiterating a more concrete, more down-to-(this-) earth politics of relationship-making.

Markets are often publicly held municipal institutions whose real management is within the purview of various associations and networks, sometimes formally constituted, at other times not. Far from offering the simple selling and exchange of goods, markets are constituted and become sites of complex performances, not easily, if ever, congealed into a coherent, unified machine. The demands of proximity, fair exchange, accommodation, delivery, maintenance, visibility of transactions, setting prices, packaging, storage, allocation and authorization are addressed through practices that simultaneously have to be choreographed, stay out of each other's way, and assert their independence. But these practices also act as if they are indeed subsumed by an overarching framework, which exists only by virtue of these practices acting as if such a framework does exist.

Individuals and associations secure a place in the market through negotiations with networks and contracts, which specify a given location and terms for operation. This means that, even though sellers largely pursue their own economic interests, the very practices needed in order to make this pursuit work give rise to what John Law (2011) calls "collateral realities." These are realities of collective entanglement created in the background, incrementally and "silently," as the visible and "official business" of the market is put together. These "collateral realities" make markets collective forces. The market may appear to be simply a place to provide an occasion for buying and selling based on price advantages, sourcing of products, and individualized calculations of both the pressures of supply and demand and other larger price-setting mechanisms. But behind such appearances is an intricate infrastructure of understandings and practices that enable them to operate in concert.

This infrastructure is exemplary not necessarily of social solidarity but, rather, of what Tim Ingold (2007) would see as a meshwork of lines and knots. These lines and knots act as a composite, drawing things along without clear standpoints or positions. They thus necessitate vigilant monitoring, a way of everything paying attention to everything else, of witnessing and of bringing things into appearance. To unload, deliver, park, invoice, sell, clean, buy, repair, instruct, smooth over, enforce, inform, circulate, allocate, juxtapose – all essential practices in the market – may be distributed across specific roles and individuals. But in the many situations in which we have worked, these roles can also be assumed by anyone operating within the market. In this way, practices interpenetrate each other, as do those that perform them. This is why markets do not work well when, for example, municipalities try to administer them from above, imposing hierarchies of authority and specific rules and procedures about how those practices are going to work with each other. Nevertheless, many municipalities persist in constructing formal markets, often as a way of managing the eviction of residents from one part of the city and resettling them in another.

This is why the "real authorities" of markets are often weakly or completely undesignated clusters of individuals who appear to have no formal role, but who everyone knows to be somehow "in charge." The basis of their authority rests with the story lines they are able to discern from and engender for the market. In other words, these are characters that pay a great deal of attention to how all of the non-coherent practices work or do not work with each other, the oscillations of transactions and performances, the affects that a wide range of actions and behaviors seem to exert on each other.

All of these intermeshing and frictions elaborate various story lines. For the "real authorities" need to be the avid collectors of stories. They listen to various reports and observe the wheeling and dealing of the assembled characters engaged with the various affordances, infrastructure and routines of the market. The power of the market is largely concretized in unsettling the dominance of any one story, a story that might break the ongoing line of one story leading to another (Simone 2014). This is why governments often perceive markets to be dangerous places, since they are never really able to impose one story about what the market is and should do. One reason why markets do not demonstrate the kinds of social solidarities to which they might otherwise give rise is that governments often have to resort to extra-parliamentary measures in order to constrain them. They do this through shakedowns, extortion and under-the-table payoffs. States also sometimes intervene by turning the market into a space of exception. In other words, the market is rendered exempt from the enforcement of laws around such practices as counterfeiting, smuggling, illegal labor, and even theft, in return for a portion of its proceeds.

While the market may then endure as a place where participants continue to believe that certain stabilities can be attained and routines exercised, this form of intervention – where the state intervenes by not intervening as the official state – breeds mistrust and misapprehension, warding off the consolidation of social collaboration. When the state makes the market a space of exception, it attenuates the exceptionality of the market, as well as its capacities to generate realities and possibilities that exceed a narrowly defined economic function.

Most traditional markets in Africa and Asia draw thousands upon thousands of people on a daily basis, not to sell or buy anything in particular but, rather, to take their chances in the market. They insert themselves in the interstices, that nexus of binding and unbinding all of the "background" practices that are necessary in order to make the market run. They do so in order to make themselves known, to garner or spread information and impressions, to offer specific or amorphous services to customers, sellers and managers that confront unusual circumstances, or to participate in a kind of generalized "espionage." For these "hangers on" also pay attention to all that is taking place in order to convince others, who have access to more resources than they do, to make a move, to buy or sell particular items as variegated bundles and special deals.

Markets are sites for proselytization, prophecy, exegesis, rumour, speculation, conviviality, entertainment, mobilization and networking. So they are always spilling over from their established confines, which is what makes them powerful attractors. It is never clear what future they might portend. Whatever orderly buying and selling of specific goods at specific, reliable prices under the roughly fair conditions of exchange they do stabilize, the very practices that bring this about are always "circling" each other, being reworked even as their relations appear highly routinized. This means that the market can always be "done" differently. It is not subject to a big picture. Its efficacy is not dependent upon a series of sequential steps or a harmonized vision.

Such operations stand in contrast to the widespread deployment of urban strategic planning in today's urban governance. Strategic planning attempts to "round up" different kinds of actors regardless of their background, to get them to enumerate their own distinctive perceptions and uncertainties, and then to broaden these discrete particularities into a "big picture." This big picture is then presented as the thing which individual actors have not been seeing, which they now need to see and which, once seen, provides the overarching mechanism that connects divergent positions (Kornberger 2012). By pursuing a sequential series of steps, each contingent upon the completion of what comes before, the contested, uncertain and fragmented experiences of the present are aligned as *the* future.

Strategy is, of course, never true or false, but it is the precondition for making judgments. It concerns making a decision that best captures the prevailing unfolding of the future in the present. It operates as a framing device that covers up the fact that it is a device, as opposed to a window onto the harmonizing totality which it purports to be. The framing folds the details of individual and collective behaviors into "communities," whether they are communities of interest, identification or location. In all cases these communities are abstractions which obscure the textured ways individuals and groups relate to each other at different times and circumstances. With strategic planning offering itself as the mechanism through which different communities can reach and complement each other, constituents of the strategic planning process are simply added up to make a visualization of a whole, a panoramic view of the city or region, a view where once again the details fall by the wayside. This does not mean that strategic planning is redundant. On the contrary, in later chapters we make a strident case for how it can enfold new kinds of stories and new patterns of operation that can have very different outcomes compared the unjust conditions explored in chapter 2. What we have in mind here is to treat strategic planning not as a governmental fetish but, rather, as just another tool to render particular intersections and potentialities of the city more explicit and desirous without succumbing to the conceit that the strategy is all that is going on, or needed.

In fact, no matter what big pictures are drawn, details "leak" from the frame. Urban life is replete with secretion – things overflowing their boundaries and things being hidden away, kept from use or made secret. In the process of re-describing what is taking place, how much do, or should, the narrators show, make evident? Under what visibility or guises does the important work of remaking urban life take place? What kinds of mixtures of evidence, fabrication, visibility and invisibility can be choreographed as political tools? In the following chapter we attempt to demonstrate the conundrums involved in getting any such balances right.

4
Secretions

To inhabit the urban is to inhabit a paradox. Even when scarcity of basic materials may diminish, hardship seems to increase. Greater access to the multiplicity of urban experiences at times seems to heighten a sense of insufficiency. The harder that people work, the more they seem to fall behind. The urgency to solve problems, to make life improve as fast as possible, often seems to militate against the capacity to act in a meaningful way. Rather, taking seriously all of those legacies of life-making practices that never quite knew exactly where they were heading, but nevertheless often produced new breakthroughs and livelihoods, urban residents often opt for standardized choices, accruing debt for assets that may have a short shelf life or limit their future capacities to act creatively in face of new challenges. In many respects, even as many cities have mushroomed into mega-regions, they have lost density.

For the density of the city was never just that of human bodies. The creativity and ethical attainments of urbanization were predicated on density as a mode of efficacy through variation, as the intermixing of devices – measures, angles, calculations, impulses, hinges, screens, surfaces, soundscapes, exposures, folds, circuitries, layers, tears and inversions. All are instruments for associating things, bringing things into association, where things get their "bearings" by having a "bearing" on each other. City life was propelled by this possibility of creating sets of "bearings" by things having a bearing on each other. The bearing down of things as an impression, as the impact of force, could walk a thin line between inciting adaptation, and thus new capacities, or a wearing away of desire and ability.

But the difference between inhabitants "getting their bearings" and being rendered "bare" is not always clear, and this reflects a persistent conundrum in urbanization. Urbanization is a process that has been caught in the crossfire since its inception. On the one hand, it makes possible a circulation of things across any border that would delimit them – such as habitats, niches, territories or scales (Adams 2014). It is not only that bodies, things, machines and institutions brought together in dense interactions operate as a gravitational force, drawing materials inward, but these interactions also constitute platforms for making materials move, whether in the shape of resources, commodities or information. As they move, their potentials and values change.

As such, urbanization entails not just circulation but stability and security as well. Populations are secured into territories that operate as domains proper to the particular characteristics of their inhabitants. For too much circulation poses a danger to the ability to know who people are, what they are capable of doing, and what can be demanded of them. So urbanization points to continually revisable structures of working out relationships between circulation and security. Who and what should move under what circumstances, then is always an issue that entails relations of force, constraint and contestation. One of the reasons we consider infrastructure to be a political force in its own right, and why we attempt to work through infrastructure as a way of reiterating the importance of socio-cultural dimensions to urban operating systems and a matter of concern through which to mobilize grassroots action, is because infrastructure points to its own "leaks." It suggests how things could be "otherwise," even as if it engineers the coming into existence of defined spatial and social bodies.

Infrastructure exerts, channels and constrains force. Take a neighborhood. Imagine all of the actions, events, gestures, exertions, speech and operations that take place simultaneously at any given time. No one situated in or outside of this neighborhood can possibly be aware of all of these occurrences. What they can be aware of, as well as the kind of impacts they can register among them – the impact each has upon the other – is largely a matter of the infrastructure available to them. For this infrastructure provides specific ways of witnessing or sensing what the intersecting trajectories of force bring about. Infrastructure establishes specific channels of interaction among these occurrences, specific trajectories of impact. As a result, what we come to know, feel and be is largely a matter of infrastructure. However, force also can exceed the bounds placed on it. It leaks, radiates and affects in ways that cannot always be anticipated and controlled (Simondon 2009a, 2009b).

Thus, any of these occurrences can ramify across each other, affecting and being effected in ways that exceed whatever infrastructure is available. Volatility is a default position, and, in this sense, infrastructure is always built upon turbulence. This turbulence may be largely constrained but it does not go away, it is always there – the undertow of the contemporary city.

This chapter looks at various dimensions of secretion. We have several senses of secretion in mind that concern the interplay between processes of leakage and flow and those of withholding and opacity. Part of the logic of normative urban management has been to open up spaces so that they can be properly read, made transparent. In his discussion on the transformations of postcolonial Singapore, Daniel Goh (2015) points out that poor and working-class neighborhoods, with their convoluted built environments and living arrangements, were considered repositories of secrets and dissimulation. Thus, even when residents seemed to express their support for the developing state and its intentions, the state could not really trust these neighborhoods. Even if the spaces of slums or popular neighborhoods could be contained, set off from the rest of the city, their ways of doing things, their illicit economies, collective rituals and not easily discernible collaborations could "leak" across the city, infiltrate and thus compromise the coherence of state institutions. The proper management of space required the remaking of built form so that secrets could not take place.

This preoccupation with secrecy reflects a larger concern with the force of the political. As Michael Dutton (2012) points out, the political is always a potentiality, expressed through the flows of affective intensity, buried within the circuits of power. The machinery of politics draws out and then channels flows that can assume many different potentials and dispositions into the realm of the homogeneous and rational. Yet the intensities of affective energy leak through the infrastructures of containment. All the current tropes of possible human extinction – uncontrollable rising sea levels, extreme weather, rapid desertification, the immanence of the uninhabitable – become shrouded warnings about the inadequacies of infrastructures of all kinds, including states and moral and regulatory institutions, to stem the "tidal bore" (Dutton 2012) of the political.

Then there is what Édouard Glissant (1997) calls the "right to opacity," which he sees as the very *right to existence* – all of the flailing, rubbing against, working through, clashes and caresses, promiscuous mixing and friction that keep bodies, times, memories and cultures moving, without having always to take a reading of position or imaging the source of problems or potentials. The engagements of people, places and things take place through multiple languages, manoeuvres, tricks and gestures that exceed clear representational capacities. Excesses often mistaken for secrets become secretions moving in all directions.

Secrets also entail a play of visibilities where possibilities of commonality and connection among different populations and places in an urban system are modulated by the way different users of the city position themselves in relation to each other – that is, the ways users of the city are positioned in different angles from each other, with different possibilities of paying attention to what is going on, about how much and what can be seen and felt (Shapiro 2010). The question is how do these angles and possibilities switch? How do they remain in place? So there is an experience of things leaking but also being held back, of exposures and cover-up. It is a matter of how opportunities are secreted across the boundaries, as well as secreted away outside of general use.

So enactments of secretion also concern the messy oscillations between how residents are able to stay constantly on the move but also limit the exposures that circulation entails. How circulating residents can be sufficiently visible to grab opportunities when they appear, to be sufficiently visible to be themselves grabbed and included in opportunities, while also not being exposed to all of the "elements" that can throw a person off, draw too much scrutiny, yet still enable a person to "hack" into the tools that are available. In what follows we give some examples of how this takes place in order to concretize the broader argument.

Moving to stay in place

ITC Cempaka Putih is one of Jakarta's largest low-cost retail markets. Like many of these so-called international trade centers that have been around for decades, Cempaka Putih remains an economically dynamic place and hires thousands of young workers, most female and largely between the ages of sixteen and twenty-five. At 10 p.m. at night, when their twelve-hour shifts are finished, they pour out of the ITC, hop onto motorcycles and spread out, supposedly heading for home. But where is home? When is home reached? Home for these young people is enacted in varied scenarios and compositions across hundreds of nearby rooming houses and houses with extra rooms, with the aim of keeping rent under $25 a month – essential given that most of them make perhaps no more than $100 per month. They canvass the city, often looking for nothing in particular, often frequenting the 24/7 convenience stores where they can sit for hours with a coke and noodle soup and watch what other youth are up to. They move back and forth, usually on "back roads" and side streets, populating the shadows of Jakarta with attitudes, behaviors and sensibilities that run counter to the prevailing conventions.

But, in doing so, they continue to sustain various off-the-books economies that are, for the most part, tolerated, sometimes even depended upon by the institutional "faces" of those conventions – local authorities and commerce of all stripes. It is not that these youth are without aspirations, plans or methods for pursuing specific trajectories. For example, YouTube is used constantly as a medium through which to learn new skills, such as those of the coffee barista, web designer, chef, sound mixer, hacker or electrician. Rather, they do not conceive of any occupation as a destination, but simply consider it as something to pass through, as if the city were a proliferation of doors – devices that hinge rather than hedge futures, marking trajectories simultaneously connected and detached.

In Jakarta's main textile and clothing market, Tanah Abang – the largest in South-East Asia – many young men have fairly stable work as sellers in stalls owned by others. But a large number never stay at any particular stall for very long. Most also never leave Tanah Abang. In order for the bosses to retain labor, deal-making becomes more intricate. Different formulas of compensation are negotiated – daily, weekly, monthly and varying combinations of these – accorded on the basis of flexibility of hours and tasks. This deal-making is not the product of any self-conscious mobilization on the part of the bottom tier of the market's workforce. Still, young laborers talk to each other and, through these interchanges, get a sense of the market's atmosphere – the fluctuations of prices, the capacity of owners to respond to new trends and volume, the capacity of owners to bundle their goods with others to offer wholesale prices to buyers coming from all over Indonesia and also pooling their money together.

The young sellers get a reading of who is in debt and who is making a lot of money. Then, they try to find ways to get closer to the real action. Of course, there are a lot of failures in what the owners do, either collectively or individually, and there is always a sense of urgency to recover from these failures. This happens not only by reducing costs but also by taking on energetic labor equipped with new ideas and solid experience. These are situations to be "harvested," as some young laborers put it. Most of these young people will never make enough to become owners or ever substantially increase their eventual earnings. But this circulation through the market at least creates the semblance of trajectories, of going somewhere, even if it is not necessarily going forward.

Youth in Jakarta frequently talk about how it is necessary to keep moving in order to retain some semblance of stability. There are those who stay put, either by choice or through desperation, those who hold onto whatever anchorage they can find. But many in a new generation of youth claim that to stay put for too long in any given job or residence is inevitably to miss something important. For the trajectories of viable livelihood no longer seem to depend upon building strong and long-term relationships with a particular place and imbuing it with a gravitational force able to draw in resources. Rather, it is seemingly more important to try to capture opportunities in motion, to try to be at the right place at the right time, because what is critical or advantageous inevitably moves on. In many ways this echoes the practices and dispositions of young people in Kinshasa whom we encountered earlier, who stretch themselves across a number of footholds in a "bizarre" effort to be in many places at the same time.

Slim margins

Despite the proclamations that point to a growing middle class across urban Africa and Asia and the inclinations of residents to consume as much as possible, most households across very different kinds of cities – Bangkok, Chongqing, Jakarta, Nairobi, Karachi and Hyderabad, for example – are living within slim margins. They are compelled to provide for basic consumables whose costs inevitably rise. They put money away simply in order to maintain their place, as this small saving is invested in education, small enterprises, one-off opportunities, essential repairs or strategic social relations. Efforts to keep costs down are coupled with opening new windows of opportunity. Even if households remain the integral unit of accumulation, management and expenditure, the balancing of plural needs and aspirations requires intricate collaborations with others. As a result, residents turn at various times to a wide range of modalities for such collaboration, from place-based affiliations to kinship to occupational clusters to shared school attendance. In other words, these operations of trying to keep costs affordable as well as investing in new opportunities require material platforms, infrastructures. These platforms do not always easily coincide with grids, private property, zoning or clear demarcations of function.

For instance, keeping food expenditures down requires circumventing conventional commercial mediations, acquiring commodities in bulk, and arranging appropriate storage spaces. Entrepreneurial experiments require low-cost workshops, low-risk deployments of venture capital raised through aggregating small household surpluses, warding off extractive intrusions from authorities and police, securing sufficient markets, disseminating information, and arranging trade-offs with potential suppliers. Built environments need to be repaired. They often need to be infused with additional value without their being rendered unaffordable. Particularly important, built environments become the objects of reshaping so they might mediate the multiple provisioning of various affordances – i.e., to act alternately as residences, markets, community centers, workshops, storage spaces, retail outlets and social hubs.

A good illustrative example is the central city district of Utan Panjang in Jakarta. There are some areas where buildings snake around each other, twist and turn their walls and spaces in ways where it is difficult to tell whose place is whose, where the entrances and exits of a specific household unit might be. There are areas where nearly stately suburban-looking homes have their backyards jam-packed with makeshift dwellings, where you have to walk sideways in order to navigate the connecting lanes, while the frontages of these same properties are profusely decorated with greenery and open air. Contiguous households are often composed very differently – a conventional family, the employees of a single commercial enterprise, the self-grouping of individuals in similar occupations but working for different firms, the sellers at a nearby district market – while other residences are used completely for commercial purposes.

Within a single lane, then, a wide range of different actors and resources are put into possible play. Each household continues to live a "separate," life but the proximity of others induces sufficient contrasts that precipitate the need for everyday negotiations in terms of managing the immediate area. It is these negotiations that open up the possibilities of mutual discovery and tentative collaboration. The diversity of the built environment reflects the multiplicity of land statuses, the consolidation and dividing of plots, the possibilities of supplementing household incomes with additional rents, and the elongation of holdings to include workshops, small factories, restaurants, stores and storage spaces.

There are areas where people have built above-ground extensions across lanes and adjoining buildings; there are entire blocks of three- to five-story buildings where it would appear from the front that the insides correspond with a standardized neat row of aligned front doors, but once you enter one of those front doors you zigzag in all kinds of directions as residents have tunnelled their homes into each other in all kinds of strange designs while still managing to live and work together. These arrangements of the built environment reflect the accommodations that have been made to intersect affordances and affordability, to intensify the complementarity of residents with different backgrounds and access to opportunities and resources. The makeshift quality of these arrangements also reflects the incremental character of such intersections – that various labors have been undertaken over time, adapting to each person's relative usefulness and inadequacy.

Figure 4.1 Utan Panjang, Jakarta
Source: AbdouMaliq Simone.

The arrangements also reflect a "muddying of the waters." It is not clear what space belongs to whom. Although in the everyday occupation of such buildings residents have a fairly certain idea about where they can put their bodies and under what circumstances, and who may own what, the actual patterns and practices of habitation and the understandings residents have of them rarely match any official cadastral. The interpenetration of everyday residence makes it difficult for outside developers to pursue their common practice of "picking off" households one by one in order to assemble large plots to work with. So there is an intentional making secret here of something that is evident to everyone.

These are arrangements that have clearly taken a great deal of effort over long periods of time and require large expenditures of collective attention to maintain. They often hang together through constant adaptations and negotiation. Like a "matchstick construction," they could easily fall apart with the withdrawal or repositioning of the smallest components. In districts where local economies, relative political autonomy and elastic labor markets are built upon individual residents circulating through multiple roles in different kinds of associations and collectives – be they religious associations, savings groups, political parties, commercial networks, sport clubs or street associations – claims for rights are not situated in specific, overarching formats. Rather, claiming becomes a means of configuring different vantage points from which to "get an angle" on what is going on. It is a way of diversifying access to resources and opportunities and a means of opening up new kinds of networks.

And so districts such as Utan Panjang operate as a series of parallel formations. Residents and others who run businesses in or help manage the district do not feel they have to know everything about what everyone else is doing. People can pursue highly particular agendas through provisionally connecting with all of the different kinds of collective formations taking place, but without a sense of owing anything or having to align agendas. It doesn't mean there is not conflict. But what usually happens is that particular "projects" – economic activities, uses of facilities, streets and labor – spin off in different directions. This is made possible by the past history of the district and efforts to replenish or remake that history, so that lots of different things can go on at the same time. This is why the formulaic policy prescriptions for upgrading, tenure security and particular kinds of social formations that stem from the urban policy literature are unhelpful and acontextual. It is not possible to figure out how to intervene in these kinds of spaces without understanding the existing dynamics with all of the inevitable opacity and secretions.

In Utan Panjang, all of these multiple uses of land and the built environment have been made possible partly by the ambiguous status of land. Land may be bought and sold, but there is no overarching legal framework of private property. So, in this district, working out a delicate balancing act between pluralizing affordances and keeping things affordable required a material base where things were not consolidated or pinned down, as well as a large number of residents willing to forego the possibility of making a great deal of money to keep all of these "projects" going.

The flip side of this dynamic is the difficulty entailed in holding any specific individual or group accountable in the end for overseeing things. There may be residents whose job it is to "represent" the area to the outside world, and, in doing so, they deliver abstracted pictures of what the place is in its entirety. These "pictures" usually reflect the pragmatic functions of managing the interfaces between a particular district and the larger city, of regulating external scrutiny and accessing attention and resources from the outside. The circulation of residents through different versions of themselves in various collective formations may be an important manoeuvre for making sure that opportunities and resources get around. But it also may mean that longer-term planning and commitments to follow through on the management of specific infrastructures and institutions may be difficult to achieve over time.

Clearly, there are many urban districts in Jakarta and other cities that don't come close to Utan Panjang in terms of operating with such dynamic recalibrations of space and bodies. Many areas are stuck, exhausted, and their residents are ensconced in prolonged inertia. There are districts where it is difficult for residents to do much of anything with each other. And, while it is possible from our research over the years to attribute particular reasons for why some districts are more dynamic than others, the equations between success and specific variables are difficult to generalize. The legal composition of land and the flexibility of its use; the location of a district in larger urban fabrics; the heterogeneity of the material and social environments; the definitiveness of governmental decision-making and regulation; the histories of resident mobilization; the possibilities for incremental development; and the availability of a district to new inflows of residents and residential turnover can all be critical components in the dynamism of local quarters. But how and to what degree these dimensions are combined opens up all kinds of possibilities that districts will in all likelihood go down different roads. This pluralism militates against any kind of singular reading or obvious political or policy response.

Paying attention to the details

In Hyderabad, India, even in districts that seem stuck and full of internal bickering, some youth see such places as resources to be harvested with small gestures. Ayeesha is a sixteen-year-old girl who says that she really feels neither inside nor outside home and school, where she spends most of her time. She describes the housing tenement where she lives as a "body somewhere between the living and the dead," as a "relic" in the city to which everyone desperately tries to hold on. In a world where "everyone watches" but "no one pays attention," she views her everyday life as taking small advantage of all the things that "don't really fit in."

In the increasingly desperate attempts of the nearly impoverished to maintain the integrity of their households in close proximity with others, there are varying mixtures of enforced conformity and letting things slide. Wayward children or spouses may be temporarily locked out of their quarters, while hurried exchanges and random affections are left to settle in the cracks, becoming information that can be hoarded and perhaps used later. Things are always spilling over, and, instead of ignoring it all, Ayeesha prefers to find a way "to take it all in," even if it has nowhere specific to go. She doesn't expect much of her life. She tries to avoid contact with relatives so as to avoid pressure to get married. She has to invent reasons – part of the surplus of paying attention to the information economy of the tenement – in order to circumvent her mother's rage when she attempts to attend the social functions of friends. She imagines ways of being independent without "being made independent" as a result of extended family disapproval of any autonomous action. She relishes the unexpected opportunity she has to attend college and diligently does everything she is expected to do at home. She fetches water in the middle of the night, even if it potentially drains her of time and energy for her studies. But it is the mostly routinized navigation of the spaces between school and home that she particularly values, that she "saves up for a later occasion." Many youth fashion these multiple worlds and emotional navigational structures as they act as intermediaries between tradition and modernity, expectation and anticipation, keeping the peace and letting all hell break loose.

The everyday churning of banal disputes and surveillance that act as immunization for some districts against the threatening volatilities of the larger city can also be contrasted with the dystopian nightmares of living in lurid neighborhoods full of opaque complicities among gangsters, cops, politicians and big business figures. Here, Lyari, the old working-class district of central Karachi, abutting port, industrial zones and central business district, stands out as a common example of an overcrowded place replete with constant turnovers of residents living in fear.

This fear leads them to circumscribe their daily routes and routines to self-constructed shadows so as to avoid the eerie and violent politics that rules everyday life. It is not unreasonable to expect that a district with such strong locational advantages for speculative development and such strong historical roots in ongoing contestations about the political control of Karachi would exude violence. But the dystopian renditions of this violence act as a lure for easy generalizations about what ensues when an intensely heterogeneous population overcrowds a particular site in the city headed for massive redevelopment, and where the contestations about the trajectories of the future of this development are not quickly categorized and resolved (Kirmani 2015; Vigar 2014).

Indeed, as Adeem Suhail (2015) points out, Lyari is full of idiosyncrasy in its multiple strands of religious, cultural and economic practices rarely found in other parts of Karachi. Long-honed collective accommodations enable residents to sidestep each other while keeping each other in view, taking bits and pieces from each other but largely keeping the integrities of these practices intact. Mutual accommodations and complicities are then overgeneralized by assuming there are no differences among gangsters, cops and politicians. The general assumption is that all are corrupt; all simply extract parasitically what they can from residents urgently trying to locate scarce accommodation, authorizations of all kinds, jobs and other resources.

Lyari demonstrates the ways in which complex transactions become cartoon figures of danger. These are then mobilized as justifications to bring the right kind of rule and order to the area. But this "curating" of Lyari as something unknowable, where no one can be trusted, ends up occluding ways of dealing with mundane institutional practices that are actually well known and accessible. This lure of the purportedly unknowable creates a kind of common blindness. It forces people to lose their way and then be gratuitously guided by the "benevolent" hands of bureaucrats, patrons and developers into new homes in the far outskirts of the metropolitan area. In the same vein, residents are hearded into highly circumscribed and overarching identities, such as "the marginalized," "the fundamentalist" or "the gang member." Even when a plurality of other designations exists, still behind "the nurse," "the shop owner" or "the teacher" lurks one of these more overarching identities.

This is not to deny the ways in which the "militarization" of local urban communities is sometimes generated by growing mistrust among residents, as well as their inability to sift among all of the things taking place and decide which of these events have something directly to do with their own lives. As Diane Davis (2010: 409) indicates:

> In the absence of any certainty about which armed actors or state/non-state institutions are most likely to guarantee security or inflict harm, and in the face of growing violence,

a multiplicity of armed actors offer their own services to ever larger but disaggregated numbers of clients, with the most complex array of coercive forces particularly visible in cities. The existence of a wide range of individuals and groups using coercive force either defensively or offensively helps to undermine the state's longstanding monopoly over the means of coercion, even as it allows varying disaggregated networks of individuals and communities to look inward for identifying and guaranteeing their own quotidian needs.

To use Dilip Goankar's (2014) formulation, residents of popular districts such as Lyari have been "hailed" so many times – mobilized for so many different campaigns, political ideologies and feigned emergencies – that they are no longer anchored as any clear or stable political subjects. As such, what they need to know are the highly idiosyncratic trajectories, opportunities and dangers posed by the immediate surrounds or the generalized abstractions of a more global view. Neither way of making things visible has much traction in the other. Knowledge about what exists between the very particular and very global is tentative and fragmented, reflecting the very nature of those in-between spaces. Cut off from the mediations and portals of a viable "middle," residents figure out ways of immunizing themselves from the uncertainties of such disjuncture as well as ways of operating under the radar in order to extend themselves beyond the confines of the immediate surrounds.

For many residents, lives can unfold simply by keeping one's head down, doing what one is told, and fitting into whatever program seems to be in operation. But, for others, the sheer fact that they live in a city makes such an option intolerable, and they sometimes go to great lengths to do something very different from what they are expected to do, or even expect from themselves. The various intermixtures of such actions and choices make each city intensely peculiar; they piece together a patchwork reality from which it is difficult and dangerous to generalize. Clearly, taking everyday urbanism seriously can induce epistemic madness to the point that any hint at generalization or action that seeks to engage these thick contingencies can take on a phobic power.

Stepping beyond the details

Yet even if generalizations are problematic, it is difficult to avoid them if new political debates and imaginations are to be possible. We can't avoid them if we are to ensure work for growing urban populations and to elaborate the material platforms of urban life that are necessary in order for residents to enact new ways of being urban. To be urban is something largely to be created, as it is not something that comes with pre-set conditions or terms of reference. There are intimations of what is required, and one of the key paradoxes is that those urban populations that presently don't have much access to rights, resources and opportunities actually prefigure, in their making something out of difficult conditions, what many urban futures may need to look like.

This is not to say that such practices within precarity are "best practices" for planning prospective viable urban lives. Rather, the incessant managerial ethos, which professes that urbanity will manage its way out of the conundrums of disappearing work and infrastructural crisis, persists largely because it "impersonates" the capacities of poor and working-class districts by abstracting the specificities of what they actually do under the rubric of "resilience" (Braun 2014; Nielsen 2014). So, instead of paying attention to the details, however varied, complex and often dysfunctional they might be, those that manage cities too often simply characterize such details as evidence of a population's capacity to adapt to difficult circumstances. This capacity is either to be left alone or marshalled as evidence that shifting these same populations across different spaces and circumstances is plausible and cost-effective because, after all, they will be able to handle it all resiliently.

Instead of learning from local economies, socio-technical relations and popular cultures that have usually been reworked over long periods of time – and thus have provided new specificities and dimensions – national and municipal managerial apparatuses tend to undermine them completely. They do this by treating them as "natural flexibilities" essentially to be left alone, as if their capacities did not rely upon productive articulations to contexts beyond themselves. The challenge is not to ascribe a generalized state of resilience to volatile urban conditions and populations. Rather, the challenge is how to *re-describe* the specificities through which they collectively constitute themselves – with all of the ambivalences and ambiguities entailed in how they access land and shelter, how they put noodles on the table, how they pay attention to each other, how they fight and cooperate – in ways that project these local realities outward into larger arenas of deliberation and decision-making, to re-describe them in ways that can be understood and usable by other actors, thus opening up new horizons of possibility.

Just where are the secrets?

In the previous chapter we looked at acts of re-description in terms of how the habitable and the uninhabitable are *re-described* in terms of each other. This notion of re-description is like hinges on a door, modulating the various angles and apertures of what can be seen in a play of angles. This notion of hinging is important because it concerns the kinds of connections that can be both joined and modulated among different urban spaces, where doors constitute both boundaries and openings. If a certain part of the definition of the uninhabitable entails the extent to which a particular place is closed off from access to a larger world or is, in turn, relatively impermeable to incursions from the outside, then in this respect no place is uninhabitable. Even in the most seemingly depleted cities – Maiduguri, Bangui, Juba, Homs or Gaza – there are doors to walk through. There are ways in and out, but who can use them and under what conditions, at what price and scrutiny, and where particular bodies can go once they either arrive or leave are the critical variables. It is also a matter of proportion – how many of city's residents are trapped in narrow spaces of manoeuvre in relationship to how many are floating across a larger world with no real place to land, and what impact these apparent extremes have on how the city "sees itself."

In a world where every inch of the earth's surface can be surveyed, from which information can be drawn and specific persons or buildings targeted, little remains unknown. This is why the hinge, as a metaphor for the act of making generalizations, is important. Where can the experiences of particular kinds of urban residents and places lead? How can they open up onto new surrounds, help constitute those surrounds, and inform the shaping of the larger infrastructures of material and discursive flows that constrain how far they can go, how much their ideas and bodies can circulate?

Once it was a matter of what surveying eyes were interested in paying attention to. Vast interiors of supposedly uninhabited neighborhoods were not worth the effort required to know or engage with. For long periods of time, important population centers in major cities were not even designated on maps because they were bastions of illegal occupation and poverty. It was simply not worth paying attention to the *bidonvilles*, peri-urban settlements, shantytowns, or even long-honed popular working- and lower-middle-class districts because there was nothing going on there of any importance.

Such occlusion sometimes could operate to the advantage of a particular part of the city. In the outer regions of Khartoum's Omdurman district, just before the city met the desert, there was a densely compacted maze of mud structures that from the air appeared like the crumbling remains of some vast and abandoned way station. Yet, Souk Libya, as this place was known, was a pounding market where virtually everything was for sale, from the latest East Asian electronics to surface-to-air missiles to herds of sheep and camels. Brokers of at least fifteen different African nationalities controlled specific sectors of the market, and traders came from as far as Nigeria, the Democratic Republic of Congo and Tanzania, brokering deals across the Middle East. Everyone in Khartoum claimed to know about the market, had gone there once or twice, but it still acted as a public secret, a place beyond regulation and policing because on its surface it always exuded the sense that nothing happened there.

Now we live in an era where nothing is to be missed, where the prevailing assumption is that something is going on no matter how a place looks, that all places are prospects for making money, and, the higher the risks, the more money to be potentially made – or lost. Of course within specific towns and cities there is great variance in the availability of particular doors, as many inhabitants are relegated to highly circumscribed spaces of operation. They may barely know anything outside their immediate vicinity, let alone anything about a larger world. No matter how much the world may come to them, through media, cell phones, the internet, information and rumor, most of the doors available are to the same room. There are times when these doors are tightly controlled, as if, in a larger world of operations, it is important to keep many prying eyes away in order to protect the little you have or to exert a semblance of control over a capacity to reach beyond it.

Just like Chungking Mansions in Hong Kong, that warren of "guesthouses", small restaurants and trading stalls one square-block long, which has for long served as a favorite metaphor for the opacities of "old school" international trade and is divided up into different turf, where exits, stairwells and elevators are "secured" by various groups, much conflict in cities is also about "controlling the doors" – the entrances and exits (Mathews 2011).

In Maiduguri, Nigeria, for example, the intensity of violence deployed by Boko Haram is largely about controlling where the doors will go. In its seemingly pathological fear of education and public institutions, it senses that the extinction of the poor is through a door right around the corner and that the only thing they have to work with is an adamant and stark rendering of faith (Agbiboa 2014). But, at the same time, behind doors that open at midnight and are locked shut until 6 a.m., Maiduguri hosts one of Nigeria's most active party districts.

Walking through doors has left many urban inhabitants feeling that their lives are situated in the middle of the doorway, that, no matter how much knowledge they may have about any given place in their city, no matter how many thresholds they cross, they are somewhere in the middle between the habitable and uninhabitable. This is an ambivalence that all the information-saturated tagging of environments will not undo. No matter how available regression analyzed correlations between real-estate values, the availability of amenities, public services, the history of property transactions, rates of growth, demographic profiles, capital investments, and local government budgetary allocations may be to any smartphone user inquiring about a specific location, a gnawing sense of uncertainty may remain. Uncertainty is hardwired into the phenomenology of popular districts in many of the cities across Africa and Asia.

In Bangkok, for example, the city always tries to "retain face" throughout all efforts to deface it. In other words, the city remains full of markers and reminders that take the shape of the surfaces of shrines, palaces, historical monuments, sex tourism, all-style shopping malls and low-cost, high-quality medical care – in one of the world's most popular and most visited cities. In a city full of contrasts and divergent temporalities, full of hip designs, political anachronisms, cosmopolitan flair and overbuilding, these markers would appear to provide an unyielding sense of history and orientation. It is a city full of distinctive doors that allow fluid passage from one markedly different experience to another. Yet, maintaining this disposition of doors that interconnect different spaces of life into what looks to be a seemingly virtuous symmetry entails a responsibility to forget. The Bangkok resident must forget that this need to retain the calmness of surfaces, this sense that one door leads to other – from the king to the monk to the shopkeeper to the businessman to the sex worker to university students to motorbike drivers to the tourist – has wreaked havoc on the city in terms of its infrastructure, natural resources and built environment (King 2008).

Across many of the cheap condominiums where many Bangkok residents now live, there is an incessant anxiety concerning the appearance of ghosts, spurring discussions about the yearning for the happiness of an earlier time, however entangled with poverty and messiness it may have been (Johnson 2013). At the same time, there is an abiding fascination with all of the hyper-sexualized and disembodied digital landscapes of the city that would seem to suggest that the cultural references through which that former happiness is expressed have come undone.

Such ambivalence suggests a critical conundrum in working through the politics of habitation. For who is to determine what is habitable or not, and according to what criteria? How do we take the present distribution of habitation across many places normatively considered to be inhabitable and decide where people can live or not, and under what circumstances? In the exigencies to raise money for needed infra-structure, to provide work for a more youthful urban population, to work out more functional balances between maximizing the value of physical assets and assuring that the city remains affordable for its residents, the standards used in constituting normative habitation become more homogeneous. They become more constrained precisely during an era where we are more aware than ever of the sheer plurality of situations that people inhabit. Again, finding ways to re-describe the relational skills of residents into new mediums and at new scales is critical. Over time, this empirical, lyrical, poetic, artistic, analytic and pedagogic epistemic project will prove to be the elusive core of new theoretical dispositions rooted in the becomings of the global South, but at home in the world.

Working in secret

To give an example of such re-description, we want to tell a story about some colleagues of ours, and we tell it in a particular way in order to ensure that these colleagues are not in harm's way. This story offers an illustrative insight into the kinds of story lines that need to be unravelled if one wants to apprehend secretions and distil insights for re-description. In a third-floor walk-up apartment in a now crumbling residential complex that spans an entire square block in inner-city Phnom Penh, a young university lecturer, who inherited the flat from his parents, has crowded the only bedroom he has ever known with hand-written diagrams, full of lines that chart relations that have been repeatedly scribbled out and redrawn. A bank of laptops sit on a make-shift table along the wall closest to the window, allowing the power source to connect directly to the wiring system that runs across the fringe of the external roof. The room is packed with documents, newspapers, random notes and the leftovers of fast foods purchased at the end of the stairs that open onto the street full of shops and restaurants. Here is the "headquarters" of what we will for purposes of discussion here call the "Prama Group."

Sitting in the room is a tight-knit network of long-term friends, all fairly well educated, as was possible for lower-middle-class Khmers in the few decades after the city struggled to "get on its feet" following the evacuation of much of its population to the countryside during the Khmer Rouge period of 1975–9. Most are junior faculty likely to languish in over-worked and underpaid jobs. A few are fairly well-paid and more gratified NGO staff always prepared to adapt to the whims of funders. But in this room there is an almost messianic devotion to detailing how the roughly forty families who run the country continue to acquire land, companies and service delivery systems and their resultant economic power and stranglehold over the urban population. Given that the acquisitions are performed with an inflated indifference to public opinion and profitability, the underlying opacity of what these transactions actually do and how they are interconnected to others render this task much more than simply trying to get to the bottom of things. For there seems to be a bottomless pit of deals that appear to be mere fodder for the almost arcane rituals of a super elite inventing their power as they go along (Menzies et al. 2008).

It is well known that Hun Sen, the current long-term head of state, and his family have acquired enormous wealth by stripping the country's forests of wood and selling it on parallel markets, as well as controlling oil, gas and coal reserves. Within Phnom Penh itself, economic muscle is displayed through attempts to exert significant control over the distribution of goods and services. The family owns pharmaceutical distribution networks, transportation companies, shopping centers, shipping services, private universities and power companies; in addition they either own vast amounts of urban land outright or control it by virtue of governmental positions. As is the case with the monopolization of services, prices rise while, at the same time, the interlocking connectivity of the different assets can reduce costs through enforcing particular pricing mechanisms in the transactions among these discrete sectors.

The investigative resources available to the Prama Group come nowhere close to those of organizations that have managed to detail the regime's extensive economic control and corruption, such as Global Witness, the international research NGO on natural resources and politics, or national human rights NGOs such as LICADHO. But what the group does have is a determination to find out how the consolidation of urban assets in the hands of the elites plays out in terms of how these businesses are run and the city itself is actually managed as a result.

Despite the massive acquisition by the ruling families of ordinary urban services, the group has used its information gathering as a way to target particular points of intervention, often with the sheer disclosure of information. Phnom Penh, like many cities undergoing rapid and uncertain change, is a place where conversations among strangers have a particular character. There is a pervasive sense of equanimity still present in the psyche of a people that survived where a large proportion of its population did not, and that the subsequent reoccupation of the city could not be based on widely divergent claims of legitimacy or right. So there is a certain dignity afforded to everyday exchange, a willingness to disclose something, even if it is insignificant or a matter of small gestures.

When state-owned companies are put into private hands, the almost total absence of legitimate procurement instils a widespread belief that there are always more powerful forces lurking and waiting for individuals to slip up and thus lose whatever minimal control they might exert over their modest trade. So the diffusion of just how extensively elite control reaches into the ordinary real economy potentially intensifies an already widespread anxiety.

But the Prama Group tries quietly to popularize a "common sense" that acquisitions come and go without those who activate them paying a lot of attention. For example, the acquisition of the main bus companies by an ex-wife of Hun Sen's first cousin was mostly used as a way to increase her borrowing privileges in offshore banks. The owner was not interested in maintaining an operation that had to keep a large number of drivers on the payroll or maintain the conditions of vehicles and preferred to split up the company into a series of competing yet interlinked sub-companies. The Prama Group channelled this information through a relative who worked as a clerk in the company office and, using this connection, convinced the drivers to approach a household in the Prama block who had just sold their street-level commercial property for an enormous sum of money and was now interested in investing it in something. Thus an asset picked off from a quasi-public agency and fractured into parts was in turn picked off by a collective of drivers.

Retailers in markets are usually beholden to particular trading brokers who advance money for wholesale purchases. These brokers play off different retailers by spreading misinformation about customs duties and payoffs, and sometimes they will intentionally under-invoice supply chains in order to collect on accruing interest rates tagged to the debts of retailers. The political party of Hun Sen usually takes a cut of these extractions as a way of funding the party machine across the city – a presence that stands out everywhere.

These dealings go back to the mid-1980s, when Cambodian Chinese were encouraged to reactivate long-term trading networks in order to spur accumulation for the city (Verver 2012). While marketing remains largely the purview of the Cambodian Chinese, many of them, in addition to a new substrate of Khmer retailers, are eager to break out of highly restrictive wholesaling networks, even if they are fearful of doing so. Additionally, the management of what takes place within actual markets remains fairly opaque, as the financiers and wholesalers tend to set up shop on the market's periphery.

While henchmen of the regime may criss-cross the width and length of trading spaces, they concede the actual operations to more informal groupings. These groupings become responsible for loading and unloading goods, sorting out traffic and parking, cleaning and maintaining facilities, assigning floor space, collecting market fees, and supervising commodity sales. The authority of such informal groups rests primarily on how much they come to know the intersection of all of these activities, how they can be most proficiently brought together. This means continually making concessions and social repairs, issuing promissory notes and exemptions from agreed-upon rules, and forging agreements for a set of provisional, unwritten yet real regulations. Even if traders remain dependent on various forms of indebtedness and supply chains, this opening in the midst of the market, this "void" at the heart of the market, allows for small performances that go against the grain. As a result, a whole range of small trials and errors exist where retailers access particular goods "off channel."

Working with relatives, friends of friends, contacts in particular syndicates and ministries, the Prama Group connects small groups of retailers in the market with drivers, customs officials, or relatives working in Bangkok or China to access small supplies of both conventional goods and items new to the city so as to experiment with different ways of selling things. The stall in the market is then used as a ruse, a gathering point, to plan for the issuance of goods at some other point and time – a function that is not uncommon in the history of such stalls across different cities.

Perhaps the efforts of the group to try and gather the most intimate details of the ruling families have been the most audacious and risky. They start from the presumption that the rewarding of absolute loyalty also is accompanied by betrayal, resentment and jealousies not just among family members themselves but among the large coterie of domestics, drivers, managers, enforcers, errand boys, clients, sex workers, secretaries and personal assistants that keep the apparatus of social cohesion and deal-making together behind the façades of formal governmental positions. While specific powers of decision-making may flow downward in a strictly hierarchical fashion, the efforts of a ruling elite, cemented into the mutual availing of opportunities, wealth and obligation, also require dispersal across different sites, networks, sectors and territories, as well as opportunities to operate quickly, even erratically. Cracks and fissures in the efforts to reconsolidate, regroup, compensate and discipline may shift decisions as to what investments get pursued, even as families "circle the wagons" in solidarity.

While the juggernaut of elite accumulation and control cannot be curtailed without the consolidation of pressures from above and below, the Prama Group has attempted to precipitate greater unease in the midst of these elite dealings. They propagate rumors about large-scale foreign investment groups, about powerful Chinese mafia figures who open half-million-dollar bets at unmarked high-stakes casinos; they proficiently simulate reports of international consulting firms assessing market values for land and other aspects of the economy; they Photoshop images of individuals of the elite attending meetings or in the company of figures with whom they would not wish to be seen; they have even attempted to hack into agency computers to alter, ever so slightly, procurement orders, shipping destinations, sources of inputs and budgetary data. The idea is not to announce the capacity to hack or to leave discernible trails, but to "invisibly" alter the mundane details of governance.

They also aim to precipitate various slip-ups among the vast networks of underlings which, close enough to the daily operations of the elite to witness the abundance of wealth and power, sometimes strike off on their own. For they realize that their present position will likely never exceed that of receiving the "crumbs." Feeling protected just enough by this proximity to power, they may enter into all kinds of risky ventures, such as drug dealing, child trafficking, smuggling, corruption and theft. By making sure various Armenian, Iranian, Chinese and Nigerian gangs, for example, are fed with up-to-date information about the profiles of various functionaries working in close proximity to the ruling elite, approaches may be made, and then tip-offs provided, to contacts in the police or military who usually see various illegal rackets as their own prerogative. Messes have to be cleaned up and attention diverted – once again, there is the proliferation of unease. The Prama Group knows that the regime is relentless in its repression and does not hesitate to kill or detain. So the planting of information and the development of dissimulation unfolds cautiously through various substrates of contacts and layers of dissemination and provocation.

Again, what is important here is the notion of performance. Dissimulation and trickery, long the weapons of the so-called weak, are cautiously experimented with here as a means of puncturing small holes in the otherwise seemingly seamless veneer of total control. When there is a consolidated indifference as to what actually happens to the majority of a city's residents as a result of the wholesale grabbing of the fundamental asset of land, thus undermining the basis on which residents have elaborated complex interchanges and livelihoods, the city becomes populated with excess uselessness. But perhaps the city is productively useless after all. You cannot exchange it, cash it in for something else, or leverage it for bigger acquisitions. Maybe the city has gone rogue, secreting leftovers from which we must try to find nourish-ment while it is on "the run."

In this chapter we have deepened the discussion concerning the complexity and indeterminacy of everyday life and social networks through a deployment of the concept of secretion. In the process we have made an epistemic point about what the possible implications might be to take seriously both the banal and occult folds of everyday urbanism. We made this point through a number of cryptic and extended stories that emanated from the folds of numerous African and Asian cities. Despite the overwhelming density of opaque social practices and cultures, we also insist that, by taking secretion seriously, it becomes possible to re-describe the relational and institutional potentialities of these cities. In the next chapter we shift the register away from ethnographic invocation and explore the kinds of prospective and speculative politics that can be mobilized through the theoretical sensibilities explored in the last two chapters.

5
Horizons from Within the Break

> We cannot say what new structures will replace the ones we live with yet, because once we have torn shit down, we will inevitably see more and see differently and feel a new sense of wanting and being and becoming. What we want after "the break" will be different from what we think we want before the break and both are necessarily different from the desire that issues from being in the break. (Halberstam 2013: 6)

In chapter 2 we referred to a number of recent interventions which remind us that, despite the neoliberal onslaught of the past three decades, the rolling back of the state, growing inequality and theft, it is possible and essential to think in much more radical terms about alternatives for the near to mid-distant future.[1] Considerations of such possibilities cannot be delinked from the imperatives of a *grounded* politics that pays attention both to popular everyday practices as explored in previous chapters and to the more systematic organization and advocacy of democratic social movements of the city.

From these previous chapters we attempted to elaborate the multiple temporalities and transversals of connection that operate across and through urban spaces. Within the rubric of the "real urban," it is difficult to sustain clear demarcations among functions, flows, territories and events. Institutional life has been largely distributed across a network of seemingly divergent practices and actors, prioritizing the non-contractual, and the disavowal of overly congealed forms of inhabitation. Popular practices of the "make+shift" relied upon large measures of dissimulation, manifesting important practices of provisioning, care and mobilization within rubrics and places not readily recognized as appropriate to them.

At the same time, we live in urban conditions that perhaps require drawing new lines around and between particular spaces and things and, as such, to give them the appearance of some kind of cohesiveness. While collective forms of any kind are never definitive, it is important to find ways of bringing to the fore new forms of congealment, articulation and conveyance that enable otherwise divergent residents, places and activities in urban space to feel concretely implicated in, complemented by, or even dependent upon each other. Of course the drawing of lines always marks something that is kept out, but here line drawing doesn't so much mark distinctions of value or identity. Rather it concerns a means of finding the forms through which people and things can appear to each other in ways that articulate a common operational space.

As such, we argue that it is opportune to clarify various policy/political perspectives and tools that might animate conceivable objectives. Since so much of critical urban studies rightfully maps unequal power relations and various systems of oppression and exclusion we want to offer a different contribution to the larger urban studies project. We want to project what alternative urban claims and modalities of organization could look like so as to chime with the transitional and militant moods of our times. The argument unfolds in five interlinked steps. First, it is possible to concretize claims for an increasingly inclusive and just city by specifying the "how" of the adaptive pathway presented in the last part of chapter 2. Second, for the claims to be strategically informed and holistic, or, more appropriately, latticed, it is useful to think of the city as an assemblage of five operating systems: infrastructure, the economy, land, governance and cultural systems. In each of these domains, it is possible to project the dimensions and dynamics of more inclusive and just forms of city functioning, which is a useful policy/political tool to critique and reimagine the status quo. Third, in exploring and defining the transition pathways from the status quo to alternative trajectories, it is handy to operationalize two metrics – resource flows and intensity per capita and carbon emissions per capita – but disaggregated to reflect differential class contributions.

These measures do the work of drawing lines between mainstream formal policy architectures shifting at a rapid pace and the agendas of insurgents who continually experiment with alternative ways of city-making. Hackers cannot do their viral work unless they intimately understand the system they wish to undermine and can speak its code fluently and, at the same time, have the hard skills to put it to very different uses (Ratti and Claudel 2016). Similarly, effective urban activism requires getting up close and "dirty" to mainstream urban institutions and politics to understand fully where the most strategic opportunities for subversion might be. The fourth step, on the back of this strategic political-policy positioning, is that it is possible to spell out very specific parameters of an alternative system which then becomes the discursive and hegemonic reference point for urban politics and governance, especially if done with careful thought. The function and power of parameters are spelled out in chapter 3, but here we try and extend that critical reading into a tactical politics of possibility.

Once the parameters are marked, then the real work can begin, in a fifth step, to *create* a prefigurative universe of these alternatives, which could be implanted in the bowels of state practices or wild outriders who prefer their specific anarchic patch where they can make and say whatever the hell they feel like (Scott 2012). Both are essential to guarantee fertile conditions for a culture of experimentation and transgression. In any envisaged city, both state actors and wild outriders will be needed, and the latter can often only be discerned through paying attention to the affective folds pulled back in the previous two chapters. These chapters sought to find ways of re-describing present conditions in terms of what might be taking place already, or at least the insinuations of different modes of urban living which find their way within and across the fissures and contestations among different practices of inhabitation, secretion and governance.

For the adaptive city

In chapter 2 we introduced the idea of competing urban scenarios (figure 2.4) as a mechanism to differentiate between the green new urbanisms that seems to dominate the discourse of mainstream actors in both the North and South. At the same time we laid claim to the rights-based insistence on universal access to basic services and the elaboration of the commons in conjunction with regenerating vital ecosystem services, which requires a fundamentally different form of economic accounting and care. We suggested there that real transformative action is embodied within the adaptive city scenario. This agenda seeks to reconcile the potential of ICT innovations with political claims to advance the right to the city and the commons, premised on the imperative of meaningful work, economic inclusion, ecological regeneration and cultural flourishing.

We also argued that this political terrain should be pursued in tandem with a critical engagement with the "next generation" private-sector interests that gravitate around the smart-city agenda linked to the emerging discourse of sustainable infrastructure. This is because there are significant overlaps between how to rethink the routine functioning of the city and the importance of more efficient urban forms and resource dynamics.[2] Also, unless one is able to exploit the tensions and cracks among various fractions of capital, it is not possible to secure the political or ideological space to advance and concretize alternatives at scale. And surely, given the scope and scale of routinized injustice, we need to take large-scale alternatives a lot more seriously (Amin 2011; Ferguson 2011; Harney and Moten 2013). Nevertheless, the challenge remains: how to drag that agenda into contexts where the urban majority cannot afford to buy into the smart city and, more likely than not, will be expelled by its real-estate ramifications, as discussed at considerable length in chapter 3.

Addressing this requires *three* political imperatives. First, it is important to understand in a much more differentiated way the profound economic crisis we are living through and how it reflects the contradictions between entrenched capital and the new sources of wealth creation that form the core of the so-called cognitive economy (Perez 2014b; Rifkin 2014). In this game, fierce battles and conflicts play themselves out. In the confusion about where the real power and influence resides, crucial opportunities exist to push these clashes beyond elite disagreements about the most sensible portfolio of investments. On the contrary, the very determinants of fundamental concepts that drive calculation, "rate of return," "risk," "value proposition," and so forth, are ripe for reframing as mainstream development discourses embrace oxymoronic concepts such as sustainable production and consumption. Such reframing, or resignifying, is of course the oldest trick in the radical political playbook. But it is one we tend to neglect from the perch of moral certitude. The recent politicization of tax havens and tax evasion is but one flicker manifesting these conflicts.[3]

Second, it is crucial that progressive urbanists remain focused on material improvement and wellbeing for the majority of urban dwellers. In all of the convoluted political philosophy that presages most specialist areas within urban studies, the fundamental questions about how to ensure improved health through better sanitation, access to potable water, affordable care, and security from gendered violence tend to become obscured if not ignored. In a time of unprecedented financial wealth, readily available information, expanding state bureaucracies, the expanding adoption of socio-economic rights in national legal frameworks and constitutions, and endless forms of civic organization and exchange, a lot more can be achieved in terms of the basics. This almost banal political imperative deserves greater airplay and action. It also points to a domain of everyday practice that can be enfolded into the routine functioning of popular communities in terms of its core functioning and expansion of capabilities as a potential platform for engaged citizenship and political literacy. These domains are too easily written off as reformist or welfarist practices that are merely sites for forms of biopolitics that promote technologies of self-regulation.

Third, we need to rejuvenate insurgent coalitions of social movements and support NGOs, communities and community associations that form the living tissue of everyday spiritual, economic and cultural practices. Similar attention must be devoted to action networks that can forge epistemic communities, which opportunistically draw relationships across the state, civil society organizations, universities and the private sector. Activist institution builders are vitally important to ensure that insurgent pressures are suitably translated into the "market signals" that formal bureaucracies and political dynasties can understand. They are also indispensable in formulating the necessary experiments to figure out how to supplant the status quo. However, action networks do not achieve very much in the absence of clamorous civic organizations, reasonably competent public institutions and self-respecting media. With these imperatives in mind, we now want to explore one way of framing the urban agenda that we believe can animate public life and agonistic politics.[4]

Operating system assemblages

There is now an established literature that sets out how cities can be thought of in substantive analytical terms as a dynamic assemblage of various interacting and interdependent systems.[5] This literature lives at the intersection of complexity theory, systems thinking, actor-network theory, Deleuzian philosophy and the recent turn to the affective domains of urban life (Bennett 2010; Berlant 2011; Connolly 2014). Considering the diverse origins of these perspectives, there is no consistent interpretation as to what constitutes a system. But, for our purposes, it is instructive that everyone agrees on the ontological idea that large-scale systems *do* exist and are co-constitutive of each other and the larger urban whole. This is not the occasion to review and discuss this extensive literature, but, in the interest of the argument, we want to foreground the notion of operating systems with specific internal properties that form part of larger path-dependency dynamics of contemporary urban spaces. This matters because the anticipatory politics we seek to foreground demands a long-term perspective that endeavors to activate new kinds of dynamic, adaptive *directionality* toward more just, inclusive and sustainable horizons.

The infrastructural operating system can be divided between social-cultural and bio-physical network infrastructures. The latter refers to roads, transportation, information-communication technology, energy, water and sanitation, food and ecological system services (which in turn can be connected to landscape infrastructure) that underpin the built environment and make urban life and movement materially possible. The concept "flow management" provides a useful lens on how these infrastructures can be viewed as conductors of resource flows that are always the product of socio-technical processes (Moss 2001). We'll return to the question of resource flows in setting out a method to connect this systemic understanding of path dependencies with identifying strategic entry points to reorient the underlying logics of the urban system.

Socio-cultural infrastructures refer to the social development investments that forge identity and community and that guarantee a degree of social reproduction – e.g., cultural services, education, health care, public space, libraries, food gardens, green spaces, housing, sport and the arts. It is of course not a given that the state is the sole or primary provider of these services. On the contrary, in most Southern contexts, especially those dominated by informality, a variety of social institutions step into the breach (Bayat 2010; Roy 2011; Scoones et al. 2015; Simone 2010). Social infrastructures by definition need to be tailored to the molecular street- and neighborhood-scale dynamics, which implies, potentially, a substantial degree of community involvement and control in their execution and maintenance. These are potentially critical moments of democratic enrollment and citizenship enactment (Buchanan 2013; Rojas 2010). A quick scan of the literature on urban innovation through strategic design-based acupuncture falls into this category of urban social action (Inam 2014; Tonkiss 2014). It is often painted as the "sexy" end of the contemporary urban agenda in the mainstream incarnations of Jaime Lerner (2014) but typically without much critical interrogation (Cruz and Forman 2015).

In contradistinction to this design-based acupuncture, network infrastructures often imply scale dynamics that cover the larger urban system in all of its territorial expansiveness. This substantive and qualitative difference holds profound implications for how political engagement is defined, structured and connected downward to the neighborhood or community scale. In fact, as is demonstrated by the expansive work on splintering urbanism (Graham and Marvin 2001) and urban political ecology (Heynen 2013), the lack of appropriate democratic oversight and engagement on "invisible" network infrastructures produces conditions where city-wide infrastructures are tailored and routed to service only those sections of the population and economy that can contribute to the investment and maintenance of such systems (McFarlane 2011). This is indisputably one of the primary drivers of large-scale service deficits across cities of the South.

The economic operating system involves production, consumption and market systems that underpin the exchange of goods and services. Importantly, these systems span formal and informal institutions and commonly involve their entanglement. In an era of intensifying globalization, this is an intermeshing not only of formal and informal but also of vast criminal and illicit systems (Naím 2005; Neuwirth 2011). This meshing is particularly important given that formal economic systems in the urban South absorb less than half of the labor force (see chapter 2). The rest eke out an existence in the informal economy or are completely disconnected from any gainful economic activities (Huitfeldt and Jütting 2009; UN-Habitat 2010). Those "lucky" enough to engage in informal work often have to put up with extremely low, and mostly irregular, income which confines them to the category of the working poor (Chen 2008).

In a broader context of the ever deepening global integration of national economies and value chains, it becomes more difficult for national governments to protect jobs, provide support to the working poor, and induce employment because such actions are, ironically, perceived as undermining competitiveness (UNRISD 2010). As long as the intensifying financialization of economic value continues apace, it will be difficult to promote labor-absorptive and equalizing economic policies, despite the reiteration of the discourse of economic growth through job creation that forms part of the SDG mainstream consensus.

Most urban governments have little control or direction-setting power over the economic operating system of cities. However, to avoid looking impotent and feeling redundant, extraordinary effort is expended on local economic development strategies, competitiveness ranking, reducing the cost of doing business, and so forth (Kilroy et al. 2015). As various new seductive discourses surface around the creative economy or smart economy, city governments are further encouraged to benchmark themselves against metrics that stand as proxies for their relative "creativity" or "smartness" (Peck 2005).

Of course, when assuming that a so-called formal economy predominates, these games continue to be blind to the broader spectrum of economic life and work. This "blindness" in turn limits what can be considered as valid and reasonable urban politics and policy, even when city-based regional economies in the global South are so clearly manifested as unequal, extractive and exploitative of people and natural resources. By thinking of the economic operating system in more dynamic and enfolded terms, it becomes possible to explore how to reconcile the imperative for new path dependencies with a deep understanding of the sticky socialities and contradictions of the real economies of these places (Simone 2014).

Infrastructure and economic operating systems depend on land markets and the concomitant spatial forms of the city to function and metastasize. The physical spatiality of the city is structured and conditioned by the economic systems that define and activate land markets. Since the ideal of land-use productivity – maximizing value through floor-space ratios and ground rent – has dominated neoliberal assumptions about urban management for over three decades, we are left with narrow and impoverished conceptions of the spatial operating system of the city (Harvey 1989).

During the last decade, however, there has been an important rethinking of the urban land question in relation to the normative ideal of the commons and how important this value and practice is for inclusive and just city-making (Marcuse et al. 2009). In the Northern literature this has often centered around anti-commoditization debates and in celebration of open public spaces to animate social mixing and exchange in the city as a way of restoring a certain urban vitality (Mitchell 2003). The related debates about urban expulsions, rabid gentrification and the securitization of public and private space all speak to the profound constitutive importance of land markets in shaping urban experience and possibility.

Politicizing operating systems

In figure 5.1, four of the five operating systems have a normative qualifier bracketed before the descriptor. This device of differentiation among five interdependent operating systems helps us to think analytically not only about the assemblage of the systemic drivers of urban life but also about how we can recast each of these domains in the direction of particular philosophical horizons that have become broadly accepted by progressive urbanists (Amin and Thrift 2013; Davis 2006; Harvey 2010). At the heart of this conceptual device is the institutional imperative of governance and its lifeblood: the political. None of the operating systems can exist and have purposive momentum without active governmental regulation, or at least an implicit stance on how not to interfere or be

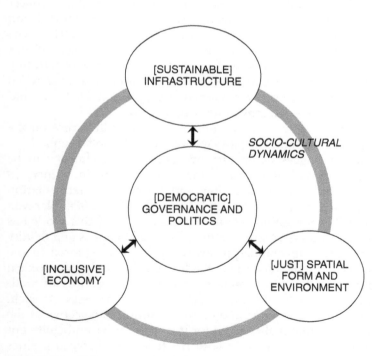

Figure 5.1 Urban operating systems
Source: Adapted from Pieterse (2011: 45).

perceived to be at arm's length. Whether there are strong local states or not, infrastructure, economic life and land-use decisions remain profoundly embedded within structures of rule, coercion and consent, which in many African cities involve forms of authority rooted in traditional systems of rule and regulation (Beall 2006; Rakodi 2002). Even where states have adopted extremist neoliberal practices, the invocation and legitimation of those self-same practices imply a strong, determined and interventionist state (Mouffe 2009). Even when the "official state" looks pared down, the functions of rule and administration and decision-making regarding public funds are increasingly distributed across a network of administrative sectors, logics and agencies which for all practical purposes constitute an interoperable state (Martin 2014).

The final operating system points to the social. It denotes the fact that all four operating systems that tend to preoccupy urbanists and policy activists are profoundly enmeshed in the sticky cultural beliefs which structure individual and collective identities that invariably stretch across corporeal and spiritual worlds (De Boeck 2011b; Howe et al. 2015). The rich and expansive literature from anthropology, science studies, development and political science offer penetrating insights into all that goes wrong in formal planning when cultural specificities are ignored or suppressed (De Boeck and Plissart 2004; Romaya and Rakodi 2002).

At the same time, the now equally vast literature on the virtues of democratic participation in public policy- and place-making suggests that effective political enrollment can be designed and orchestrated through sufficient investment in the right kinds of institutions and practices of intermediation (Goetz and Gaventa 2001; Hickey and Mohan 2004; Narayan and Kapoor 2008). However, what a lot of this work has failed to contend with are the myriad ambiguities and fluidity that invariably underpin everyday life (as explored in the preceding chapters). This fluidity and intensely paradoxical setting will always mutate beyond the prescripts of well-ordered, predictable and legible political processes. As such, how can we imagine and evoke a cultural perspective of the everyday that makes room for this constitutive ambiguity but also articulates it to some of the formal and staged politics of city-making and invention? The exploration of radical localization in the later part of the chapter picks up this thread.

Metrics for transformation

Quantifiable metrics have a special place of disdain for the left (Rose 1999; Swyngedouw 2009; Touraine 2001). Such metrics purportedly reek of an instrumentalized politics manipulated for a multitude of nefarious ends. Furthermore, by definition, quantifiable indicators narrow the field of vision to one or two vectors, excluding or repressing all that flourishes beyond calculation. We appreciate this sentiment and are of the same opinion about all of the dangers associated with calculable rationalities and their recent morphing into algorithmic governance (Greenfield 2013). That said, an effective politics that manages to shift stubborn power relations is not pretty or nuanced. It demands a sharp point, a sliver to pry open. It needs a moment of controversy or, better still, crisis, so that new ways of thinking and organization can be proposed and institutionalized. Concomitantly, struggles can unfold on a different plane, with broader discursive parameters (Scoones et al. 2015). In thinking through how the politics of adaptive urbanism can be anchored to ensure a more explicit commitment to social justice and radical inclusivity, it is useful to appropriate some important environmental metrics that find resonance with ecologists, economists, developers, financiers, activists and political parties of the left.

In a vital work, Mark Swilling and Eve Annecke (2012) suggest that progressive urbanists can build broad-based coalitions for radical urban transformation around two social justice benchmarks: CO_2 emissions per capita and resource consumption per capita. Their argument works with the scientific consensus established through the International Panel on Climate Change (IPCC), which recommends that total carbon emissions per capita per annum should average 2.2 tonnes. The protracted negotiations around the work of the IPCC that manifests in the annual Conference of Parties (COP) seeks to restrict overall temperature increases to below 2 degrees Celsius, which translates into this per capita figure.[6]

Since it is possible to disaggregate the proportional contributions of countries, cities and, within cities, different income groups, the argument that a per capita envelope of 2.2 tonnes per capita per annum holds the potential to be a powerful rallying call for environmental social justice. For example, Swilling and Annecke (2012) disaggregated the households of Cape Town into nine income segments and calculated the carbon footprint of each class of household to prove that the poor contribute a fraction of the total emissions compared with the wealthier households, which exceed their fair share by up to fourteen times.

In a related vein, Swilling and Annecke also argue for working with the analysis and recommendations of the International Resource Panel (IRP), which is concerned with the level of material and resource consumption associated with economic growth. The IRP follows a similar methodology to the IPCC and arrived at the conclusion that a sustainable and equitable global metabolic rate would depend on contracting material extraction to an average of 6 tonnes per capita per annum (Fischer-Kowalski and Swilling 2011). Again, on this score, rich countries and wealthy classes within cities dramatically overshoot this level of consumption. These two metrics – carbon emissions and resource consumption per capita – potentially open up a politicized discussion about the tensions between continued unsustainable economic growth, ensuring access to basic services for all, and taking the necessary policy decisions to reduce carbon emissions and resource consumption per unit of economic output. Given the technocratic nature of these indicators, there is a sound basis for getting large firms and corporations to engage in these debates as an extension of their professed commitments to good corporate citizenship, as ensconced in various globalized "ethical business" standards.[7]

From metrics to infrastructural claim-making

Figure 5.2 isolates the different structural elements of a broader analysis about how to change the "carbon intensity" and "resource efficiency" of a given city. These factors are deter-

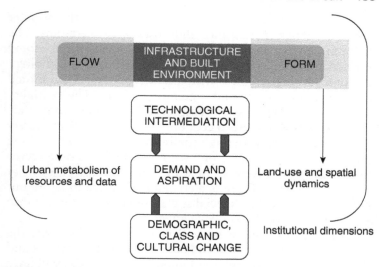

Figure 5.2 Dimensions of material reproduction of territories

mined by the aggregate resource consumption of the city, which in turn is shaped by the types of infrastructure and how resource intensive or efficient it is in conducting urban flows. The nature of land use and associated markets (formal and informal), mobility systems, and relative densities drives the *form* of the urban system. Thus, if a given coalition of urban actors latches onto blunt proxy indicators of resource efficiency and carbon envelope per capita, it potentially creates a broad-based platform on which to make specific claims about how urban infrastructure systems, land-use provisions and planning regulations need to be changed to systematically move a given city toward a more just and equitable future position.

Furthermore, such a perspective is also consistent with an aggressive argument for a transition to a green economy that is resource-efficient, low-carbon, economically and socially inclusive, and spatially just. This definition of the green economy extends the approach promoted by the United Nations Environment Programme in their influential green economy report (UNEP 2011). But, by adding the spatial dimension to their framing, it becomes possible to connect the mediating role of socio-technical systems to the broader concerns with the substance and flows of the economy. The literature on dematerialization or decarbonizing the economy is often apolitical, aspatial and focused mainly on technological innovations coupled with incentive systems promoted through public policy and regulatory reform. The spatiality of resource flows, emissions and social inclusion is what effectively politicizes the green economy discourse. Unfortunately this broader perspective is usually lost in the claim-making politics of progressive actors, who tend to focus on a sector (e.g., energy or movement or water) or a specific part of city at the micro level. There is a crucial imperative to figure out how best to articulate specialist claim-making and resistance with a larger political-policy canvas.

Urban justice cannot be achieved without addressing the politics of spatial injustice and access to essential services and the commons. Most high- and middle-income cities will have overshot their sustainable endowment of resources consumption per unit of economic output. They will also demonstrate a degree of inequality that shows a considerable proportion of the population earns well below the average income (Swilling 2006). Furthermore, disaggregated analysis of most cities in Africa and Asia reveals that the urban poor endure completely untenable residential densities in precarious settlements, whereas the middle classes and the elites enjoy overly generous densities that skew the average for the city (Angel 2012).

Put differently, spatially blind infrastructure modernization can worsen class divisions and exclusions in the city even when it is framed as inclusive city development. A more politically astute perspective is called for that can draw explicit connections between the need for infrastructure investment and its resource efficiency, distributional effects, and impact on the unsustainable and unjust path dependency of the operating systems of the city. This line of political reasoning opens up every single infrastructural system, land-use plan and economic investment to close public scrutiny in terms of whether it contributes to aggregate resource efficiency and whether it deals with differential densities in a way that can foster spatial justice for all. It is precisely in such a political arena that the contextualized imperatives and drivers of adaptive urbanism can come to the fore and be translated into historicized and spatially specific claims for socio-technical reforms and the re-regulation of land markets and land use.

Furthermore, new ICT-based tracking applications also equip coalitions with accessible tools to ensure that the politics and contestation around these metrics remain in the public eye and the basis of continuous contestation and debate. For example, the Peta.Jakarta program mobilizes social media to crowdsource real-time data on flooding in the city, which is also underpinned by a continual tracking of water flows across the city crossed-referenced to indexes of landownership. All of this information is then provided as open-source data. Figure 5.2 also signals that these metrics and concomitant technological and regulatory innovations are not simply quantifiable objects. On the contrary, it is essential to pay very close attention to the culturally rooted patterns of aspiration and demand. These patterns are in part about deeply embedded ideological assumptions and the prospects of the new that can address previously unknown desires and aspirations. Also, even where there is an absence of formal access to essential infrastructure, there are complex embodied enactments to compensate and find ways to make do (De Boeck 2012; Lancione and McFarlane 2016).

On account of technological intermediation, important hybrid opportunities are emerging to extend routinized community practices into new forms of infrastructural technology and organization. The example of micro solar energy grids is a good case in point. For a long time, the most effective and common encroachment strategy in popular neighborhoods has been to tap existing electricity cables and hack pre-paid meters. The former strategy is dangerous and creates a repair and maintenance burden that reduces the lifespan of that particular equipment. However, through careful intermediation and subsidies, it is possible for micro grids that are locally owned and maintained to become a more desirable alternative. This bodes well for extending access to power across larger proportions of the population, and it is compatible with the continual expansion of base-load power, in the form of either new hydro or renewable systems, which are being rolled out with great urgency.

Infrastructural horizons and claims

Similar "infrastructural land-use" service delivery design scenarios can be developed for sanitation, waste management, transportation, water, and so forth (Allen et al. 2016). Table 5.1 provides a rudimentary overview of conventional (modernist) infrastructure approaches contrasted with more environmentally sound alternatives. It is important to understand that the conventional and alternative approaches imply very different technologies and forms of organization, all of which induce a different spatiality (Allen et al. 2016; Rydge et al. 2015; UN-Habitat 2012). The fundamental point is that new political horizons are available but require a deep understanding of existing infrastructure institutional practices and how they are embedded in the preferences and aspirations of urban residents. An understanding is also required as to how these institutional practices of popular aspirations are articulated against new sustainable infrastructural innovations that are affordable and well suited to the fluid livelihood dynamics of popular neighborhoods – i.e., fundamentally adaptive. This analytical work is starting but requires expansion to reflect the diversity of practices and trajectories across urban regions.[8]

Sequencing and calibrating urban claims

A perennial problem for urban activists and leaders is that the city often feels like everything and nothing at the same time. Conceptually, philosophically, everything can be returned to the city in one reading or another. It reflects the sum total of our greatest fears and desires as so evocatively sensed in literature (Bacigalupi 2015; Cole 2014; Okri 1986). Inevitably, the city always oscillates between terra firma and quicksand. Since everything matters, and it is impossible to think about the totality in one swoop and act on it comprehensively, it is extremely hard to figure out an existential or political angle on the city. As soon as a target is fixed, the whole thing morphs into unrecognizable proportions and angles. The emergence of systems thinking, complexity science and sustainability has not helped matters because, ontologically,

Table 5.1 Selected conventional vs. alternative infrastructure systems

Sector	Conventional technology	Resource intensity	Alternative technology options	Resource intensity
Electricity	Coal-fired power stations	Coal Water	Concentrated solar power	Solar
	Nuclear	Water	Photovoltaic wind farms	Solar Water Wind
			Wind Turbines	Water
Water	Large dams, beyond the urban functional region	Rainwater catchment at scale	Water tanks/urban water harvesting for low-quality demands	Rainwater
			Desalination	Seawater energy
	Ground water aquifer exploitation	Groundwater	Sustainable aquifer recharge	Treated wastewater
	Wastewater treatment works	Large-scale treatment and disposal into natural water systems	Decentralized systems Dual systems Vertically integrated systems	
Solid waste	Landfill	GHG gas Soil and water contamination Land use	Avoidance, reuse and recycle	Solid waste
	Incineration	GHG	Composting/anaerobic digestion Gas capturing	Organic materials Solid waste CO_2

Source: Hyman (2016).

everything is interconnected in the human/non-human webs of life; and not only is everything connected, but everything is important. Yet, if politics is anything, it is about choices, trade-offs and navigating the consequences.

In light of this, the current discursive political openings encapsulated in the SDGs, which seek to draw a connection between unsustainable production and consumption, inequality, structural poverty, climate change, weak governance and systemic discrimination in terms of gender, ability and other markers of identity and class, point to the possibility of a fresh political-technical agenda. This agenda uses the imperative of sustainable infrastructure as the entry point into debates about socially just levels of resource consumption and pollution. Infrastructure systems in particular mediate the flow of resources through the urban system and refract patterns of consumption.

By unveiling the socio-technical underpinnings of infrastructural armatures it becomes possible to pose novel questions about the politics and costs of access, regimes of production and maintenance (whether they are capital or labor intensive), technological choices and time-frames within which universal access to essential services can be guaranteed. Moreover, by starting with infrastructure configurations, it becomes possible to reconsider the differential value of land use and how that structures urban opportunity and exclusion. These insights are essential to make political judgments in a given city about how best to prioritize and sequence infrastructure and land reforms. Whatever a given context demands, it will always be necessary to work at both a molecular and a meta scale in order to forge the appropriate articulations between the everyday and the systemic.

Molecular imperatives

Etched into the psyche of the left is a deep and romantic attachment to the state. The current that runs through the waves of neoliberalization analyses in urban studies over the past three decades boils down to an intellectual project to prove that market ideologies drive the continual withdrawal of the state from the provision of essential services and the guarantee of equality. Within this frame, such withdrawal is patently unjust, and instead our political desires must remain trained on a strong, capable and redistributive state. Given the dramatic changes in forms of rule and institutional architectonics with the coexistence and blending of hierarchies, markets and networks, critical scholarship has simply refused to move on from a culturally limited Keynesian conception of the state (Mulgan 2005). Meanwhile, in most of the global South, very different arrangements of state building, forms of rule, institutional design and networking established alternative (not necessarily better) practices and possibilities (Boudreau et al. 2016). The point is that so much urban scholarship has been in mourning for a past that never existed in the first place, except in very different contexts that owed much of their existence to imperial connections with the territories of the global South (Comaroff and Comaroff 2011; Connell 2007).

This stance has given rise to a political outlook of deferral and waiting. In this mindset, because of the "cunning" of powerful elites, the possibility of a radical Keynesian or democratic developmental state is always deferred, always delayed by the inability of a unified working class to challenge and upend neoliberalism. By extension, because this mythical future state is meant to deliver material wellbeing and the commons, you wait for the better life to come and focus all political passions on a militant politics of opposition and resistance. Work that seeks to improve the living conditions of the urban poor in the present is then often read as ameliorative, piecemeal and fundamentally apolitical. This is a grave conceptual and political error (Appadurai 2002; Ferguson 2011).

Urban transformations are most likely to arrive when ordinary citizens amplify their abundant agency, rooted in the dense everyday politics of livelihood and spirituality, to make connections with city-wide (meta-regional) agendas, which are most potent in the form of network infrastructures and symbolic circuits of meaning. Thus, it is arguable that a fertile seam of urban politics can be found in the practices of placemaking that are attuned to the fundamental relationality of urban space. The emerging debates on resilient communities and sustainable infrastructures offer a wide range of vital political openings to push forward a less nostalgic and more creative politics of the city. Let us get more specific.

Adaptive urbanism as a political praxis is first and foremost about doing, about action. On the basis of the materiality that emerges from such practices, it formulates contingent claims that are able to speak to different temporalities and scales. In the global South, the politics of adaptive urbanism therefore first and foremost confronts the crisis of work and all of the associated social-spatial dynamics that accompany precariousness, vulnerability and makeshift practices. In order to connect with the possibility of meaningful work that can also address the insecurities of everyday life, it is important to be as empirically specific as possible. In parsing the politics of work in the makeshift city, a crucial scale of praxis is the neighborhood. Figure 5.3 offers a stylized hierarchy of essential investments that structure the routine reproduction of neigh-

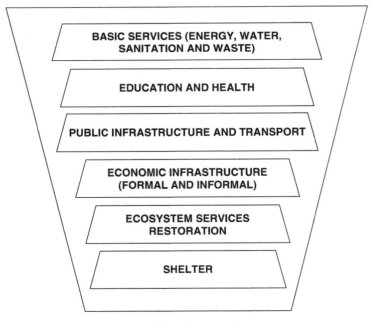

Figure 5.3   Drivers of neighborhood wellbeing
Source: UN-Habitat (2015).

borhoods and communities. Rooted in the contextual understanding set out in chapter 2, it proposes that the bare essentials of everyday life are not arbitrary or disconnected. On the contrary, it is possible to infuse this typology with an appreciation of spatial justice.

The logic behind this hierarchy is that the basic needs of all urban residents must take number one priority over everything else and goes to the heart of fundamental wellbeing and dignity. This is followed by key investments to optimize the capabilities of all residents. In a knowledge-driven globalized economy, this imperative becomes more important if people are able to access employment, which in turn is the fundamental driver of household wellbeing and social mobility. Since many urban dwellers live in slums marked by overcrowding, it is essential that the public realm (the street and key social and mobility nodes) is optimized as a social space, an economic artery and a primary cultural domain.[9] The vitalism of the street is a theme that we have explored on previous occasions (Pieterse 2011; Simone 2004, 2010). But there are other vitalities potentially unlocked when a focus on the public realm is combined with a concerted public transport and mobility strategy.

Building onto an activated public realm entails a commitment to optimize logistical infrastructures that can enhance and diversify urban economic life. Here, a holistic understanding of the economy is critical (Amin 2010; Friedmann 2002; Moulaert and Ailenei 2005). Informal economies and everyday livelihood practices are the dominant modes of economic life in most African and Asian cities. Furthermore, the formal and informal systems are structurally interdependent and fated to evolve in tandem. Thus, the crucial policy objective should not necessarily be formalization; rather, it should be enlarging the economic room for manoeuvre in these communities, which demands an approach of openness even when public authorities do not know exactly what is going on or how things get done.

Once a rounded understanding of the local economy is established, attention can shift to ecosystem services. In a variety of international development policy frameworks, blue and green economic sectors could become the fundamental underpinning of Southern economies over the next few decades

(Floater and Rode 2014; UN-DESA 2013; UNEP 2011, 2013). This potential will only be harnessed if local authorities and citizens realize that the restoration and protection of natural ecosystem services is vital to their wellbeing, their sense of community, and the overall quality of life of the urban system as a whole. More importantly, the pervasive indigenous and traditional cultural institutions that suture popular neighborhoods are often compatible with these approaches, pointing to grounded synergies. A large number of public works opportunities can be shaped around ecosystem services restoration, which is arguably the missing conveyor belt that will enable urban economies to transition youth into the labor market and entrepreneurship, especially in sub-Saharan Africa and the environmentally precarious cities of Asia.

Importantly, in this schema, shelter investments come last. This is contrary to the way in which the urban development agenda was framed at Habitat I in 1976 or affirmed with the focus on slums at Habitat II in 1996. However, this approach does not to diminish the importance of consolidating the right to housing but, rather, insists that urban majorities need support with the enabling armatures of urban life while they take care of the shelter needs, even if in a makeshift manner. Across Latin America and Asia examples can be found to demonstrate that improvements in the public realm prove much more important to the wellbeing and livelihoods of poor households than starting off with public housing provision (Cruz and Forman 2015). This approach may then represent a departure from the urban policy fixation on shelter and tenure security, or, rather, put these two dominant agendas in a more expansive and grounded policy frame.

Service delivery as hinge

Beyond this stylized hierarchy of local investment areas, it is possible to get even more concrete by focusing on the *de facto* systems of service delivery in popular neighborhoods. In most places, residents have very little confidence that public authorities can or will deliver or that militant struggles to shift the status quo will produce the concomitant improvements to warrant the effort. Instead, most residents understand the importance of getting on with what it takes continually to work as many angles, connections and opportunities that could possibly come their way. This means foregrounding every conceivable social connection – ethnic, religious, craft, caste, musical lineage, familial, regional, linguistic – and whatever else can be mobilized as a source of social connect.

A major part of what lubricates these social ties is of course a deep distrust and disbelief in the capacity, or propensity, of the state to care until election time comes around. Furthermore, it is very clearly understood that active participation in political parties is but one pathway in the larger hustle of the "hood" – one potentially productive avenue to explore if the opportunity presents itself. Within this highly dynamic and opportunistic social structure, it is almost inconceivable to configure an imaginary that correlates with leftist militant desires (Perry 2004). Importantly, as the work of Sylvy Jaglin (2014, 2015) demonstrates, amid this reality, very poor households do access basic services, even if it is at a premium and premised on a rhythm of day-by-day consumption. Jaglin draws the veil on situated hybrid systems of delivery whereby local entrepreneurs secure essential resources in bulk and sell on to other local intermediaries or poor households. These systems pilfer from the formal grid, but at the same time they represent an informalized economy of provision, maintenance and repair that is beyond the accounting system of the state (Bayat 2010). Out of these schemes grow expansive systems of exchange, reciprocity, extortion and obligation which serve as the social infrastructure of urban reproduction for urban majorities.

The service delivery dynamics and logics set out by Jaglin remind us that it is important to establish a fine-grained institutional map of the highly localized hybrid architectures – i.e., some formal government provision, combined with formal and informal private suppliers, held together by a host of intermediaries that continually calibrate supply and demand for neighborhoods, households and micro businesses. This configuration tends to reproduce the status quo indefinitely. It chains popular neighborhoods to expensive, erratic and vulnerable delivery systems. It also creates levels of indebtedness for poor households that hijack the best-laid plans for the future.

Even if the vulnerabilities of such hybrid provisioning are well known, its apparent efficacies allow the state continually to defer paying attention to such neighborhoods. These efficacies "buy time," attenuate the sense of emergency, and instead hold popular neighborhoods as sites of waiting that will eventually flourish. Instead, states tend to prioritize creating favorable landing pads for international and local capital keen to enlarge real-estate interests that circulate around retail, service industries, and suburban developments. These developments enable the upper middle class to withdraw from the city at large and deepen their connections with globalized circuits of exchange and consumption. In other words, airports, ports, highways, skyscrapers, securitized gated condominiums or estates, glitzy shopping malls and private leisure spaces (golf and polo estates) become the only investments and cultural priorities that matter, with the promise that, as these investments grow the veritable cake, investments in slum areas will also take off.

Even if continually subverted and tested, highly gendered power inequalities persist at the neighborhood level, as key intermediaries who run and finance the hybrid systems extract optimum rents for their services. It is fairly common for there to be considerable overlap between this class of "system operators" and powerful actors within the political party system that anchor the public and private accumulation opportunities surrounding the development enterprise. In this context, it means that people can access some of the basics within a livelihood rhythm that is sort of affordable (often structured around daily transactions and short-term futures trading schemes), but they are effectively prohibited from engaging in dangerous political acts that could destabilize the routinized way of doing things.

Of course these transactional power landscapes do not negate the overall dynamic of "quiet encroachment" evoked by Asef Bayat (2010). Asymmetrical power dynamics overdetermine service delivery hybrids, but at the same time people are continually pushed to the edges of what they can get away with in terms of occupying land and pilfering power, water and advertising space. As Bayat points out, the sheer scale and constant glacial encroachment does add up to very significant "occupations" of what is considered the domain or property of the state or elites. This is the cumulative power of incrementalism, which of course does not represent a disjunctive break with the overall patterning of injustice. Our interest is to fashion a speculative imaginary about how best we can inhabit these dynamics, drawing on the insights of Bayat (2010), De Boeck (2011b), Elyachar (2011), Jaglin (2014) and Simone (2010), among others, and explore how the imperatives of service delivery, social justice and cultural transformation can best be articulated. This suggests a number of concrete steps.

Place-making as politics

Start with an accurate account of how services are delivered: the configuration of the value chain; the actors enrolled and activated in these hybrid architectures; the cost structure of both supply and consumption; the nature and dynamics of the surplus value extracted; the degree of "satisfaction" with the terms and pattern of provisioning; and what does not work and requires dramatic improvement from various perspectives – e.g., efficiency, cost, reliability and reticulation with related services and operating spaces. Extrapolate an account of the political economy of these hybrid systems in terms of the formal management system, the role of major private-sector players and the nature of the incorporation of the so-called informal. This is crucial because it would allow one to triangulate the relationship between resources flows, institutional control and power.[10] This kind of knowledge project implies purpose-built collaborations between knowledge intermediaries, social movements, grassroots associations and key allies in the state.

Through various dialogical processes, embark on some speculative institutional mapping about how aspects or entire service delivery value chains could potentially be reconfigured, rewired and remade without rendering households and communities more vulnerable. Instead, create possibilities for enhancing the potential of better synergies in terms of the functioning of a neighborhood. Such mapping and its attendant potential neighborhood enhancements can become the political incentive for questioning the larger system of service delivery and resource allocation (Bebbington et al. 2008).

If one's starting point is the extremely low and erratic incomes of poor households, combined with the absence of

Table 5.2 Socio-technological options available when creating institutional hybrids

	Local	Network	National and regional
Energy provision	Off-grid micro solar systems interoperable with smart grids; efficient biomass stoves, community grids; neighborhood-scale waste to energy systems, articulated with the network system; subsidies for demand-side management	Off-grid micro energy (solar, biogas) interlaced with a city-wide expanding grid fed by an dynamic energy mix; bilateral power-sharing with industry connected to appropriate building regulations, extension of access, retrofitting public buildings	Integrated energy planning involving coal, hydro, gas, liquid fuel, renewables and demand-side management; increased supply, decarbonizing utilities, better integrated regional power pools, reduced transmission losses, implementing policies that prevent anti-competitive behavior from multinational hydro-carbon companies so as to allow new renewable entrants

Water and sanitation	Hand-held and community water purification, bio-centers, community-run biodigesters and biogas projects, permeable paving locally manufactured and installed, aquifer recharging	Water treatments and sanitation, effective water pricing, biodigesters for purification, preservation of wetlands, rainwater harvesting, greywater recycling, composting toilets and showers	New dams (linked to energy), inter-basin transfers, trans-boundary water-sharing agreements
Waste management	Waste-picking and recycling, school programs, waste-to-energy	User-pays waste charges, demarcation of space for recycling, biodigesters, upcycling, composting	Packaging legislation, hazardous waste legislation, waste transport legislation
Mobility	Densification, dedicated mass transport lanes, connecting pedestrians with retailers, vehicle parking restrictions, secure bicycle parking facilities	Taxis, car-pooling, ICT and virtual business, motor/bicycle delivery services, electric bicycle facilities, bike-share schemes, bus rapid transit system	Inter-city connections, regional transport hubs, rail freight, fuel-quality control

Source: Cartwright (2015).

formal work and an almost total reliance on piecemeal and low-wage work, the driving question must be how alternative service delivery modalities can take these issues into account and provide a basis for an enlarged relational politics that connects the molecular dynamics of place-making with larger city-wide questions of distribution of public resources. In addressing this question, the potential power of environmental politics comes to the fore. In almost all infrastructural sectors related to the social reproduction of (poor) households, it is possible to rethink and reconfigure these systems in ways that are labor-intensive, ostensibly favorable for the regeneration of ecosystem services, and catalytic for social learning and deepening politicization. In elaborating the potentiality of adaptive urbanism, Anton Cartwright (2015) points to a number of possibilities for adopting low-cost, labor-intensive approaches to urban infrastructure at the local level, but articulated with city-wide networks and national systems. This typology (table 5.2) is particularly suggestive because it hints at the expansive opportunities for local innovations while nesting these in larger scales of reform and action. It goes without saying that none of this is possible without a highly politicized public sphere within which the terms and focus of urban investments are problematized and contested.

Meta imperatives

One of the dangers of the approach proposed here is that the larger systems of rule, exclusion and exploitation remain undetected and unproblematized. Paradoxically, counteracting this danger is able to commence with street-level engagements only as they register the effects of larger distributions and circulations of power. Once urban dwellers get stuck into the molecular politics of fashioning alternative delivery systems, two institutional imperatives come into view. First, the need to articulate various sectors (energy, water, waste, sanitation, public space, transportation, economic service) into a spatialized whole that becomes increasingly molded to the aspirations and agendas of local households. To safeguard and deepen such an understanding demands organization, democratic oversight, deepening accountability and a willingness among emergent leaders to represent the interests of the neighborhood in larger political forums.

Second, the expanding understanding of the nature of the institutional systems that structure underinvestment and exclusion provides a practical insight into the relations between the neighborhood, its larger immediate surrounds, and the city in its full regional expansiveness. Put differently, once a community decides to embark on a shared endeavor, for example, to create localized biodigesters connected to communal restaurants, school feeding schemes and community gardens inside school grounds, the larger political economy of energy provision, licencing, investment and access becomes much clearer, creating opportunities for relational politics.

Ultimately, in the bigger scheme of things, the kinds of urban transformations invoked in this book require regional innovation systems anchored in "action networks" (Carley and Christie 2000) that knit together radicals in all domains of the city – the local state, social movements, universities, business, trade unions, mass-based associations and think tanks. Regional innovation networks are the backbone of experiments in adaptive urbanism. In practice one can imagine city regions (or smaller-scale town-centered agglomerations) committed to low-carbon, resource-efficient and inclusive growth paths working in concert to consolidate intra-Asian and intra-African trade and solidarity. Over the longer term, the economic competitiveness and autonomy of Africa and Asia will have to be rooted in the next generation of infrastructure technologies that are consistent with the criteria of the green economy involved earlier: resource-efficient, low-carbon, economically and socially inclusive, and spatially just.

Strategically, the regional transformation agenda is most effectively advanced through a focus on how four meta-urban reforms cohere:

1 transitioning to a sustainable energy system that allows for affordable distributed systems to be articulated with a grid that becomes progressively less carbon-intensive;
2 transitioning to a public-focused mobility system that places non-motorized transport imperatives at the apex, followed

by affordable mass public transport, at the expense of car-based mobility;

3 accelerating the adoption of ICT infrastructures that can ensure universal access to affordable and secure internet access to lower daily transaction costs and radically enhance economic and political participation; and

4 a radical land-use reform agenda to use the acceleration of these three technologies to anchor the rapid emergence of truly mixed-income and cosmopolitan fabrics of the city.

The elegance of these mutually reinforcing scales is that they obviate the need for rigid blueprints but at the same time underscore the value of strategic line-drawing and road-mapping, which provide an orientation for how different experiments and innovations can best be articulated and horizontally distributed. Moreover, they point to the beginning of a new urban sensibility and disposition that we believe will only grow in visibility and relevance.

6

Experimentations

At the core of arguments running through the book is a deep belief in agency rooted in the mundane routines of social reproduction and culture-making, the tactical capacities of institutions, and the political potential to remake the terms of urban recognition, social justice and aspiration. However, there is no obvious program or stable ideological edifice that can be invoked to establish an orderly modern politics of city-making or rights, even though all kinds of manifestos and tabulated claims can of course be conceived, as demonstrated in the previous chapter. Instead, what is called for is a commitment to experimentation, unlearning, shedding habits of thought, and always figuring another angle despite the odds.

In this chapter we want to restore experimentation as a normative aspect of living in and running cities and to think about how concretely to create space for such experimentation. To make this case we turn to a number of stories from the coalface of diverse sites of practice: international policy circuits and associated architectures; national policy platforms that call on diverse stakeholders and actors to find common ground on how to comprehend urbanization; social movement repertoires and cultures of learning; and, finally, various mechanisms to invent and shape publics concerned with urbanism and its unruly potentialities.

Our practices stem from a very particular political sensibility honed over decades of moving between activism, intermediation, cultural work and scholarship. In brief, we insist on a deeply relational reading of urban politics and imaginaries (Pieterse 2008; Simone 2004, 2010, 2014; Simone and Pieterse 1993). Specifically, it is important to differentiate between formal and insurgent political institutions. Formal systems typically involve an amalgam of the representative local government system (elected domains and the supporting bureaucracy and associated agencies), as well as corporatist forums where mandate-carrying representatives of business sectors and civil society organizations convene with the (local) state to carve out medium- and long-term plans, or at least set priorities. It goes without saying that the mechanics of effective corporatist pacts turn on highly informalized networks and agreements, often lubricated by varying degrees of culturally meaningful forms of patronage, clientelism and extortion when needed. This is urban politics as "a game," as powerfully evoked in dramatized stories such as *The Wire*, *Luther* and *Narcos*. These formal institutional domains are reinforced by various discursive regimes that are typically projected through the media and other forms of symbolic communication.

Insurgent dimensions cover the full spectrum of non-state passions and actions – e.g., resistance, cooperation through critical partnerships, collaboration, and so on. In democratic polities, most insurgent institutions are keen on recognition and therefore tend to play by the rules established in law and formal government. However, those who understand the intricate dance of power and counter-power are most interested in a much more opportunistic game that pushes the formal system as far as it can bend, while stoking radical passions in order to continually alter the terms of engagement. This is a manoeuvre that enables new, formerly unthinkable possibilities to become visible and debateable – properly political. However, the unmistakable disjuncture between institutional dysfunction on the part of the formal urban management system and the dramatic scale of "developmental" requirements in African and Asian cities demands an unconventional approach to the political. These conditions demand a political awareness that is both *subtle* and *timeous*. It is by inhabiting this sensibility that the kind of commitment to urban knowledge and practice as a permanent site of experimentation comes into relief.

The unvalued art of subtlety

There is no quick fix or grand gesture to democratize urban life and instantiate full socio-economic citizenship. In order to advance a cumulative, slow-brew politics attuned to the popular and rooted in an ethic of care, particular knowledges and political sensibilities need to be cultivated as central to the practice of research and theory building. The advancement of such a politics requires an endless capacity to live with seemingly contradictory double-moves that demand counter-intuitive capacities to thrive amid frictions. It is not about resolving the dialectic. Instead, it is about holding contradictory impulses in deliberate tension without losing one's political or cultural footing. This can best be evoked through the following propositions regarding *doubleness*, which we argue is an appropriate sensibility to enter and inhabit urban political life conjured throughout the book.

First, urban actions should always seek both to "connect" *and* to "weave" different scales of being and action, but in a manner that treats scale not as a hierarchical ordering of materiality but, rather, as a topological dynamic of co-constitution and multiple kinds of extensions and contractions (Thrift 2008). Practically this means that the long-standing political/policy obsessions to figure out what is best done nationally versus locally, or vice versa, or how the local can ensnare the global or the regional tend to lead down culs-de-sac. Any intervention will have resonances in a multiplicity of ways that hold the potential for specific culturally informed mobilization in concrete settings. Figuring out what the most powerful resonances might be is essential to forging a grounded, and therefore more promising, politics that can reverberate well beyond the local. The idea that there is an optimal calibration of organization and regulation across different hierarchical scales is a bit of a red herring in urban geography debates.

Second, it is essential to keep both "the systemic" and "the acupunctural" in view when urban interventions are designed and operationalized. Molecular actions may seem acupunctural, but they are unlikely to find sustenance unless they feed into and off broader systemic actions that can generate durable transformations over time. In chapter 5 we explored our understanding of the assemblage of interdependent systems calling out for a strategic politics of transition. Similarly, large-scale ambitions need to be tempered by the micro impacts and ramifications that they will carry in tow. However, it is much harder to accentuate the cultural and popular significance of the systemic, since everyday life gains shape through the intimacies of acupunctural actions. The masculinist claim that only large-scale systemic interventions that shift the political economy of access and citizenship count as real politics amounts to hubris if it is unable to recognize the power of micro transformations in the domain of everyday living and psychological dispositions (Appadurai 2011; Biehl et al. 2007; Pieterse 2011).

Third, building on the previous point, urban interventions need to pay astute attention to both "the intimate" and "the public." Indeed, the commons is most likely to be enlarged through a more robust agenda to amplify and enrich public space and shared infrastructures such as streets, markets, parks and other social groundwork, but these should never be defined without a deep engagement with the requirements of secrecy, obscurity, privacy, autonomy and interior (psychological) room to breathe. In the political clamor for a celebration of the commons and its recuperation, there is often a tendency to gloss over the unavailability of room to be fundamentally contradictory and psychically incomplete. Religious and spiritual movements are growing across the global South precisely because they offer various kinds of respite to social density and claustrophobia.

Fourth, these propositions demand a creative sensibility that seeks to articulate "the designed" and the "organic-emergent." Put differently, there is little gain in valorizing informality for its own sake and adopting a live-and-let-live attitude to urban life. There is much that thoughtful and politically alert design thinking (Boyer et al. 2011; Sinha 2012) can bring to the larger project of remaking the city. But, as a rule, if this flattens the finely honed organic practices of livelihood and association, it will simply fail and produce even more oppressive (unintended) consequences. So, a mode of thought and design is called for that can draw inspiration and orientation from the kinetic city, while molding it into experimental transformative interventions that are both acupunctural and systemic.

Fifth, none of these dispositions and artful practices can find a footing if our political imagination continues to pit formal political chambers against the street. As intimated earlier, urban politics is constitutively relational in that it spreads across formal political structures, governmental bureaucracies, corporatist forums, backroom deal-making, militant sentiments embodied in practices of direct action, developmentalist institutions and the public sphere instantiated by the media, public discourses and symbolic representations (Pieterse 2008). This makes for dynamic and unpredictable relational fields where formal and insurgent governance institutions – typically in conflict – seek to shape each other by drawing on different forms of legitimacy and power. The formal domain seeks to envelop and discipline the emergent systems, whereas insurgent practices typically seek to elide or neutralize the ambitions of formal efforts. However, formal governance institutions are not necessarily democratic or inclusionary even if such institutions espouse the values of participatory governance. Similarly, insurgent organizations are not innately democratic or inclusionary either. In these settings, the *real city* is often marked by quasi-authoritarianism, variable forms of clientelism, patronage and populism; it takes on the form of "a game" that demands a hustler's cunning (Hansen and Verkaaik 2009). It is up to patient and far-sighted activists in both domains to forge the appropriate mechanisms and spaces for collaboration and systematic transformation, typically anchored to vital urban development issues such as safety, food security, shelter, access to basic services, livelihoods, and so forth, that can be pursued along molecular and regional lines of experimentation.

Lastly, visionary, pragmatic and programmatic political passions demand an approach that can engage with the full gamut of material necessities in terms of work, income, security, shelter, health, learning, leisure, mobility, technology, connectivity, and so on, as well as with the spiritual and symbolic underpinnings of these imperatives. Urban policies and programs often run aground because of technocratic heavy-handedness and a modernist conceit distrustful of indigenous and tacit knowledge systems that underpin routine survival. As we have argued throughout the book, everyday life holds the key to both urban theory and practice, which in turn means that the remaking of the city must, by definition, be driven by the urban majority.

As an ensemble, these propositions constitute a *doubleness praxis* that is audacious and nimble. It also intimates an expansive political repertoire that can accommodate and extend insurgent politics comprised of militant resistance as well as prefigurative development work to attend to urgent livelihood imperatives. At the same time, it is able to take in the dull, reformist, potentially reactionary work of bureaucratic rewiring, enhancement and consolidation as manifest in state institutions and the endless permutations of co-producing formations that live somewhere betwixt and between the state, the market, civil society, academia and households. It is patently patient, open and generous without abandoning an insatiable hunger for social justice and transgression. However, for such a cultural milieu to emerge and deepen, there has to be a shared commitment to radical experimentation as a source of sustenance.

Experimentation

Although essential most of the time, the inbuilt optimism of design can greatly complicate things, first, as a form of denial that the problems we face are more serious than they appear, and second, by channeling energy and resources into fiddling with the world out there rather than the ideas and attitudes inside our heads that shape the world out there.

Rather than giving up altogether, though, there are other possibilities for design: one is to use design as a means of speculating how things could be – speculative design. This form of design thrives on imagination and aims to open up new perspectives on what are sometimes called *wicked problems*, to create spaces for discussion and debate about alternative ways of being, and to inspire and encourage people's imaginations to flow freely. Design speculations can act as a catalyst for collectively redefining our relationship to reality. (Dunne and Raby 2013: 2)

This sober reflection on the limitations and potentiality of speculative design captures aptly the spirit of experimentation we have in mind. As explained before, it is imperative to confront the urgency of large-scale routinized deficits that frustrate the wellbeing of urban majorities, which cry out for more effective politics, intelligent policy and institutional efficacy – the ingredients of what is often decried as a form of "policy-fix." We think it is a mistake to abandon this vital terrain of struggle, thought and experimentation. However, to make effective incursions into the worlds of formal politics and policy, a commitment to an experimental politics must be nurtured. This in turn demands a sustained engagement with the full spectrum of public life, everyday practices (as elaborated in chapters 3 and 4), and organized resistance politics that takes rhizomatic power and potentiality seriously (Hardt and Negri 2011; Massumi 2015). However, as explained in chapter 5, the task at hand demands an articulation of the urban moment with multiple temporalities to activate the potential of transitions toward adaptive urbanism. Figure 6.1 illustrates the zone of experimental practice that this points to.

By thinking in these institutional, cultural and relational terms of urban life, it becomes possible to respond to the invocations of Ferguson (2010) and Amin (2011) not only to narrate what is wrong and oppressive in our times but also to instigate ongoing experiments that can concretize alternative urban futures. Put differently, it is possible to *occupy* imaginaries about the future. But this makes sense only if such occupation shapes a politics of the present about current investment priorities and systems of delivery. Stitching together the future and the present is vital and ultimately requires an experimental disposition.

Tales from imperfect practice

As rogue scholars, we find that our most useful interventions fall in the domains of enriching and enlarging discursive frameworks. In this section we will reflect on various examples of this practice, moving from macro policy frameworks to

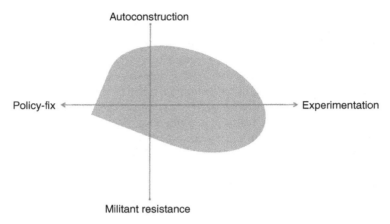

Figure 6.1   Sphere of experimental practice[1]

the grounding ideologies of social movements and the fostering of different kinds of publics through various interstitial publications, deployed from the platform afforded by the African Centre for Cities.

Sculpting discursive architectures

World Cities Report

A long-standing concern and critique of ours is the way in which the desire for consensus in urban politics has dominated the mainstream policy discourses about urban governance ideals (Pieterse 2008; Simone 1998; Simone and Pieterse 1993). In these narratives there is no room to appreciate the constitutive importance of dissent and agonistic conflict (Mouffe 2000) in strengthening democratic appetites that can deal with systemic drivers of routinized urban injustice and cruelty. Thus, when one of us was asked to help with the backroom drafting of the chapter dealing with urban governance in the *World Cities Report 2016* – a UN-Habitat biennial flagship publication – we jumped at the opportunity. Given the ways in which the United Nations and the discourse of the Habitat Agenda of 1996 remain deeply wedded to a deliberative democracy model that is premised on consensus between the "holy tripartite" cooperation of business, government and civil society, it was worth exploring the potential to embed an agonistic model of democracy.

Given the discursive elasticity entailed in the drafting of a such report, which has to convey both a sense of "the groundbreaking" and "the politically plausible," the notion of democratic agonism was pushed to the hilt. For, at the same time, one also knew that such a notion would invariably be diluted or potentially erased in the final version that was published in the run up to Habitat III. Yet, it still seemed worthwhile to see what the political edge of this discursive machine might be. In the final version of the *World Cities Report*, the following concession is made:

> The Habitat Agenda, along with most policy agreements emanating from the UN system, rests on a consensual model of modern democratic politics. This approach operates on the assumption that it is possible to differentiate societal institutions along distinct categories: public (government), private (business) and community (civil society organisations). These institutions come, in turn, under the influence of distinct interests that must be brought into harmony for the larger societal good.... However, this model of planning and politics is running against some criticism. This includes claims that elite interests can adopt formal resolutions that embrace the precepts of democratic, transparent and inclusive local governance – but still manage to perpetuate elite-driven processes of decision-making and control. It is, therefore, imperative to recast governance systems in order more explicitly to acknowledge the necessity of agonistic (i.e. friendly rule-based competition) debate as a necessary fuel for effective local governance. This calls for both legal and cultural acceptance of pluralistic civil society engagement with the local authority, which can range from close collaboration and cooperation around service delivery to an adverse relationship expressed through non-violent action and protest. (UN-Habitat 2016: 115)

Given the ways in which the placid discourses on "good governance" have sought to tame and delegitimize militant social protests, it is important to appreciate how this seemingly innocuous acknowledgement creates a foothold for a radical reframing of the terms of urban recognition, claim-making and a more dynamic relational politics that can more easily move between protest, cooperation, co-production, experimentation and further protest when this is called for in terms of the democratic calculations of urban movements and their networks. Its radical potential is further strengthened when read alongside another important acknowledgement in the same chapter that urban planning, even if participatory, can be ineffective and complicit with the systems that reproduce urban inequality and expulsions. Promoting the centrality of planning and urban strategy when the historical limitations and dangers of planning are acknowledged is an important political opening. Moreover, this provisionality is connected with an explicit conceptual and political acknowledgement of unequal power relations in the city.

Drawing on the work of Gaventa (2013) and Pettit (2013), the chapter foregrounds the ways in which visible, invisible and hidden power coexist and co-constitute routine political and administrative practices of local governments, which calls for more radical processes of contestation in order to shift these dynamics. *Visible power* is the manifest capacity of actors in formal decision-making bodies and public spaces to present and advance their interests, (ideological) perspectives and priorities.

Hidden power denotes the ways in which the formal political and policy deliberative processes and forums are not on an equal playing field – the ways in which numerous voices and interests are systematically excluded from the debate. Hidden power explains how official political and policy arenas are constructed and hemmed in by specific discourses. Furthermore, hidden power works effectively because it is culturally underpinned by *invisible power*, which stems from subjectivity – i.e., how a person understands and enacts a sense of self as an expression of self-esteem, confidence, self-worth, dignity and corporeality – one's relationship with one's own body in terms of reproductive health and sexuality.

In highly stratified, patriarchal and unequal societies, those at the bottom of the pile are systematically devalued and considered inferior, in part on account of their material and educational deficits and in other senses because of their membership of "inferior" classes. Thus, for Gaventa (2013: 12), invisible power "involves the ways in which awareness of one's rights and interests are hidden through the adoption of dominating ideologies, values and forms of behavior by relatively powerless groups themselves. Sometimes this is also referred to as the 'internalisation of powerlessness' in a way that affects the awareness and consciousness of potential issues and conflicts, even by those directly affected." It is clear how this problematization of power relations within a policy frame can allow various subaltern categories to enter the fray on their own terms and potentially contest the terms of urban prioritization, investments and future projections.

Echoing the current dominant sensibility of urban policymaking, the *World Cities Report* also makes the case for explicit national-level policies that can proactively engage with urbanization processes and propose a multi-level governance system to deal with its implications (UN-Habitat 2016). In keeping with this discursive preoccupation, South Africa has also been engaged with a multidimensional policy process since 2012 to formulate an Integrated Urban Development Framework (IUDF) for the country, which, again, involved one of us.

South Africa's Integrated Urban Development Framework

South Africa confronts a tough urban policy challenge: the more the state increases its redistributive investments in the form of free public housing for all households below a predefined income threshold, the more spatial inequality and economic marginalization intensifies. The reason for this is that the 100 percent public housing subsidy has to cover the costs of land, the structure of the house and the internal infrastructure. Since land markets are highly uneven, the only way in which the policy can be implemented is if the land acquired is sufficiently cheap, which invariably means being marginal in the larger urban land market. Once families take up occupancy, it means they are saddled with a host of new problems in comparison with living precariously in a makeshift dwelling. For example, transport costs become very expensive, and the neighborhoods in which they now find themselves are devoid of clinics, schools, and a host of other social infrastructures. However, since the new house represents an asset (which can in theory be traded informally) that provides the prospect of improved security and/or financial liquidity, the demand for public housing is seemingly insatiable. Since 1994, the government has processed over 4 million subsidies.

However, the spatial effect of this policy since that time has been that the segregationist apartheid planning effects have effectively been reinscribed. Furthermore, the public housing program transmogrified into a *de facto* urban development policy in the absence of a more considered one. In December 2012, Pieterse was invited and appointed to head up the "Panel of Experts" established to support an inter-ministerial committee to draft a formal urban development policy framework for South Africa. Knowing the inherent limitations of these processes, which are very similar to the ones expressed at the international level with regard to UN processes, it did seem that the potential was there to shift the discursive and political parameters of the practiced political debates on the future of South African cities and towns.

In terms of an insurgent approach, it was important to secure four policy assumptions. First, informality in the economy and living conditions was a more or less permanent feature of the urban landscape in a context of 35 percent unemployment, large-scale poverty and extreme income inequality – all reinforced by severe spatial divides and exclusions stemming from the cumulative effects of colonial and racist planning and managerial systems. Second, it was necessary to shift mindsets on the role, function and potential of the (semi-formal) minibus public transport system that grew out of the limitations and dysfunctions of the formal public transport system, along with a commitment enabling safer non-motorized transport. Third, a move away from an (modern) engineering-dominated approach to urban infrastructure was required to appreciate the potential of sustainable infrastructure systems that are labor-intensive and conducive to a democratic politics of place-making. Fourth, there was a need to embed in urban democratic systems a fiscal and institutional commitment to invest in grassroots organizations as a precondition for co-producing urban development strategies and routine urban management. These assumptions echo the notions of radical localization and regional networks spelled out in chapters 2 and 5.

As the background research and consultations on the IUDF unfolded (2013–14), it became clear that a particularly superficial understanding of urban injustice predominated thinking and claims within civil society and the state. Predictably, the government wanted to propagate a discourse that sought to create the impression that the many urban dysfunctions could be fixed through careful policy design and consistent implementation – an institutional fix. A counter-measure was needed – one that could allow the government to take on a proactive role but also acknowledge that one policy framework cannot resolve a number of deep social, economic and spatial contradictions. Any such resolution necessitated a sustained politics that questioned the history and terms of urban incorporation. A section was introduced into the draft policy framework that made a case for confronting "deep urban logics," which were typified in the following terms.

i)   Land and property markets shape the *form* of settlements.
ii) Infrastructure networks that conduct the *flows* of people, resources, goods and data shape the metabolic dynamics of settlements.
iii) The cumulative impacts of long-term efforts to effect racial segregation and oppression live on in the DNA of settlements, reinforced by uneven patterns of land values and access to resource flows.
iv) The routine movement choices of households and individuals to maximize access to urban opportunities drive settlement choices – e.g., people preferring to live precariously in a peripheral informal area in order to access better schooling than to stay on in a rural area.
v)   The imperative to maintain political (and fiscal) stability undermines the scope for structural reforms to radically alter patterns of access to urban land and other resources.

This version, minus point (v), made its way into the first public version of the IUDF (COGTA 2014) but got diluted in the final version adopted by Cabinet in May 2016 (COGTA 2016). The point is not how much it was redacted but, rather, the ways in which these policy processes can be deployed to pry open a number of political engagements on issues that would normally be inconceivable in the rationalities of the state. The value of these processes is that one can lay depth charges that can be ignited by savvy social movements and think tanks that seek to hegemonize the terms of public debate on the drivers of urban injustice and exclusion. Alas, for reasons that are well beyond the scope of this chapter, very few non-state actors exploited these opportunities, but the potential for a more radical, urgent, transformative and lyrical urban imaginary remains there for the taking (Pieterse and Cirolia 2016).

Enriching social movement practices

Social Justice Coalition

A good example of a savvy social movement is the Social Justice Coalition (SJC) rooted in Khayelitsha, which is in one of the poorest areas in Cape Town, comprising dozens of neighborhoods and home to between 15 and 20 per cent of the city's population of 3.9 million. The peripheral parts of Khayelitsha can be considered the peri-urban edge of Cape Town and therefore also the logical settlement area for new, mostly poor migrants. Most of the slum settlements in this part of the city lack sanitation and other basic services, and most areas are also marked by very high levels of routine social violence (Gurney 2014). The SJC explain their identity in the following terms:

> The SJC's main focus area is Khayelitsha (in Cape Town) – home to approximately 400 000 people, most of whom live in shacks made of wood and metal sheeting. With 11 active branches and over 40 partner organizations, the SJC promotes active citizenship through education, policy and research, and community organising to ensure government is accountable, open and responsive. The SJC is currently engaged in two primary campaigns – The Clean and Safe Sanitation Campaign and the Justice and Safety for All Campaign. (http://nu.org. za/wp-content/uploads/2014/09/SJC-endorsement-final-GIFT21Sep14.pdf)

The Justice and Safety for All Campaign has been focused on the absence of effective policing in the township. Khayelitsha and other black townships have extremely high levels of violent crime and mortality rates related to interpersonal violence. Yet, in per capita terms, these neighborhoods are short-changed by the South African Police Service in terms of the number of officers per head of population, physical infrastructure and the capacity for investigative work. In order to address this deficit, SJC opted for an interesting strategic approach. They courted the premier of the Western Cape government led by the Democratic Alliance (DA) Party, which is the official opposition to the ANC at the national level. The DA has been keen to secure more authority and resources for municipal policing and greater oversight over the national police service.

Thus, when SJC approached the premier to establish a formal judicial commission to investigate the experience of crime and violence in Khayelitsha, she responded with enthusiasm. At the same time, the national minister of police opposed the commission on the basis that its establishment was beyond the powers of the premier. After a number of court battles, the commission – known as the O'Regan–Pikoli Commission of Inquiry after the two leading commissioners (Ndifuna Ukwazi 2016) – was set up and allowed to complete its work.

The findings were damning in terms of the utter disregard for basic rights and decency in terms of the experience of the by now nearly half a million citizens living in Khayelitsha. It pointed to a culture whereby the most exhausted, burnt-out and demoralized police got stationed there as a hardship post, where their impossible caseloads exacerbated the deeply entrenched culture of disregard. Throughout this process, SJC worked tirelessly to gather affidavit after affidavit to bring the full horror of insecurity into the public domain. They also worked extensively with a wide spectrum of grass-roots organizations to embed the campaign and demands within the community at large and conducted original research to feed the commission and make the political claims irrefutable. Once the commission report[2] was finalized in 2014, vindicating most of their claims, they proceeded to work very closely with the various components of the security establishment to figure out how to address the recommendations in practical terms, while reserving the right to take to the street if implementation is lacklustre or underfunded.

The parallel campaign focusing on clean and safe sanitation took on a similar multidimensional mode. But now the target of advocacy and militant mobilization was the City of Cape Town metropolitan government, which is run by the DA as well. In other words, while they were working closely with the DA on the commission investigating policing in Khayelitsha, the SJC opted to challenge and oppose the same party on their track record with regard to sanitation plans and services. In both cases they demonstrated an uncanny ability to play the media and garner public sentiment in support for their work and claims. It was this capacity to move across the full spectrum of democratic activism and mobilization that struck us as highly significant and suggestive of an experimental urban politics.

During 2014–15, Pieterse began working with a core group of SJC activists. It was agreed to organize a series of open-ended sessions where Pieterse would listen to the oral histories of about ten core activists. Half of the group worked as full-time staff in the secretariat, and the other half were elected leaders of branches of the organization. The proposition of this experiment was that the speed and intensity of the work of the organization left little room for reflection, questioning, learning from international histories, and thinking through what it would take to move onto a qualitatively different plane of strategy-making. The idea was to create an open space for questioning and provocation. Pieterse would play devil's advocate by conjuring alternative histories for strategic choices made by the organization as a means of forcing greater reflexivity and connecting back to the spatiality of their practice. In other words, questions were posed about the avenues not pursued that could have produced more systemic impacts in how their communities are serviced and "seen" by the metropolitan government. The impact of this process on SJC is unclear, but it has profoundly shaped our understanding of what a grounded social movement politics could be, which is evident throughout the arguments of this book.

The operations of local "councillors" in Jakarta

There are situations where the clear distinction between the state, the private sector, and civil associations becomes largely a backdrop for competing vectors and constellations of rule that cut across institutional territories. Indeed, the state may be discerned through clearly demarcated institutional spheres, regulatory apparatuses, laws and rules. But it nevertheless is often enacted aside these structures through various forms and intensities of penetration across a heterogeneous landscape of different authorities, vernaculars and unofficial accords. Here the state itself is continually taking on an "experimental" form, but largely in the interests of competing political elites, as a means of their mobilizing financial resources, as well as commanding loyalty and collaboration. The question, then, is how ordinary residents and districts within the metropolitan arena can mobilize to address the state both in its formal appearance and in its various unofficial guises.

Jakarta provides an example of the emergence of political forms that may rely less on cascading popular support and visible contestation than on proliferating lines of collaboration that unfold horizontally across different administrative territories and types of spaces. Democratically contested politics are limited to the election of the Jakarta governor and what is known as the *rukun tentagga* (RT), which is the lowest tier of municipal governance – an administrative officer responsible for between roughly thirty-six and fifty households in a given area. Between these strata most other municipal officials are appointed, although in recent years "village councillors" have been elected as an advisory group for district administrators – each district encompassing roughly 10,000 to 15,000 residents.

Simone participated in a project to train these councillors in several districts of Jakarta, mostly in terms of managing small capital budgets granted to them, as well as watered-down versions of participatory budgeting. These tasks have been in line with the expectations of donors and administrative officers. Yet this training process became a way for councillors to use their limited official roles to broaden their capacities to operate collectively through the varied associations and networks in which they already played a major part.

Jakarta has experienced a large rate of evictions of poor households over the past several decades, and such evictions have recently intensified under the auspices of flood mitigation, traffic control and other projects of "rectification." Several important social and trade union movements have organized constituencies in various modalities so as to contest these evictions through resistance campaigns, court injunctions and political advocacy. They have had limited success, particularly as evictions have largely been justified either on account of the need for protection and the addition of crucial infrastructure or because of the state's recuperation of land for rational spatial development. Attempts to solidify political support across a burgeoning middle class that either seeks to remain or return to the urban core, and thus to avail themselves of a range of what they consider to be essential amenities, feed into the tendency for municipal government to operate in a heavy-handed manner. This heavy-handedness is only partly assuaged by government claims to provide adequate substitute housing for the poor in better conditions.

The majority of Jakartan residents have demonstrated little support for anti-eviction campaigns. This is a majority whose disposable incomes are not that much greater than those of the poor and who also circulate through oscillating periods and forms of employment. Security of emplacement, livelihood opportunities and the provision of many important services have been mediated through varying constellations of formal and non-formal authorities, collusions among politicians and local civic leaders, and extrajudicial operations of the police and military. Yet, the largely token supplement of "village councils" has provided the "veneer" or "cover" through which a growing network of local activism is being enjoined.

Here, the formal status of operating within a municipal jurisdiction – but without, with few exceptions, the encumbrance of "real responsibilities" – nevertheless allows the possibility of allocating the local populations to which these councillors already have access into continually emerging projects that cut across neighborhoods and districts. These projects might include the organization of accommodation for particular trades and workshops and their staff, resistance to the extraction of fees from local businesses and markets by police or the military, consolidating the earnings of local market associations in different parts of the city into investments in affordable housing or a range of financial instruments that constitute informal "endowments" for the development of youth training centers and other community associations.

These emerging lateral networks, operating under but yet through official administrative ambits, or at least in parallel to them, do not constitute formal political organizations. This is the case even as the councillors who largely serve as the visible nodes or anchors of these networks may be active in various political parties. For when councillors actively cultivate traditional clientelist relationships, they are usually "detoured" into agendas set by these lateral associational networks. Critically, the objective here is for neighborhoods to prevent being "picked off" one by one, neighborhood by neighborhood. Such efforts to prevent this from happening occur through extending and intensifying the circulation of information, cooperation, market exchanges and local commodity circuits across districts. Councillors acting as nodes in lateral networks attempt to find ways of articulating established "basins" of economic activity – such as textile production, furniture-making, waste reprocessing or food production – into expanded forward and backward linkages that fold in different actors connected to different religious associations, political parties, commercial networks, financial institutions and government agencies. They do this so as to insulate individual districts, now finding new ways of acting in aggregate, from attempts systematically to *devalue* the localized assets in land, social practice and institutional thickness that residents have generated over long periods of time.

Fostering multiple publics

Cityscapes

Cityscapes is a "journal/magazine hybrid" that a few of us within the African Centre for Cities initiated in 2011 based on a vision of Tau Tavengwa – an accomplished designer and astute student of contemporary urban culture and style.[3] At its core, *Cityscapes* seeks to tap an emerging vein of urban practice, thought, culture and sensibility that resonates across the global South, while keeping a firm footing on the African continent. It seeks to create a bridge between the worlds of academic reflection on urbanism, mainstream debates on urban development and culture, and broad-based curiosity of an *intelligentsia* that seeks to make sense of the dynamic transformations unfolding across cities of the global South, connected with broader interests in the arts and public culture. Thus, *Cityscapes* is consciously styled to be engaging, beautiful, tactile and deeply informative, drawing on long-form reportage as its central device, alongside strong photography, data visualization and design. It also connects with the minds of leading urban scholars and policy leaders through in-depth interviews that deliberately interweave the personal and the professional.

A key driving force behind the initiative has been to establish a beacon to attract like-minded urbanists from across the global South who can recognize the intent of the project because they have been, or wish they had been, experimenting with similar initiatives. We are certain that a powerful counterpoint can be established to the hegemonic intellectual centers of the North that is comfortable with discerning and inhabiting the *doubleness praxis* invoked at the outset. Continually exploring and manifesting the aesthetic sensibility of this praxis is essential to destabilize the cognitive rationality of the urbanism-as-theory project. Across the eight issues that we have produced to date, we have been genuinely surprised by the potential for beauty and imagination that can be unearthed if we take the time and care to curate meaningful echoes across diverse and divergent urban worlds, all caught up in a multiplicity of conflicts and generative practices.

African Cities Reader series

A closely related but very different cultural artefact is the African Cities Reader series, co-edited by Ntone Edjabe, the founder of Chimurenga,[4] and Edgar Pieterse. The African Cities Reader is a deliberate attempt to roam outside of the academy to cull the rich world of artistic practice through various forms of cultural production, especially the written word that strays between temporal planes, genres and disciplines. This gesture is premised on the assumption that, even though the academy is struggling to delineate, theorize and embrace an epistemology of practice and mundane cityness, artists and writers are simply getting on with it because their primary raw material is the world, its symbolisms and its spiritual incantations as they can be seen, heard and felt. The most telling account of this initiative is found in the first call for submissions that brought the series to life:

> We believe that a range of interventions that seek to engage the shape-shifting essence of African cities are long overdue and present this modest initiative as one contribution to a larger movement of imagination to redefine the practical work-ings of the African city. For us it is self-evident that one has to take the youthful demographic, informality and a non-conventional insertion in global circuits by African urbanites as a starting point for a sustained engagement and retelling of the city in contemporary Africa. The cultural, livelihood, religious, stylistic, commercial, familial, knowledge producing and navigational capacities of African urbanites are typically overlooked, unappreciated and undervalued. We want to bring their stories and practices to the fore in the African Cities Reader. In other words, the African Cities Reader seeks to become a forum where Africans will tell their own stories, draw their own maps and represent their own spatial topog-raphies as it continues to evolve and adapt at the interstice of difference, complexity, opportunism, and irony. In terms of focus, tone and sensibility, the Reader will be vibrant, unapologetic, free, accessible and open, provocative, fresh, not take itself too seriously, but also be rigorous and premised on the assumption that it will grow and evolve over time.... Naturally, flowing from this exploratory vantage point, the African Cities Reader will be open to multiple genres (literature, philosophy, faction, reportage, ethnographic nar-rative, etc.), forms of representation (text, image, sound and possibly performance), and points of view. (Edjabe and Pieterse 2010: i)

This experiment exceeded our wildest expectations because of the quality and diversity of submissions received, as well as the fact that most of the contributors were producing serious work but tended not to be in the academy. It obviously con-firmed the idea that we need fundamentally to disrupt the continued centrality of the university as the only legitimate locus of knowledge and cultural production in favor of a much more distributed approach. In fact, looking back over the three volumes published to date,[5] it is self-evident that the disciplinary-bounded debates in urban studies can greatly be enriched by the kind of lateral manoeuvres that many of the contributing authors make. It is therefore understandable that so much of the work has found its way into the teaching curriculum, artist residency programs, studio-based design research, and other creative mediums of expression across multiple publication platforms.

This initiative has been particularly important as a reminder that urbanists must remain committed to an epistemological adventurism that can take in numerous forms of representation, critique, proposition and, especially, provocation. It is possible to build bridges across the humanities and social sciences in ways that always leave a window open for the street to blow in. Interdisciplinarity is not only a methodological imperative but also an aesthetic resource. The African Cities Reader series points to a fascinating set of publics that swirl around, against and through the academy, signalling the importance of activating numerous and dense publics.

"City Desired" exhibition and density syndicate

Since the inception of the African Centre for Cities in 2007, we have been determined to explore alternative forms of knowledge production in order to enrich the range and scope of academic inquiry but also to engender a permanently unsettled epistemic feeling into the routines of the organization. Academic modes of inquiry and discourse building struggle to avoid the traps of (moral) certitude and judgment (Law 2004), especially politically engaged research that seeks to unveil and upend urban injustice and unsustainable practices. This sensibility is not particularly helpful for original inquiry or for fostering meaningful engagement with the variety of actors that constitute the urban realm. When ACC was established, it was deemed important to engage directly with pressing urban challenges but also to create an experimental milieu that allowed for enormous diversity in epistemic approaches and method.

Practically, this translated into a belief in fostering active laboratories of knowledge co-production. This approach moved from the assumption that academic knowledge was inadequate to understand, disentangle and "solve" a variety of tough urban problems such as structural poverty, environmental vulnerability to flooding, sprawl, climate change impacts, and so on. Instead, mongrel knowledges (Sandercock 2003) were required that emerged through structured and choreographed processes of *co-production* sustained over a substantial length of time.

The CityLabs were collaborative research programs that involved interaction between academic researchers from numerous disciplines and practitioners (from government and elsewhere) working in a wide range of sectors. These programs were generally organized around a series of seminars and culminated in a publication that included chapters/articles written by both academics and practitioners.[6] Furthermore, the experiment was incorporated into the multi-sited Mistra Urban Futures program,[7] which adopted co-production as a modality to address various categories of unsustainable urban dynamics across diverse geographies (Polk 2015). These experiments were vital to consolidate the epistemic conviction that it is possible to conduct rigorous, open-ended and problem-oriented research. However, they suffered from the same problems as traditional academic research in that they did not easily translate into the public realm, nor did they ignite public passions so that the city could recognize and explore new kinds of collective problems. Upon reflecting on this, we embarked on a new kind of experiment to aggregate and re-represent the research findings in the format of an exhibition and associated design laboratories that could conjure up potential responses to the systemic problems identified by the research.

Thus, from 2012 to 2015 a collective within ACC embarked on curatorial research to fashion a vibrant and engaging public exhibition from the raw materials of the CityLabs, the Mistra Urban Futures research, and related flotsam drifting across the university. As a result, from 30 October 2014 to 15 January 2015, we mounted an exhibition entitled "City Desired."[8] During this period a series of events were curated to bring the content to life and encourage a variety of organizations across the sector to rethink their specialist concerns through the affective prism of the exhibition.

The exhibition (which was free to the public) explored ten themes: education, work, transport, housing, land, diversity, vulnerability (especially to violent crime), wellbeing (especially health), food security and climate change. In order to bring the research to life, we commissioned in-depth narrative accounts of the everyday lives of ten Capetonians from virtually all walks of life: informal trader, domestic worker, seasoned architect, farmer, artist, and so on. As summarized in figure 6.2, the narrative stories were given visual treatment in the form of short films and photography, while radio programs (produced by high-school students, who were encouraged to script programs for their generation on the back of the data) offered another form of engagement. We worked with professional coders to generate a variety of interactive digital maps and data visualizations that enabled an intuitive

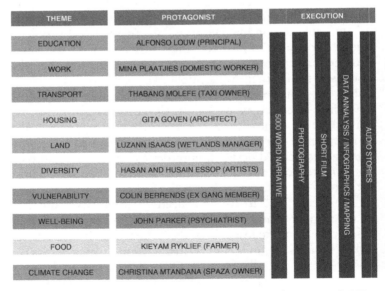

Figure 6.2 The thematic and programmatic elements of "City Desired", www.citydesired.com

touch-screen experience with some of the most important contextual and spatial underpinnings of the narratives and themes.

In addition, we undertook design studies to produce speculative proposals for how some of the most vexing issues related to urban land markets, tenure security in slum areas, sustainable infrastructure, not-in-my-backyard syndrome and gentrification could potentially be addressed. The work was done in relation to three generic conditions in Cape Town: dense informal settlements with limited infrastructure and economic opportunities; a brownfield stretch of city marked by deindustrialization and occupational vacancies; and a plump greenfield site at the cross-section where separation of class and race is maintained to this day (Provoost 2015). These speculations and their political and cultural implications are what snagged the mainstream media and enabled a broader engagement with the rest of the exhibition and, in some instances, the underlying research of the CityLabs that served as the archive for the overall program.

The exigencies of experimentation

Over the coming decades the urban world will become primarily African and Asian. It will be a world largely of youth – youth for whom there is no such thing as a career, steady work, or a coherent map of a future. A world where youth will not stand still, and where urbanization is increasingly a process of toing and froing, of incessant sutures and disjunctions, of borders erased and reinscribed. Claims will become more multiple and vociferous, as will the recognition that the old divides of here and there can no longer be places that clearly mark where violence can be exported or from which violence can be repelled. Youth will be increasingly unwilling to be "frozen in place." They will resist the easy solution of the privileged to turn them into a permanent underclass, something that will certainly impede the urgent need for people everywhere to recognize that what they have in common is the precarity of the very planet through which life is sustained.

To operate in this urban world will require an intensive politics of creating opportunities to demonstrate that conditions are not mired in exclusion or immiseration. Regardless of how incremental justice-making becomes or the speed through which places are remade, it will be crucial that this youthful population senses that "things are in play" and that there are "moves to make." Operating in such conditions can be nothing but experimental, since none of us knows quite what the game of governance in such conditions will look like. In the midst of existent megacities, whose political, social and financial complexities seem quickly to shut down or render tortuous attempts to govern more justly in the interests of the majority, it is necessary to go beyond the old antagonisms that inform how we understand and emplace residents and how we regard the built environment. It is too easy to see the mega-developments as bad and the popular self-built neighborhoods of the working class as good, to read everything in terms of gentrification, ruin, renewal, entrepreneurialism, sharing economy, cooperatives, or public or private property.

Yes, these are real phenomena. But in the emergent city we have to assume that things are entangled, that many different realities are enacted simultaneously, that these realities are "messing" with each other all the time, and that nothing can really "steer clear" of anything else in the pretence of integrity, and so we have to try to come at the architecture of these tangles from all angles. The boundaries that mark the "inside" of the slum, the institution, the government or the corporation have to be simultaneously extended and contracted. On the one hand, the experience of being inside has to be stretched to include more details and spaces, and, on the other hand, it has to be narrowed so that it is possible to see particular facets of those insides as actually and strategically part of something else. This means borrowing from the language of logistics, infrastructure and technical networks to sense things in movement and formation and to learn multiple "languages" of translation that provide access to different practices to deploy here and there, not in the same way or with the need for them to be free of contradictions. This assumes that there are vernaculars that can cut across the enactments of real estate, community building, institution management, popular practices, marketing and media which demonstrate complicities and dependencies that can feed into the dark arts of deal-making that aim to put as many judicious facts on the ground as possible.

It is especially important to get involved in urbanities in gestation – all of the small and medium-sized towns that will quickly mushroom into major metropolitan areas over the next several decades, again particularly in Africa and Asia. Here, there is less political gridlock to impede more straightforward rather than backdoor experimental manoeuvres. If a politics of experimentation is necessary as the place where the molecular worlds of everyday urban life and the proliferating apparatuses of urban rule and development productively intersect, how does such a politics endure? We have attempted to offer some concrete instances of experimentation and how they resonate across scales and sectors.

Each of these instances has entailed a process of *re-describing* what takes place in terms of what *might take place*, or be taking place in the moment, something which then needs to be made actionable if not necessarily visible, or made visible in actionable ways without giving away all of the *secrets* of its productive value. We have emphasized that this requires various instances of *doubleness*. This is the doubleness of working with different scales, vernaculars and institutions to insert, reveal or unfold aspects of their functioning that are not yet too fixed in stone, too unyielding. Doubleness also has been a way to pay attention to the inherent experimental quality in what does exist within urban conditions, no matter the disparities of power or the apparent entrenchment of injustice.

There is a tendency on the part of conventional urban politics to call for the state to do "its job," to guarantee rights, basic provisioning, and the virtuous dimensions of autoconstruction. But this call often neglects just how much the state is embedded in distributed networks of rule. Circuitries of finance capital entail a continuous reworking of the relations and contributions among retail investors, pooling institutions, dedicated real-estate and infrastructure funds, international financial centers, country-specific investment markets, and specific building and infrastructure projects. This reworking involves projects of translation and matching, where specific classifications of risk, return and liquidity are converted and materialized into particular forms and places. Governance becomes a calculation of *eventualities* – the potential to take form (spatial and temporal) – the way in which the urban built environment becomes a locus for continual recalibration of provision, consumption, monitoring, need creation, social behavior, anticipation and value creation.

So the "real state of rule and development" is not located within the institution of the "state" itself but is distributed across various logics, calculations, organizations, tasks and locations. But what this means – what is one of the main *city secrets* – is that this process, far from diminishing "the state," renders it a pre-eminent space of experimentation. As it is increasingly demonstrated not to be what we usually think it to be – a coherent consolidation of sovereignty, law-making, regulation, guarantee and administration – yet it continues to enact these roles as its dominant impression, the state is "up for grabs" in terms of what it can possibly do as it manoeuvres its ways across increasingly complex landscapes of planning and implementation. Even as state officials may be increasingly overwhelmed by the complexion of urban financial architectures, logistical systems and contentious socialities, the state still is a performance of the representation of the "common" in any given polity. It remains a performance to be experimented with, particularly if it is to endure as a viable object of people's imaginations and as a conduit of their aspirations.

As such, endurance of an experimental politics becomes a reflection of give and take. For, within crowded conditions, everyone has to find new ways of "staying clear" or "making way." The multiplicity of governmental, religious, professional and civic institutions that operate at different scales and in different forms rarely appear to operate in concert and often seem to exist simply to provide individuals with an opportunity to acquire a title, a path to some kind of cheap self-importance. But the simultaneity of the existence of these institutions does entail a mode of coordination, a sense of large-scale collective movement. No matter how much this amassing, this invisible aggregation seems to operate at cross-purposes and thus weaken its capacity to ward off the decimations of big capital or shape an overall urban agenda, its persistence ensures a multiplicity of times – continuity, rupture, full-speed-ahead, hesitation.

The complicities of government, developers and business elites can cajole, manipulate and run roughshod over the places where, and the activities which, institutions perform. They can promise new allocations and authority. Yet, in Mumbai, Cape Town, Jakarta, São Paulo and many other local institutionally thick cities, the simultaneous enactment of differentiated forms of expressions and constituencies renders the concretized summations and fixities that large-scale development seems to guarantee replete with ambiguities. There are too many neighborhoods and old housing developments to clear, too many vested interests to wade through, too many failed projects to cover up, and too many commercial activities immune to corporatization. We have tried to point out the ways in which particular political practices can take advantage of these spaces of uncertainty and make more strategically explicit the hidden reservoirs of coordination and collaboration that implicitly exist as different forms of institutional life both competing with and feeding off each other.

Speed promises the possibility of extending the metropolis across broader physical terrain: high-speed trains, highways, flyovers, optic cables, logistics for just-in-time everything. Speed spaces out the city's heterogeneities and inequities in such a way that the infrastructures that make speed possible become its content. Corporations and the economic elite steer their acquisitions and merge content and connection. The infrastructures of articulation – media, markets, sometimes even roads and ports – are turned over solely to the content generated by the same corporations that manage them. Such are the fantasies of total access – anytime, anywhere – in a mobility that does not have to worry about interruption, where physical and media infrastructures permit unimpeded journeys suited to self-aggrandizement and predictable sociality. The politics we are pointing out here attempts to "slow things down," to point out how all of the apparent seamless accomplishment of urban change are full of messy encounters, deals, and protracted and often failed negotiations, and that high-speed urban remaking is full of holes to be occupied and shaped.

We might wish for or demand intensifying and extending the public character of cities and efficient states to administer them. But, we need to understand better where and how the multiplicity of "states" are enacted now, and how those that bear the imprimatur of the state – the bureaucrats, planners, councillors, ward officers, tax collectors, police, technicians, and so forth – "perform" the state in the midst of thickly configured fields of local institutions and efforts. We need to understand how the politics of these transactions might be infused with a greater sense of common purpose, something that in many ways is already taking place but is kept out of view, out of assertion, given outmoded sensibilities and rules of propriety and eligibility. The task is to draw new boundaries that enclose disparate practices and efforts, to see them as one, and to learn to act as one.

7

Epilogue: A Story
About Stories

In a remarkable novel, *A General Theory of Oblivion*, José
Eduardo Agualusa conveys how the city is powered through
an intricate chain of stories, often organized around a withdrawn focal point, an absent center. He places a Portuguese
woman at the heart of the novel. She had accompanied her
sister and the latter's husband to colonial Angola. The couple
eventually disappeared at the advent of the revolution, and
the woman remains in her increasingly dilapidated apartment
for nearly thirty years afterwards, eking out a bare survival.
Her only contact with the outside world is a young boy who
had attempted to rob her and with whom she develops a
strange yet intimate connection. Seemingly withdrawn from
the turbulent events of the city, she becomes the nexus for a
proliferating series of criss-crossing relationships among different functionaries, profiteers, combatants and spies.

These are crossings of inexplicable generosity, parasitism
and coincidence, and they all demonstrate the extent to which
the ability to find one's way depends on the city *not working*
according to plan. As the woman, feeding off the infrastructure of her apartment and the accidental garden and aviary
she managed to shoehorn into the balcony, is unable to
find her way in Angola's violent rhythms of accumulation
and loss, she acts as the unwitting enabler of others to find
their way to and through each other. For the city is a "block-
chain" of stories held together by a fragile center of gravity,

intertwined in ways that become evident only through largely chance discoveries – discoveries that would never have been possible without enabling one story to lead to another.

In September 2016 Pasar Rumput was torn to the ground. The market in the central Jakarta district of Manggerai was a warren of beauty salons often doubling as brothels, seedy nightclubs, stalls selling cheap shoes and bags, bicycles, fruits and vegetables, and under-the-table almost anything that fell off the back of a truck. Its reputation spread far and wide as a place where anything goes in a city that has been going increasingly in one direction – i.e., servicing the expectations of an enlarging middle class. Ironically, much of this middle class has depended upon markets like Pasar Rumput to keep their expanding desires for consumption affordable and to have moments of respite from the expectations of social conformity that such a middle class ordains.

Pasar Rumput was especially well known, if not always well regarded, by the largely poor and working-class districts that surrounded it. Jakarta's government, in tearing down the market, announced its intention to replace it with 2,000 units of social housing for 8,000 poor residents who have been evicted from a long-standing community on a riverbank not far away. This is part of the government's plan to control the river more effectively in order to mitigate flooding. A new market will be built, under the strict authority of the municipal agency that is supposed to manage markets but which hasn't really done a good job of it in the past. The market is intended to accommodate all of the small-scale trading that the new residents were conducting in the areas surrounding their soon to be demolished homes. Integrated social housing and commercial facilities is a major step forward from the usual practice of consigning the evicted poor to the outskirts of the city in towers that neither provided commercial space nor were close to any sufficiently populated area for hawking, repairing and fabricating to take place in a viable manner.

Pasar Rumput was in many ways a useless place, an eyesore and an affront to the sensibilities of an expanding central business district. But few places in Jakarta generated so many stories. Many of these stories centered on how the surrounding lower- and working-class districts were really run, on the shifts in local power, and on the behaviors and tastes of local officials. The market was the site of all-night card games where brokers, military guys, favor-seekers and political hacks would come from all over the city, spreading news and gossip, hatching plans. It was the place where prostitutes could be "trained" to infiltrate opposition political parties to provoke scandals or to blackmail big shots. It was the place where brokers who provided labor for large construction projects would initially meet to get their stories straight before fanning out to the fancy hotels to meet with developers. It was the place where teenagers with little money in their pockets could go to get their hair done for almost nothing and then hang out at shopping malls, passing for acceptable middle-class kids. It was the place where youth riding around the city from different neighborhoods would meet to organize their itineraries for the night. Pasar Ramput, rundown and naughty, was a story-making machine. Stories were built upon, revised, connected – always finding a way to keep going.

Keeping multiple stories in play

In our argument about emerging new urban worlds in Africa and Asia we have attempted to avoid any kind of overarching theoretical story about urbanization processes. We have attempted to avoid subsuming a vast heterogeneity of urban experiences and forms to a structural narrative, even as we appreciate the creativity and importance of recent efforts to understand better how urbanization processes actually work. Instead, we have tried to find a way to keep multiple stories in play, realizing that the exigencies of the way in which urbanization is taking place in our regions of concern require an enhanced capacity to work with all of the tools at our collective disposal, even while acknowledging their limitations. But too often the nearly inexplicable capacity of the most resource-challenged urban areas to hang together (barely) beyond reason becomes the sacrificial "lamb" through which new urban agendas and developments take place.

So we have attempted to tell a story that values *both* the resourcefulness of urbanization processes that remain a highly contested meshwork of influences, articulations, circuits, itineraries, impositions and collective efforts *and* the substantially plausible prospects for bringing new sensibilities, political justice and material sustenance to urban life. That this "both–and" is a relationship replete with paradoxes and conundrums is an essential aspect of both the impediments and the possibilities. But why do we place this emphasis on stories?

We are not arguing that to keep things as they are represents the integrity or authenticity of a particular way of urban living. The lower classes across urban spaces do not belong to any particular built form, and no particular form belongs to them. After all, the processes of self-construction that produced much of the urban built environment across Asia and Africa occurred incrementally, step by step, without the definitive imagination of a specific destination. What would completion look like? Even if those who built their own quarters looked toward concretizing particular dreams or norms of place worthy of them, many would run out of money or motivation. To leave things incomplete was often the wisest thing to do – so as to avoid taxes, leave room to address different contingencies, or bring others into the production process. What was important was a sense of forward momentum; that the efforts were worth something, not necessarily in monetary terms but in the ongoing capacity to build relationships with the "surrounds" – with other inhabitants, human and non-human – that afforded a range of different possibilities for action.

When conditions don't seem to be taking you anywhere, when you constantly battle to keep your head above water, and when most of the efforts you make, both individually and as part of a larger collective, at best manage only to repair breakdowns of all kinds, then the particular format or mode of living the urban doesn't really matter. It doesn't really matter regardless how much it is familiar or embodies cherished memories or attainments. As such, indifference sets in; inhabitants wait for seemingly inevitable displacements or eagerly jump at opportunities to acquire new assets, new property, new lifestyles, if the price is right.

What is important, though, is the capacity to keep going. What was productive about many instances of self-constructed urbanization was the way in which the things that were built could be translated into each other in many different ways. Housing, work, sociability, caretaking, service provisioning and livelihood were all connected to each other. A house wasn't simply a house; a place of work wasn't simply a workplace; a religious institution wasn't simply a church, temple or mosque; a neighbor wasn't simply a neighbou; water, sanitation and power weren't simply material resources coming out of the blue. They were woven through each other, continually combined in different ways. In other words, what was important was the capacity to keep telling stories and for stories to lead to other ones – multiple story lines, where inhabitants could see themselves "written" into the fabric of urban life in various ways. In this manner, inhabitants had recourse to concrete exemplars of different versions of themselves, as well as to different versions of what was possible.

The character of the self-constructed was a space for many characters, a space where the many could become one, and the one many, in a back and forth movement that ensured that there were a sufficient number of different ideas and ways of doing things in circulation. But, at the same time, these differences did not rule out people paying attention to each other and, as a result, making them an integral part of the stories they would weave out of their own lives.

To be clear, it is not so much a matter of the capacity to tell stories requiring specific built environments or vernaculars. People can create stories regardless of where they are. But our concern is with the tendency of built environments to be created with the purpose of inhabitants keeping their stories "straight." Under the auspices of inclusion, of providing inhabitants with a viable level of affordances, built environments become a one-size-fits-all narrative. Now, we do understand the difficulties in rolling out housing and service provision that is affordable and manageable. In order to service the largely underserviced populations of urban Africa and Asia – long accustomed to "make+shift" infrastructure of all kinds – intricate regulatory frameworks specifying eligibilities and conditionalities appear to be common sense. Redistribution is difficult in settings that do not have all that much to distribute in the first place, and, where demands are so great and the landscape to be governed so messy, there has to be at least the impression that there are devices through which administrators can get a handle on things.

This is why we have emphasized those aspects of our work that engage policy-making processes. That is why we have spent many days of our careers negotiating the wording of documents and cajoling support from government officials for pilot projects and commitments to line items in municipal and national governments. Negotiations over the language of accords at any scale may seem to be tedious exercises condemned to fall short. But they are about the politics of how to tell stories, to provide different kinds of actors with story lines through which they can find pathways to each other. With all of the stories cities tell, there need to be moments when inhabitants of different backgrounds and responsibilities can sift through this plurality and decide which they are going to tell together – to widen the commons which is be addressed and which, in turn, will respond.

Not dissimilarly, the book has shown no intrinsic aversion to the language of finance and calculation. Financial devices end up weaving their own often incomputable narratives, configuring relationships between things and places that otherwise could be conceived only in the narratives of discrete places, cultures and materials. New "neighborhoods" of proximities are brought into existence, as well as the sense of things not being what they seem to be. The problem with such devices is their use and control for capital accumulation, for the manipulation of value, and for maximizing the uncertainty and turbulence that allow hedging and leveraging, shorting and longing, to exert profitability from vulnerabilities of all kinds.

The notion of price, long thought to eliminate consideration of messy external conditions, also can be thought of in different ways. What does it mean, for example, that one thousand exactly similar apartments in a single building of so-called affordable housing all have a different price? What stories lie behind this difference? When associations of residents of such buildings discuss the prices that they pay, or when longstanding communities go through endless negotiations over the compensation price they will hold out for before willingly conceding their land and houses to developers, how does price become a device through which to devise particular kinds of stories, particular kinds of relationships among residents?

We have shown how lower- and middle-income districts have long entered into complex relationships of borrowing and debt; how they have put together their own complex instruments for circumventing risk and building affordances based on risk. While most collective efforts were non-contractual, with nothing written down, without specific commitments or obligations, there were architectures of stories, ways in which inhabitants actively "drew lines" across discrete individual activities, assets and abilities. They conjured up imaginations of intricately sutured collective local worlds through which people and things that seemingly did not belong together ended up having some kind of connection. Much emphasis is now placed on the decentralization of money creation and control through "block chains," which are essentially collective ways of enjoining stories, of ascertaining where a particular transaction fits among thousands of others. The fundamentals of economic life, money, security, borrowing, payment, and so forth, can be marshalled into different hands, "authors" and authorities.

The politics of indifference

Much contemporary urban theory indicates that what the urban is and could be is indifferent to any particular instantiation. As a planetary phenomenon, urbanization is both an intensification of articulation and its extension across space. It takes different forms, extracts different costs. This indifference to showing itself in specific formats corresponds to an indifference that cities show to the majority of their inhabitants. Particularly in the global South, cities seem to act surprised that the majority is even still present, still kicking. They are indifferent to their needs while claiming at the same time to be the embodiment of their aspirations.

Critical political struggles in the near future will largely be centered around this indifference and the divergent reactions it is likely to provoke. Let's return to the examples of youth that we have discussed throughout the book. There will be those youth who, in face of this indifference, will be concerned primarily with trying to elicit some kind of recognition, to tie their future down, to acquire as many assets as they can, or at least to pursue trajectories that are likely to guarantee their acquisition. They will attempt to regularize themselves as much as possible in terms of the prevailing norms of success and security and, perhaps most importantly, to convert as much of their social lives as possible into a form of potential accumulation.

Then there will be those youth who will appear indifferent to the indifference shown to them. In other words, they will circulate through as many potential opportunities, places, residences, jobs and social networks as possible. They will be concerned less with being recognized as contributing members of a particular society and focused more on being ready to seize opportunities to operate somewhere else or as someone else. Of course these two divergent trajectories are not only matters of volition but life paths that are also imposed. For many, the prolongation of youth and the kinds of malleability that come with it are forced on individuals rather than being a strategic choice. For those who seem to settle quickly into particular regimens and routines, some are encumbered with responsibilities to keep their head above water where household and kin are concerned.

So the relationships between the voluntary and involuntary, the "settled" and the "unsettled," will likely produce intensely volatile stories. The well-off will run to the hills or gated communities as usual, many of the poor will simply be "wasted," and many will simply be caught up in the constant expenditure of energy in order to make ends meet. But there is a youthful population in most Southern cities today who know much more than their predecessors about the ins and outs of the city, who circulate through it in more expansive and deliberate ways.

Control is becoming much less about confinement than about interception. Dangerous circulation is targeted in the return to the primacy of government as hunt. But the hunt is always haunted by traps – both the traps that the hunter sets and the tactics the hunted use to lure the hunter into thinking that they are in charge, that the game is truly going according to their rules. For the hunted lure the hunters into showing their devices and strategies and then finds ways to have them turned against them.

Ravi Sundaram (2015) has made an important point about the shape of urban futures in the South. He indicates that postcolonial urban management was predicated on authorizing limited forms of publicity, of managing populations through putting them in place and then providing for them, enabling specific and regulated circuits of visibility. But now everyone, no matter how settled they may be, possesses and lives through various media devices, making things public in ways that cannot be controlled, as individuals circulate through various experiences and information whose dispositions are difficult to anticipate. Sundaram talks about how provisional networks form around temporary connections, citing the examples of bluetooth sharing of media by sailors, urban proletarians and migrants; shadow libraries moving via USB drives; hawala transfers via text; and neighborhood shops that refill phone memory cards with pirate media. Everyone seems to be trapping everyone else, as well as avoiding traps of all kinds.

The future population of Africa and Asia will be much more mobile, no matter how many closed borders or surveillance systems there are, or whether they actually go anywhere physically or not. They will produce stories, many of which will make empirical validation irrelevant, and cities will remain vast layers of impressions, claims and dissimulation. They will remain places of secrets, of stories always in waiting, to be told.

Stories are not clean slates

In our previous discussions on experimental design, we have pointed to a vast range of potentialities that exist to do urban development differently. We have pointed to all of the consolidated and distributed knowledge about how to work with materials, how to build, how to renew, and how to curate different intersections among inhabitants of different backgrounds, incomes and skills. Thousands of pilot and demonstration projects seemingly wait to be upscaled, to be financed and to become objects of successful political mobilization. Potentialities have to be rooted somewhere; they have to be attached to existent and ongoing stories, made to be part of the sensible of the present, to resonate with experiences of which actors feel assured.

Too often municipal officials, urban researchers and financiers argue the need for a clean slate. In the recent prelude to the Habitat III meeting in October 2016, there were many invocations on the parts of mayors, researchers and planners to "get things right," and that the only way to get things right was to start with a "clean slate." What they usually meant by this was the systematic extension of the city beyond its conventional conceptual and territorial demarcations in order to effectively design the appropriate proportions and affordability of things such as public space, transportation, network infrastructure systems, incubators and institutions.

While we certainly agree that such expansionary mechanisms are viable trajectories of urban change, it is this notion of a "clean slate" and "getting things right" that worries us. It worries us in terms of its residual modernist impulses, its repetition of the need always to start again, a starting predicated on eliminating or at least evacuating the stories that came before and their architectural embodiments and residues in built and social environments. It is the abandonment of intersection, of figuring out how to splice new forms and ways of doing things onto what already at least tries hard to work. It is the abandonment of a process of recomposing, of what Fred Moten (2003) has called "ensemble work," of how to do different things in concert, even if there is no map that specifies how they will fit.

In our reading, part of the problem here again is one of stories. We always look at the city – whichever version of it we may be using – and think we know what we are looking at. But, as we have emphasized in our thoughts about *re-description*, spaces and processes that seem to be divergent *really* are divergent. At the same time, however, and with a different story, they are connected to each other in ways that are not apparent. To take yet another example from Jakarta, the rapidly enlarging CBD seems to encroach upon and eviscerate long-standing working-class districts. This sets up what seems to be a troubling interface, full of frictions, unequal power relations, disrupted lives and cut-throat real-estate competition, where developers attempt to offer ever more spectacular "experiences." Indeed, a large volume of displacement of existing inhabitants has taken place over the past decade, a process which seems to accelerate as a kind of "herd effect" that takes place among corporate entities eager to maximize locational value and the purported synergistic effects of many different kinds of services in close proximity to each other.

But, at the same time, different stories can be told. The uncertain relationships of this interface between CBD and "popular" neighborhood can become a different kind of epistemology, one where each territory becomes a device to discover unattended dimensions inherent in both. For example, within the "popular neighborhood," it is possible to tell stories about the ways in which various constellations of actors and residents operate as "holding companies," develop local forms of "securitization" on land that still has an ambiguous formal status, where it is not clear who exactly owns what. Or, more importantly, where tenancy, ownership and property are conceived not on a plot-by-plot, building-by-building basis but across a patchwork of multiple "properties" and "residencies." One plot of land may be officially registered as another, several buildings may be registered in different places under different names, or several places may be viewed as the "property" of groups of extended families or a local association. As evictions and displacement frequently take place through "picking off" one "plot" at a time, it is important to learn more about how to concretize the use of these practices to develop such popular districts in different ways.

At the same time, these neighborhoods act as extensions of the CBD. They house and feed thousands of workers, and there are many instances where corporations have been enticed into applying pressure to keep some of these neighborhoods intact, since they see the benefits of having a workforce close by, always available to show up on time, and able to save some of their usually meagre salaries. More invisibly, it is also important to demonstrate how the CBD, itself, acts as an extension of the popular neighborhood. We know that the high-rise towers and shopping malls could not function without all of the low-end service workers that keep these machines going. But we know less about all of the off-the-record informal businesses and deal-making that take place among them in association with different syndicates and brokers, and the ways in which many of the infrastructures and affordances of these places are used during the night or out of hours to support "illicit" economic activities.

Additionally, vertical living does not necessarily put an end to the popular district or a process of autoconstruction. While prefabrication and large towers indeed do not leave too much room for physical adjustments and incremental additions, the ways in which individual apartments may be acquired and occupied, and then lived in, reflect, in many instances, a reinvention of collaborative work. In many so-called affordable housing projects, apartments are acquired in blocks, extended families and associations may occupy an entire floor, and floors initially sold for residential purposes may come to house many different functions.

The point in all of these examples here is to look productively at what we think we know for sure and use this apparent certainty as an incentive to look once again, and perhaps generate a parallax view, a way of seeing things as *both–and* rather than *either–or*, and to use the interstices of these views as a way of figuring out how to reinvent valued characteristics of neighborhoods in new formats.

Responsibility and instigation

To tell stories entails responsibility. People can come up with any kind of story, but if it doesn't make an appeal to others, if it doesn't take into consideration their conditions and sensibilities, the story ends up conveying more about the person telling it than having an incitement or pleasure in its own right. Stories attempt to draw lines between a "here" and a "there" or a "then and a now," as well as imagined future places and times. Part of the problem of urbanization as a process of capitalist reproduction is that the stories that get told in this process tend to abdicate any such responsibility. The city is treated as something that is to be the site of simply willing a new world into existence. The daily routines, sociability and aspirations of popular neighborhoods may have contributed to *eventualities* – i.e., where something comes to life that is not planned and where the shape of what comes cannot be foreseen or described in clear terms. At all times, however, there was a link acknowledged between what people did and how this uncertain eventuality – difficult to put into words – turned out.

But, increasingly, urbanization becomes a vehicle through which capital attempts to consolidate everything that exists in urban space and deploy this consolidation as means of controlling the very process of eventuality. In other words, capital is interested less in the profitability of development projects, less in getting people to stay put, less in developing precise calculations about future scenarios. Rather, it wants to control a capacity to give rise to eventualities no matter what, regardless of what shape or behavior they might assume. It is as if capital desires finally to realize itself fully as magic.

Here, it doesn't matter how stories connect to other stories or how they connect to those who might be their recipients. In fact, the story here is that recipients basically don't matter. They don't matter in part because, as we have pointed out several times, folding everything into the capitalist game generates eventualities that can become incomputable, and the best way for those most powerful at managing the game to position themselves to this situation is to be prepared for anything and not to worry about the interests and identities of those who are affected.

An example might clarify better what we have in mind. Take the fact that across many urban regions of Africa and Asia there is a rush to build. Politicians, developers, investors, bureaucrats and ordinary residents seem to talk of little else but the need to build things – from new freeways, transit systems, luxury sub-cities and flood canals to thousands of small houses and commercial buildings. We have described aspects of this rush to build earlier as well as the large number of contingencies involved these days in developing projects. Even if contracts, policies, projects, technical instruments and brute force hold in place the constitutive components of roads, rails, housing developments, flood mitigation conduits, water reticulation or sanitation treatment systems, each of these components is also enmeshed in a plurality of other relationships and statuses that can throw any project off schedule, even off the map entirely.

As we indicated previously, this rush to build is something that goes beyond speculation. It not only operates within the rubrics of the financialization of risk as a means of hedging a multiplicity of probable futures for how a specific infrastructure will operate and the value it will have. This instigation also aims to posit infrastructure as *detached from reason*, within a scenario that cannot be fully calculated now, and which imbues it with an adaptability to futures where no matter what happens there is a possibility of recouping something which itself cannot be specified. This implies stories that have no responsibility to point to predictable destinations. It confirms that stories work best when they are full of surprises and unanticipated twists and turns. But the surprises, the instigations of imagination and new ideas, work through their ability to connect to those facets of everyday life to which people continue to feel belong to them. They need not hang onto life's familiarity or the particular look and feel of their surroundings. But inhabitants want to have a sense of the story as a kind of journey, to feel the movement as a passing along through and from discernible places and things.

It is like when John Coltrane starts with a tune almost universally familiar – *My Favorite Things* – and then takes a journey where everything about that tune is taken apart, recombined, spread out, and then almost inexplicably returns to the melody. You have a sense about how Coltrane "left the home of the tune," but you don't know how he got back until sometime after he arrived there, because you are drawn to listen again and again, where the itinerary of the journey becomes clearer without attenuating the surprise. Capitalist urbanization as practice largely forgets about such journeys and how they are produced with ensembles, calls and responses, and the rapid-fire reciprocities of ideas and feelings. Perhaps the city was only ever a shadow of such creativity and improvisations. Maybe too much was made and expected of it all along. But in this book we have attempted again to tell other stories – stories that provoke the capacity to keep on going, but knowing that providing viable homes and platforms of operation are still critical. The intricacy of everyday life can be part of the story of structural change and urban governance, just as the details of administration and finance are part of the fabric of everyday life. In this sense the book is a polemical call to abandon the disciplinary and thematic stories that weigh urban studies down, leaving it unable to contemplate the imbricated nature of emergent urbanisms.

Ensemble work is perhaps more metaphor than method. But it does point to the ways in which urban residents in Africa and Asia address many possible futures at once. If one considers multiple municipal histories, the repetitions of long-time spans of contested space, governance and jurisdictions, and the incessant insufficiencies of resources, it is clear to see how the predominant processes of urbanization occurred in the interstices of definitive patterns and authorities. Residents had to constitute themselves – and their assets, plots and networks of belonging – as "ready-made" facets of any possible development trajectory or system of governance. They prepared themselves to be part of many different stories, where no overarching narrative prevailed in the present.

Narrative lines of course will have to be drawn, spaces articulated, and provisioning made more systematic, effective and just. But just what these lines are and how they are to be drawn must take place within a reality of many possible dispensations and weighting. As a great deal of the dynamism, uncertainty and growth of urban systems today occurs at the so-called periphery, it is here where contestation and potential inventiveness will transpire. For the expansion of industrial land, often at inflated prices, the relocation of the poor evicted from the urban core and near-suburban areas, the roll-out of large swathes of so-called affordable housing in varying vertical and horizontal forms, and the persistence of agricultural activity all sit in an uneasy contiguity, with rarely any clear lines of articulation among them. The disjunctions are not easily subsumed by conventional spatial development strategies, as their different histories, exigencies, financial substrates, sustainability and associated political interests all push against each other without clear vernaculars or images of mediation.

It is here where maintaining a multiplicity of story lines will be most important, for there are limits to how far urban systems can extend themselves, how far populations can be pushed away from existent centers of gravity, and limits on how quickly new ones can be constituted. Metros can only go so fast and so far, ecological footprints already exceed sustainable levels, and competing agendas run out of capacity when the primary strategy for accommodating them is to space them out. Divergences will have to be part of the same story, a density of stories, and, even though urbanization may no longer rely upon density as its defining trope, density – of the relationships among all things – is the only urban future.

Notes

Chapter 1   Paradoxes of the Urban

1 There is an important aspect of urban development that proceeds not so much by the rational, modernist assumptions of linear progress as by the almost metaphorical resolution of substituting one matter of concern or way of thinking about urbanity for something else, another problematic, another thing to be solved. In this way the city becomes an interminable cycle of metaphorization – different ways of associating things simply are converted in other ways of doing so, and, in this way, there is no specific teleological trajectory of urbanization. Rather the urban is simply a locus of incessant substitutability. This is borne out in various investigations: Nuijten 2013; Parker 2004; Robinson 2016; and Söderström 2014.

2 A substantial literature has been produced on issues of evictions, peripheral urbanization and particularistic forms of gentrification in the global South. Much of this literature has focused on the conversion of the commitments to the public city accompanying nationalist development programs to the city as a locus of private accumulation. Eviction concerns not only the extrusion of the poorest residents from the urban core but also the removal of the use of the city as a locus for national cohesion. See Bahn 2016; Ghertner 2014; Obeng-Odoom 2015; and Shin 2016.

3 While neoliberal urbanization may suggest the standardizing of what counts as viable forms for generating livelihood, making investments in assets and security, creating and occupying urban space, these authors indicate that there are many routes toward what look like similar destinations – methods that could be

deployed in many different ways: Allen et al. 2016; Lindell and Ampaire 2016; Nyamnjoh and Brudvig 2014.

4 Even when the power of capital accumulation seems to overrun the capacity for multiple uses of urban space, the move toward the dominance of privatization and ground rent occurs through different processes in different cities. See particularly insightful accounts in Abramson 2011; Goldfrank and Schrank 2009; and Perera 2015.

5 Some of the most important literature on the urban South has focused on how neighborhood solidarities have been intertwined with different, often predatory, forms of local authority; how neighborhoods sometimes perform a sense of constant crisis in order to elicit the attention of municipal governments; about how they turn themselves into problems in order to attract resources, but how these strategies often backfire; about how attempts on the part of localities to suture relationships with the larger city can take apart long-developed internal networks of cooperation. These processes are powerfully documented in Gago 2015; Karaman 2013; Weinstein 2013; and Zeiderman 2016.

6 The following is literature that is particularly salient in terms of demonstrating how the growth and subsequent complexion of many so-called popular urban districts is the culmination of constant conflicts among different interests only momentarily reconciled through external pressures or the momentary ascendance of strong religious or cultural sentiments: Mariani and Barron 2014; Baviskar 2003; Hansen and Verkaaik 2009; and Vlassenroot and Büscher 2009.

7 The following studies are particularly salient in demonstrating the difficulties entailed in trying to establish official, legal regulatory mechanisms applicable to districts otherwise "balanced" through oscillating accords among markedly different kinds of residents and interests: Datta 2012; Elyachar 2011; Gayer 2014; Ortega 2012; and Singerman 2009.

8 Various forms of "real politics" and messy negotiations are always part of attempts to bring particular urban spaces into some kind of ordered form of management and accumulation. See Labbé 2014; Lin 2014; Lund and Boone 2013; and Ren 2015.

9 This point refers to the critiques around recent reiterations of Henri Lefebvre's notions of planetary urbanization. We acknowledge the enormous value of this work and do not wish to engage in all of the highly contentious and frequently unfruitful debates that have accompanied it. We wish only to point out that our use of the concept "secretion" here simply raises the conceptual

possibility of spaces of detachment that are immanent to, or perhaps even constitutive of, the very capacity to put together overarching explanatory contexts that account for all of the details.

10 For a broader discussion on how national states or municipal governments consolidate themselves as both the objects and the determiners of knowledge, and how they often draw upon particular ethoses, practices and imaginaries that have existed outside the realm of officialdom, see Garmany 2010; Lindell 2008; Lund 2006; and Mitchell 2002. This is a different and more interesting literature than the normative prescriptive kind that tends to underpin the policy realms invoked by the official development industry.

11 Purportedly, alternative governance can take place in a variety of different ways (with alternative here not connoting any particular ideological orientation). These include new forms of assemblies, digital platforms, the elaboration of communities of affective ties, issue-specific collaboration, the suturing together of different residents and aspirations through the broad commitments to a series of rights to the city, the use of infrastructure prototypes as a way for residents to assume greater responsibilities for the management of the physical terrain, the organization of resistance and solidarity campaigns, the use of logistics, and various forms of cross-sector cooperation. There is a rich literature to explore: Boudreau 2007; Corsín Jiménez and Estalella 2014; Lavalle et al. 2005; Maloutas 2004; Mauro and Rossi 2015; Neilson and Rossiter 2006; Purcell 2013; and Sørensen and Torfing 2007.

Chapter 2 Precarious Now

1 Andy Stirling (2015) provides a penetrating analysis of the political and cultural limitations and parameters of international discursive frameworks and events. His analysis applies to the SDG summit of 2015 and the Habitat III gathering in October 2016.

2 According to the ILO, stable employment includes wage and salaried employees and business owners. Vulnerable employment includes subsistence farming, informal self-employment and work for family members.

3 We do not delve into this issue here but want to note that, given these differences between African and Northern cities, we are surprised by the habitual ways in which the approaches of relatively wealthy cities are seen as ideals or best practice for poor

cities. Debates on gentrification, social housing, subsidies, public child care, and so forth, come to mind.

4 In 2011, the World Bank classified countries by income groups as follows: low income, US$1,025 per capita or less; lower-middle income, US$1,026–US$4,035 per capita; upper-middle income, US$4,036–US$12,475 per capita; and high income, US$12,476 per capita or more.

5 Precise estimates are difficult to make on account of gaps in the data (Bhattacharya et al. 2012).

6 According to figures from the Economic Commission for Latin America and the Caribbean (ECLAC), the region requires annual investments of between US$128 billion and US$180 billion.

7 We have in our archive the promotional brochure of this company, which one of us acquired from a meeting with the Singapore Ambassador to South Africa.

8 As an aside, in an era in which architects are powerful protagonists of green utopias, it is doubly important that the design and artistic disciplines speak to expose the hubris and opportunism of elite environmentalism. This imperative is usefully set out by Maarten Hajer (2014).

9 For two thoughtful critiques of this approach to design, see Inam (2014) and Tonkiss (2014).

10 The book is available online: www.marxists.org/archive/marx/works/1845/condition-working-class/index.htm.

11 Interestingly, as we finished writing this book (October 2016), Elon Musk launched his final banal innovation that will allow suburban lifestyles to go off the grid, representing a significant shift in markets that provide energy and mobility around the world. His announcement was the unveiling of solar roof tiles that look virtually identical to conventional slate and clay options, but each one is laced with solar panels that can capture and conduct energy to household storage devices (Tesla Powerwall home battery), which in turn can charge his Tesla electric cars. What is more significant is that, as a leading technology prophet, Musk has recently gone on record to argue for a universal basic income grant for the world to anticipate the implications of automation: http://gizmodo.com/elon-musk-we-need-universal-income-because-robots-will-1788644631.

Chapter 3   Re-Description

1 Conceptualizing relations among cities draws upon many different methodological devices – for example, using topological

relations, assemblages of policies and their transfer across different sites, the articulation of cities through logistical and commodity chains, articulations forged through the ties of colonial heritage and postcolonial aspirations, or the diffusion of planetary-scale accumulation and renewal strategies fostered by the valorization and institutionalization of particular formats of urban knowledge production (Allen and Cochrane 2010; Hesse 2010; Jacobs 2012; McCann and Ward 2011; Roy 2011; and Wyly 2015).

2 For particularly provocative discussions about just who and what inhabits the urban environment, and where the conceptualization of inhabitants goes beyond the human to include various composite entities made of varying ontologies and materials, see Haraway et al. 2016; Hinchliffe and Lavau 2013; and Negarestani 2011, 2014.

3 For particularly incisive analyses of how urban governments so frequently miss taking into consideration the "real dynamics" of what is taking place in everyday life, see Healey 2015; McQuarrie et al. 2013; and Sheppard et al. 2015.

4 For exemplary discussions about how a heterogeneity of urban practices work in difficult conditions, how they can be readapted and reshaped to meet new contingencies, and how they might constitute an emerging platform of connection among different logics of urban management, see particularly Lepawsky et al. 2015; McFarlane 2011; McFarlane and Desai 2015; and Thieme 2013.

5 Lower- and working-class districts are continually thrown off and buffeted by forces that are both external and of their own making, and particularly where the differences between these are often difficult to discern. Especially salient examples are Anwar 2016; Harms 2013; Kamete 2010; and Sen 2012.

6 An important contribution of a recent generation of urban literature about the global South demonstrates the ways in which residents make small, incremental and continual attainments in highly uncertain conditions and, in fact, use that uncertainty itself as a resource. For example, see Bayat 2010; Jeffery and Jeffery 2012; and Schwenkel 2013.

7 Particularly incisive descriptions and analyses for these processes of suturing together the discrepant as an economy in and of itself can be found in Chattopadhyay 2012; Dovey 2014; Perlman 2010; Sánchez 2008; Silver 2014; and Telles and Hirata 2007.

8 There is a growing literature that examines both how self-constructed urban districts of lower- and working-class residents actually worked and then enables a complementary analysis of

how they have been progressively transformed under neoliberal conditions, but also, importantly, how these conditions can both dovetail with and diverge from such districts' own particular aspirations for change. Good examples of this literature are Caldeira and Holston 2015; Fawaz 2008, Fincher and Iveson 2012; Guarneros-Meza 2009; Holston 2009; Hunt 2009; Raco et al. 2011; Zeiderman et al. 2015.

9 For some now classic works on urban neoliberalization and how it impacts on the spatial operations of the city and the room for manoeuvre on the part of the majority, see Banerjee-Guha 2010; Gidwani and Reddy 2011; Goldman 2011; Peck et al. 2009; and Rossi 2013.

10 For a useful, up-to-date and nuanced summary of this literature, see Deas and Headlam 2014.

11 For some of the key literature about how markets create "economy" rather than simply being economic instruments, see particularly Gandolfo 2013; Guyer 2015; Mörtenböck et al. 2015; Stillerman 2006; and Yu 2004.

Chapter 5   Horizons from Within the Break

1 We draw particular inspiration from the incisive calls for experimentation issued by the following authors, as well as their theoretical shaping of "what is possible" from an engagement of the interstices between the various infrastructures of constraint and accumulation, rather than simply the issuance of new programs or ideological commitments: Harney and Moten 2013; Mason 2015; Massey and Rustin 2014; and Srnicek and Williams 2015.

2 Following the assumption about the relationship between venture capitalists that seek out and promote emerging sustainable technologies and the imminent technological-economic transition reflected in the transitions literature (Geels 2013; Perez 2013; Swilling 2013), we envisage the practical necessity of identifying and tracking this cohort of private-sector players. It is this group that we have in mind when we refer to "next generation investors." For an insightful account of the kinds of technological sectors at play, and their market value, see the review report of McKinsey on disruptive technologies (Manyika et al. 2013).

3 One pertinent example is the Oxfam-led campaign to make tax fair, but rooted in a broader analysis of systemic inequality: https://act.oxfam.org/international/world-tax-summit.

4 This is one cut into the complexity of the contemporary city and its public sphere. We have no illusions that there are not many dangers with this approach, and it does not take in the full gamut of political and strategic opportunities. However, for us, it best captures the most strategic knife-edge of the potential role of the city in the larger story of structural economic change, within which the signs are not positive by any means of the imagination.

5 Particularly salient literature that posits the urban as an operating system, drawing from traditions of cybernetics, development biology, social systems theory and assemblage theory, includes Amin and Thrift 2013; De Landa 2006; Geels and Kemp 2007; Guy et al. 2001; McFarlane 2011; Swilling 2011; and Tonkiss 2014.

6 In November 2016, the Paris climate agreement, first struck in the city in December 2015 at COP 21, came into force. In terms of the treaty, the signatory countries are obligated to achieve national determined carbon emissions targets to ensure that worldwide emissions will remain well below 2°C above pre-industrial levels and to pursue efforts to limit the temperature increase to 1.5°C: http://unfccc.int/2860.php.

7 It is easy to dismiss the various greenwashing forums, standards, protocols and policy frameworks of the ethical business movement that come together in the World Business Council of Sustainable Development or the like-minded fora of Davos. However, these institutions are important in that they create a set of norms and standards that often lead to the formulation of legal dispensations that regulate the practices of the private sector. Among the topics that are increasingly being driven by international NGOs such as Oxfam and their partners are the issues of tax evasion and tax havens. There can be little doubt that the scope of development investment could be much greater if these resources could be captured more effectively. Defining and institutionalizing new norms with legal effect in these domains is unlikely to come about without the discursive role of the plethora of "ethical business" institutions.

8 An emergent field of critical infrastructure studies has attempted to analyze how infrastructure is a medium of political formations – about how it not only provisions and articulates distinctive entities and places but constitutes them as well; about how it enacts specific dispositions of human and technical capacities that posit specific potentialities of urban space. For example, see Amin 2014; Chattopadhyay 2012; Howe et al. 2015; Lancione and McFarlane 2016; Larkin 2013; and von Schnitzler 2013.

9 For an insightful mainstream elaboration, see UN-Habitat (2013).

10 This is not the occasion to get into a methodological discussion, but it is important to appreciate that the processes of excavating this kind of knowledge is directly connected to the prospect of establishing dialogical processes rooted within these communities, which will be the social-cultural basis of alternative proposals, experiments and political claims. The spirited work of Nabeel Hamdi (2004) on how to work with communities comes to mind.

Chapter 6   Experimentations

1 "Autoconstruction" is a term deployed by James Holston (1991), building on the work of the anthropologist Geert Banck (1986), to capture the rich aesthetic sensibilities that go into the incessant process of building and adapting informal houses on the peripheries of Brazilian cities.

2 The final report and broader work of the commission can be accessed and reviewed at www.khayelitshacommission.org.za/final-report.html.

3 *Cityscapes* as a magazine and platform is driven by Tau Tavengwa and Sean O'Toole with support from Edgar Pieterse, who acts as consulting editor. In practice, each issue emerges after many conversations and disagreements about what is most topical and how best to curate the content. It is constantly evolving. See www.cityscapesdigital.net.

4 Chimurenga is one of the most important independent radical cultural platforms where a wide variety of insurgent experiments get concocted and deployed. It is a crucial nexus of black academic, artistic, cultural and political imagination. See www.chimurenga.co.za.

5 These are available to download for free: see www.africancitiesreader.org.za.

6 For some models of academic–practitioner collaboration, see Brown-Luthango 2013, Cartwright et al. 2013, and Pieterse 2013.

7 For further information on this multi-sited research program, see: www.mistraurbanfutures.org/en.

8 The data and documentary record of the exhibition can be explored at www.citydesired.com.

References

Abramson, Daniel Benjamin (2011) Places for the gods: urban planning as orthopraxy and heteropraxy in China, *Environment and Planning D: Society and Space*, 29: 67–88.

Adams, Ross (2014) Natura urbans, natura urbanata: ecological urbanism, circulation, and the immunization of nature, *Environment and Planning D: Society and Space*, 32: 12–29.

Addie, Jean-Paul, and Keil, Roger (2015) Real existing regionalism: the region between talk, territory and technology, *International Journal of Urban and Regional Research*, 39: 407–41.

Adelekan, Ibidun, Johnson, Cassidy, Manda, Mtafu, Matyas, David, Mberu, Blessing, Parnell, Susan, Pelling, Mark, Satterthwaite, David, and Vivekananda, Janani (2015) Disaster risk and its reduction: an agenda for urban Africa, *International Development Planning Review*, 37: 33–43.

AfDB (African Development Bank) (2013) *An Integrated Approach to Infrastructure Provision in Africa*. Tunis: African Development Bank.

Agamben, Giorgio (1993) *The Coming Community*. Minneapolis: University of Minnesota Press.

_____ (2013) *The Highest Poverty: Monastic Rules and Form-of-Life*. Stanford, CA: Stanford University Press.

_____ (2014) What is destituent power?, *Environment and Planning D: Society and Space*, 32: 65–74.

Agbiboa, Daniel (2014) Boko Haram, religious violence, and the crisis of national identity in Nigeria: towards a non-killing approach, *Journal of Developing Societies*, 29: 379–403.

Agnew, John (2013) Arguing with regions, *Regional Studies*, 47: 6–17.

Agualusa, José Eduardo ([2012] 2015) *A General Theory of Oblivion*. London: Harvill Secker.

Allen, Adriana, Lampis, Andrea, and Swilling, Mark (eds) (2016) *Untamed Urbanisms*. London and New York: Routledge.

Allen, John, and Cochrane, Allan (2010) Assemblages of state power: topological shifts in the organization of government and politics, *Antipode*, 42: 1071–89.

Amin, Ash (ed.) (2010) *The Social Economy: International Perspectives on Economic Solidarity*. London and New York: Zed Books.

_____ (2011) Urban planning in an uncertain world, in Gary Bridge and Sophie Watson (eds) *The New Blackwell Companion to the City*. Oxford: Blackwell.

_____ (2013a) The urban condition: the challenge to social science, *Public Culture*, 25: 201–8.

_____ (2013b) Surviving the turbulent future, *Environment and Planning D: Society and Space*, 31: 140–56.

_____ (2014) Lively infrastructure, *Theory, Culture & Society*, 31: 137–61.

Amin, Ash, and Thrift, Nigel (2002) *Cities: Re-imagining the Urban*. Cambridge: Polity.

_____ (2013) *Arts of the Political: New Openings for the Left*. Durham, NC: Duke University Press.

Amoore, Louise (2013) *The Politics of Possibility: Risk and Security beyond Probability*. Durham, NC: Duke University Press.

Amoore, Louise, and Piotukh, Volha (2015) Life beyond big data: governing with little analytics, *Economy and Society*, 44: 341–66.

Anderson, Ben (2012) Affect and biopower: towards a politics of life, *Transactions of the Institute of British Geographers*, 37: 28–43.

Angel, Shlomo (2012) *Planet of Cities*. Cambridge, MA: Lincoln Institute of Land Policy.

Anwar, Nausheen H. (2014) Urban transformations: brokers, collaborative governance and community building in Karachi's periphery, *South Asia History and Culture*, 5: 75–92.

_____ (2016) Asian mobilities and state governance at the geographic margins: geopolitics and oil tales from Karachi to Taftan, *Environment and Planning A*, 48: 1047–63.

Appadurai, Arjun (2002) Deep democracy: urban governance and the horizon of politics, *Public Culture*, 14: 21–47.

_____ (2011) What does the nano want? Design as a tool for future-building, keynote address at the symposium "Unpacking the Nano: The Price of the World's Most Affordable Car," Cornell University, College of Architecture, Art and Planning, March 10.

———— (2015) Mediants, materiality, normativity, *Public Culture*, 27: 22–37.

Aradau, Claudia, Lobo-Guerrero, Luis, and Van Munster, Rens (2008) Security, technologies of risk, and the political: guest editors' introduction, *Security Dialogue*, 39: 147–54.

Auyero, Xavier (2012) *Patients of the State: The Politics of Waiting in Argentina*. Durham, NC: Duke University Press.

Bach, Jonathan (2010) They come as villagers and leave as citizens: urban villages and the making of Shenzhen, China, *Cultural Anthropology*, 25: 421–58.

Bacigalupi, Paolo (2015) *The Water Knife*. New York: Vintage.

Bahn, Gautam (2016) *In the Public's Interest: Evictions, Citizenship and Inequality in Contemporary Delhi*. Delhi: OrientBlackSwan.

Banck, Geert A. (1986) Poverty, politics and the shaping of urban space: a Brazilian example, *International Journal of Urban Regional Research*, 10: 522–40.

Banerjee, Sudeshna, Wodon, Quentin, Diallo, Amadou, Pushak, Taras, Uddin, Helal, Tsimpo, Clarence, and Foster, Vivien (2009) *Access, Affordability, and Alternatives: Modern Infrastructure Services in Africa*, Africa Infrastructure Country Diagnostic Background Paper 2. Washington, DC: World Bank.

Banerjee-Guha, Swapna (ed.) (2010) *Accumulation by Dispossession: Transformative Cities in the New Global Order*. New Delhi: Sage.

Bataille, Georges (1991) *The Accursed Share: An Essay on General Economy*. New York: Zone Books.

Batty, Michael (2013) *The New Science of Cities*. Cambridge, MA: MIT Press.

Baviskar, Amita (2003) Between violence and desire: space, power, and identity in the making of metropolitan Delhi, *International Social Science Journal*, 55: 89–98.

Bayat, Asef (2010) *Life as Politics: How Ordinary People Change the Middle East*. Stanford, CA: Stanford University Press.

Beall, Jo (2006) Cultural weapons: traditions, inventions and the transition to democratic governance in metropolitan Durban, *Urban Studies*, 43: 457–73.

Bebbington, Anthony, Hickey, Samuel, and Mitlin, Diana (2008) *Can NGOs Make a Difference? The Challenge of Development Alternatives*. London: Zed Books.

Benjamin, Solomon (2015) Cities within and beyond the plan, in Crispin Bates and Mio Minoru (eds) *Cities in South Asia*. London and New York: Routledge.

Bennett, Jane (2010) *Vibrant Matter: A Political Ecology of Things*. Durham, NC: Duke University Press.

Berlant, Lauren (2011) *Cruel Optimism*. Durham, NC: Duke University Press.

Bhattacharya, Amar, Romani, Mattia, and Stern, Nicholas (2012) *Infrastructure for Development: Meeting the Challenge*. Centre for Climate Change Economics and Policy, Grantham Research Institute on Climate Change and the Environment, www.lse.ac.uk/GranthamInstitute/wp-content/uploads/2014/03/PP-infrastructure-for-development-meeting-the-challenge.pdf.

Biehl, João, Good, Byron, and Kleinman, Arthur (2007) Introduction: rethinking subjectivity, in João Biehl, Byron Good and Arthur Kleinman (eds) *Subjectivity: Ethnographic Investigations*. Berkeley: University of California Press.

Booth, Derek, and Bledsoe, Brian (2009) Streams and urbanization, in Lawrence Baker (ed.) *The Water Environment of Cities*. New York: Springer.

Boudreau, Julie-Anne (2007) Making new political spaces: mobilizing spatial imaginaries, instrumentalizing spatial practices, and strategically using spatial tools, *Environment and Planning A*, 39: 2593–611.

Boudreau, Julie-Anne, Gilbert, Liette, and Labbé, Danielle (2016) Uneven state formalization and periurban housing production in Hanoi and Mexico City: comparative reflections from the global South, *Environment and Planning A*, 48: 2383–401.

Boyer, Brian, Cook, Justin W., and Steinberg, Marco (2011) *In Studio: Recipes for Systemic Change*. Helsinki: Sitra.

Bratton, Benjamin H. (2016) *The Stack: On Software and Sovereignty*. Cambridge, MA: MIT Press.

Braun, Bruce P. (2014) A new urban dispotif? Governing life in an age of climate change, *Environment and Planning D: Society and Space*, 32: 49–64.

Brenner, Neil, and Schmid, Christian (2014) The "urban age" in question, *International Journal of Urban and Regional Research*, 38: 731–55.

_____ (2015) Towards a new epistemology of the urban?, *City*, 19: 151–82.

Brighenti, Andrea Mubi (2016) The public and the common: some approximations of their contemporary articulation, *Critical Inquiry*, 42: 306–28.

Brown-Luthango, Mercy (2013) Community–university engagement: the Philippi CityLab in Cape Town and the challenge of collaboration across boundaries, *Higher Education*, 65: 309–24.

Buchanan, Peter (2013) The big rethink concludes neighbourhood as the expansion of the home, *Architectural Review*, 5 June.

Bulkeley, Harriet, Luque-Ayala, Andrés, and Silver, Jonathan (2014) Housing and the (re)configuration of energy provision in Cape Town and São Paulo: making space for a progressive urban climate politics?, *Political Geography*, 40: 25–34.

Byrd, Hugh, and Matthewman, Steve (2014) Exergy and the city: the technology and sociology of power (failure), *Journal of Urban Technology*, 21: 85–102.

CAHF (Centre for Affordable Housing Finance in Africa) (2015) *Housing Finance in Africa: A Review of Some of Africa's Housing Finance Markets*. Johannesburg: CAHF.

Caldeira, Teresa, and Holston, James (2015) Participatory urban planning in Brazil, *Urban Studies*, 52: 2001–17.

Carley, Michael, and Christie, Ian (2000) *Managing Sustainable Development*. 2nd edn, London: Earthscan.

Cartwright, Anton (2015) *Better Growth, Better Cities: Rethinking and Redirecting Urbanisation in Africa*. University of Cape Town, African Centre for Cities.

Cartwright, Anton, Blignaut, James, De Wit, Martin, Goldberg, Karen, Mander, Myles, O'Donoghue, Sean, and Roberts, Debra (2013) Economics of climate change adaptation at the local scale under conditions of uncertainty and resource constraints: the case of Durban, South Africa, *Environment and Urbanization*, 25: 139–56.

Castells, Manuel (2014) *The Impact of the Internet on Society: A Global Perspective*. Change Series. Open Mind & BBVA.

Chatterjee, Ipsita (2011) Governance as "performed", governance as "inscribed": new urban politics in Ahmedabad, *Urban Politics*, 48: 2571–90.

Chattopadhyay, Swati (2012) *Unlearning the City: Infrastructure in a New Optical Field*. Minneapolis: University of Minnesota Press.

Cheah, Pheng (2007) Biopower and the new international division of reproductive labor, *Boundary*, 2: 79–113.

Chen, Marty (2008) Addressing informality, reducing poverty, *Poverty in Focus*, no. 16: 6–7; www.ipc-undp.org/pub/IPC PovertyInFocus16.pdf.

Clos, Joan (2014) Towards a new urban agenda, LSE Cities, https://lsecities.net/media/objects/articles/towards-a-new-urban-agenda/en-gb/.

Clough, Patricia (2012) Feminist theory: bodies, science, and technology, in Bryan Turner (ed.) *Routledge Handbook of Body Studies*. London and New York: Routledge.

COGTA (Cooperative Governance and Traditional Affairs, Government of South Africa) (2014) *Integrated Development Urban Framework: Draft for Discussion*. Pretoria: COGTA.

_____ (2016) *Integrated Development Urban Framework: Implementation Plan*. Pretoria: COGTA.

Cole, Teju (2014) *Every Day is for the Thief*. New York: Random House.

Comaroff, Jean, and Comaroff, John (2011) *Theory from the South: Or, How Euro-America is Evolving toward Africa (The Radical Imagination)*. London and New York: Routledge.

Connell, Raewyn (2007) *Southern Theory*. Cambridge: Polity.

Connolly, William (2014) Freedom, teleodynamism, creativity, *Foucault Studies*, 17: 60–75.

Corsín Jiménez, Alberto, and Estalella, Adolfo (2014) Assembling neighbors: the city as hardware, method, and "a very messy kind of archive," *Common Knowledge*, 20: 150–71.

Coward, Martin (2012) Between us in the city: materiality, subjectivity, and community in the era of global urbanization, *Environment and Planning D: Society and Space*, 30: 468–81.

Cowherd, Richard (2002) Planning or cultural construction? The transformation of Jakarta in the late Soeharto period, in Peter J. M. Nas (ed.) *The Indonesian Town Revisited*. Singapore: Institute of Southeast Asian Studies.

Crandall, Jordan (2010) The geospatialization of calculative operations: tracking, sensing and megacities, *Theory, Culture & Society*, 27: 68–90.

Crescenzi, Riccardo, Rodríguez-Pose, Andrés, and Storper, Michael (2012) The territorial dynamics of innovation in China and India, *Economic Geography*, 12: 1055–85.

Cruz, Teddy (2004) Mapping non-conformity: post-bubble urban strategies, Hemispheric Institute, http://hemisphericinstitute.org/hemi/en/e-misferica-71/cruz.

Cruz, Teddy, and Forman, Fonna (2015) Changing practices: engaging informal public demands, in Peter Mörtonböck, Helga Mooshammer, Teddy Cruz, and Fonna Forman (eds) *Informal Market Worlds – Reader*. Rotterdam: NAI010 Publishers, pp. 203–57.

Datta, Ayona (2012) *The Illegal City: Space, Law and Gender in a Delhi Squatter Settlement*. Farnham, and Burlington, VT: Ashgate.

Davis, Diane (2010) Irregular armed forces, shifting patterns of commitment, and fragmented sovereignty in the developing world, *Theory and Society*, 39: 397–413.

Davis, Mike (2006) *Planet of the Slums*. London: Verso.

Deas, Ian and Headlam, Nicola Mary (2014) Boosterism, Brokerage and Uneasy Bedfellow: Networked Urban Governance and the Emergence of Post-Political Orthodoxy, in Ronan Paddison and

Tom Hutton (eds.) *Cities and Economic Change: Restructuring and Dislocation in the Global Metropolis*. London: Sage

De Boeck, Filip (2011a) Inhabiting ocular ground: Kinshasa's future in the light of Congo's spectral urban politics, *Cultural Anthropology*, 26: 263–86.

_____ (2011b) Spectral Kinshasa: building the city through an architecture of words, in Tim Edensor and Mark Jayne (eds) *Urban Theory beyond the West: A World of Cities*. London: Routledge, pp. 309–26.

_____ (2012) Infrastructure: commentary from Filip De Boeck, *Cultural Anthropology Online*, November 26, https://culanth.org/curated_collections/11-infrastructure/discussions/7-infrastructur e-commentary-from-filip-de-boeck.

_____ (2015) "Divining" the city: rhythm, amalgamation and knotting as forms of "urbanity," *Social Dynamics*, 41: 47–58.

De Boeck, Filip, and Baloji, Sammy (2016) *Suturing the City: Living Together in Congo's Urban Worlds*. London: Autograph.

De Boeck, Filip, and Plissart, Marie-Françoise (2004) *Kinshasa: Tales of the Invisible City*. Ghent: Ludion/Royal Museum for Central Africa.

De Landa, Manuel (2006) *A New Philosophy of Society: Assemblage Theory and Social Complexity*. New York: Continuum.

Derickson, Kate (2015) Urban geography 1: locating urban theory in the "urban age," *Progress in Human Geography*, 39: 647–57.

Dillon, Michael (2007) Governing through contingency: the security of biopolitical governance, *Political Geography*, 26: 41–7.

Douzinas, Costas (2014) Notes towards an analytics of resistance, *New Formations*, 83: 79–98.

Dovey, Kim (2014) Incremental urbanism: the emergence of informal settlements, in Tigran Haas and Krister Olsson (eds) *Emergent Urbanism: Urban Planning & Design in a Time of Structural and Systemic Change*. Farnham, and Burlington, VT: Ashgate.

Dunne, Anthony, and Raby, Fiona (2013) *Speculative Everything: Design, Fiction, and Social Dreaming*. Cambridge, MA: MIT Press.

Dutton, Michael (2012) Fragments of the political or how we deal with wonder, *Social Text*, 30: 109–41.

Easterling, Keller (2014) *Extrastatecraft: The Power of Infrastructure Space*. London: Verso.

Edjabe, Ntone, and Pieterse, Edgar (eds) (2010) *African Cities Reader I: Pan-African Practices*. Cape Town: Chimurenga Press and African Centre for Cities.

Elyachar, Julia (2011) The political economy of movement and gesture in Cairo, *Journal of the Royal Anthropological Institute*, 17: 82–99.

Fawaz, Mona (2008) An unusual clique of city-makers: social networks in the production of a neighborhood in Beirut, *International Journal of Urban and Regional Research*, 32: 565–85.

Ferguson, James (2010) The uses of neoliberalism, *Antipode*, 41: 166–84.

———— (2011) Toward a left art of government: from 'Foucauldian critique' to Foucauldian politics, *History of the Human Sciences*, 24: 61–8.

Fincher, Ruth, and Iveson, Kurt (2012) Justice and injustice in the city, *Geographical Research*, 50: 231–41.

Fischer-Kowalski, Marina, and Swilling, Mark (2011) *Decoupling: Natural Resource Use and Environmental Impacts from Economic Growth*. New York: UNEP.

Floater, Graham, and Rode, Philipp (2014) *Cities and the New Climate Economy: The Transformative Role of Urban Growth*, NCE Cities – Paper 01, London: London School of Economics.

Foucault, Michel (2009) *Security, Territory, Population: Lectures at the Collège de France 1977–1978*. Basingstoke: Palgrave-Macmillan.

Fox, Sean (2012) Urbanization as a global historical process: theory and evidence from sub-Saharan Africa, *Population and Development Review*, 38: 285–310.

Friedmann, John (2002) *The Prospect of Cities*. Minneapolis: University of Minnesota Press.

Gago, Verónica (2015) Financialization of popular life and the extractive operations of capital: a perspective from Argentina, *South Atlantic Quarterly*, 114: 11–28.

Galloway, Alexander (2012) *The Interface Effect*. Cambridge: Polity.

Gandolfo, Daniella (2013) Formless: a day at Lima's Office of Formalization, *Cultural Anthropology*, 28: 278–98.

Garmany, Jeff (2010) Religion and governmentality: understanding governance in urban Brazil, *Geoforum*, 41: 908–18.

Gaventa, John (2013) Understanding the power cube and related concepts, in *Power Pack: Understanding Power for Social Change*. Brighton: Institute of Development Studies, University of Sussex; www.powercube.net/wp-content/uploads/2011/04/powerpack-web-version-2011.pdf, pp. 6–28.

Gayer, Laurent (2014) *Karachi: Ordered Disorder and the Struggle of the City*. Oxford: Oxford University Press.

Gazdar, Haris, and Mallah, Hussain Bux (2013) Informality and political violence in Karachi, *Urban Studies*, 50: 3099–115.

Geels, Frank W. (2013) The impact of the financial–economic crisis on sustainability transitions: financial investment, governance and public discourse, *Environmental Innovation and Societal Transitions*, 6: 67–95.

Geels, Frank W., and Kemp, René (2007) Dynamics in socio-technical systems: typology of change processes and contrasting case studies, *Technology in Society*, 29: 441–55.

Ghertner, D. Asher (2010) Calculating without numbers: aesthetic governmentality in Delhi's slums, *Economy and Society*, 39: 185–217.

―――― (2014) India's urban revolution: geographies of displacement beyond gentrification, *Environment and Planning A*, 46: 1554–71.

Gidwani, Vinay, and Reddy, Rajyashree N. (2011) The afterlives of "waste": notes from India for a minor history of capitalist surplus, *Antipode*, 43: 1625–58.

Glaeser, Edward (2012) *Triumph of the City: How our Greatest Invention Makes Us Richer, Smarter, Greener, Healthier, and Happier*. New York: Penguin.

Glissant, Édouard (1997) *Poetics of Relation*. Ann Arbor: University of Michigan Press.

Goankar, Dilip (2014) After the fictions: notes towards a phenomenology of the multitude, *e-flux*, no. 58, www.e-flux.com/journal/after-the-fictions-notes-towards-a-phenomenology-of-the-multitude/.

Goetz, Anne Marie, and Gaventa, John (2001) *Bringing Citizen Voice and Client Focus into Service Delivery*, IDS Working Paper no. 138. Brighton: Institute for Development Studies.

Goh, Daniel (2015) Singapore, the state, and decolonial spatiality, *Cultural Dynamics*, 27: 215–26.

Goldfrank, Benjamin, and Schrank, Andrew (2009) Municipal neoliberalism and municipal socialism: urban political economy in Latin America, *International Journal of Urban and Regional Research*, 33: 443–62.

Goldman, Michael (2011) Speculative urbanism and the making of the next world city, *International Journal of Urban and Regional Research*, 35: 555–81.

Gottschalk, Marie (2014) *Caught: The Prison State and the Lockdown of American Politics*. Princeton, NJ: Princeton University Press.

Graham, Stephen, and Marvin, Simon (2001) *Splintering Urbanism: Networked Infrastructures, Technological Mobilities and the Urban Condition*. London and New York: Routledge.

Greenfield, Adam (2013) *Against the Smart City*. New York: Do projects.

Guarneros-Meza, Valeria (2009) Mexican urban governance: how old and new institutions coexist and interact, *International Journal of Urban and Regional Research*, 33: 463–82.

Gupta, Akhil (2012) *Red Tape: Bureaucracy, Structural Violence, and Poverty in India*. Durham, NC: Duke University Press.

Gupta, Akhil, and Sivaramakrishnan, Kalyanakrishnan (eds) (2012) *The State in India after Liberalization: Interdisciplinary Perspectives*. New York: Routledge.

Gurney, Kim (2014) Edge design: urban form and social change in Khayelitsha and Dunoon, *Cityscapes* 5: 34–49.

Guy, Simon, Marvin, Simon, and Moss, Timothy (eds) (2001) *Urban Infrastructure in Transition: Networks, Buildings, Plans*. London: Earthscan.

Guyer, Jane (2015) Markets and urban provisioning, in Célestin Monga and Justin Yifu Lin (eds) *The Oxford Handbook of Africa and Economics*, Vol. 1: *Context and Concepts*. Oxford: Oxford University Press.

Hajer, Maarten (2014) On being smart about cities: seven considerations for a new urban planning and design, in Maarten Hajer and Ton Dassen (eds) *Smart about Cities: Visualising the Challenge for the 21st Century Urbanism*. Rotterdam: NAI010.

Halberstam, Jack (2013) The wild beyond: with and for the undercommons, in Stefano Harney and Fred Moten, *The Undercommons: Fugitive Planning & Black Study*. New York: Minor Compositions.

Hall, Suzanne, and Savage, Michael (2016) Animating the urban vortex: new sociological urgencies, *International Journal of Urban and Regional Research*, 40: 82–95.

Hamdi, Nabeel (2004) *Small Change: About the Art of Practice and the Limits of Planning in Cities*. London: Earthscan.

Hansen, Mark (2012) Engineering preindividual potentiality: technics, transindividuation, and 21st century media, *Substance*, 41: 32–59.

Hansen, Thomas Blom, and Verkaaik, Oskar (2009) Introduction – urban charisma: on everyday mythologies in the city, *Critique of Anthropology*, 29: 5–26.

Haraway, Donna, Ishikawa, Noboru, Gilbert, Scott F., Olwig, Kenneth, Tsing, Anna L., and Bubandt, Nils (2016) Anthropologists are talking – about the Anthropocene, *Ethnos*, 81: 535–64.

Hardt, Michael, and Negri, Antonio (2011) *Commonwealth*. Cambridge, MA: Harvard University Press.

Harms, Erik (2013) Eviction time in the new Saigon: temporalities of displacement in the rubble of development, *Cultural Anthropology*, 28: 344–68.

Harney, Stefano, and Moten, Fred (2013) *The Undercommons: Fugitive Planning & Black Study*. New York: Minor Compositions.

Harrison, John, and Hoyler, Michael (eds) (2015) *Megaregions: Globalization's New Urban Form?* Cheltenham, and Northampton, MA: Edward Elgar.

Harvey, David (1989) *The Condition of Postmodernity*. Oxford: Blackwell.

_____ (2010) *The Enigma of Capital*. London: Profile Books.

Healey, Patsy (2015) Re-thinking the relations between planning, state and market in unstable times, in Jean Hillier and Jonathan Metzger (eds) *Connections: Exploring Contemporary Planning and Practice with Patsy Healey*. London: Ashgate, pp. 169–78.

Hesse, Markus (2010) Cities, material flows and the geography of spatial interaction: urban places in the system of chains, *Global Networks*, 10: 75–91.

Heynen, Nik (2013) Urban political ecology I: the urban century. *Progress in Human Geography*, 38: 598–604.

Hickey, Sam, and Mohan, Giles (2004) Towards participation as transformation: critical themes and challenges, in Sam Hickey and Giles Mohan (eds) *Participation: From Tyranny to Transformation?* London: Zed Books.

Hinchliffe, Steve, and Lavau, Stephanie (2013) Differentiated circuits: the ecologies of knowing and securing life, *Environment and Planning D: Society and Space*, 31: 259–74.

Holston, James (1991) Autoconstruction in working-class Brazil, *Cultural Anthropology*, 6: 447–65.

_____ (2009) Insurgent citizenship in an era of global urban peripheries, *City*, 21: 245–67.

Howe, Cymene, Lockrem, Jessica, Appel, Hannah, Hackett, Edward, Boyer, Dominic, Hall, Randal, Schneider-Mayerson, Matthew, Pope, Albert, Gupta, Ahkil, Rodwell, Elizabeth, Ballestero, Andrea, Durbin, Trevor, el-Dahdah, Farès, Long, Elizabeth and Mody, Cyrus (2015) Paradoxical infrastructures: ruins, retrofit, and risk, *Science, Technology, & Human Values*, 41: 547–65.

Huchzermeyer, Marie (2014) Humanism, creativity and rights: invoking Henri Lefebvre's right to the city in the tension presented by informal settlements in South Africa today, *Transformation*, 85: 64–89.

Huitfeldt, Henrik, and Jütting, Johannes (2009) Informality and informal employment, in POVNET (ed.) *Promoting Pro-Poor Growth: Employment*. Paris: OECD, pp. 85–108.

Hull, Matthew (2012) Documents and bureaucracy, *Annual Review of Anthropology*, 41: 251–67.

Hunt, Stacey (2009) Citizenship's place: the state's creation of public space and street vendors' culture of informality in Bogotá,

Colombia, *Environment and Planning D: Society and Space*, 27: 331–51.

Hyman, Katherine (2016) Sustainable urban infrastructure: the prospects and relevance for middle-income cities of the global South, PhD thesis, University of Cape Town; https://open.uct.ac.za/bitstream/item/23204/thesis_ebe_2016_hyman_katherine_rose.pdf?sequence=1.

ILO (International Labour Organization) (2013) *Global Employment Trends for Youth 2013: A Generation at Risk*. Geneva: International Labour Office.

_____ (2014) *World of Work Report 2014: Developing with Jobs*. Geneva: International Labour Organization.

_____ (2015) *World Employment and Social Outlook 2015: The Changing Nature of Work*. Geneva: International Labour Office.

Inam, Aseem (2014) *Designing Urban Transformation*. New York and London: Routledge.

Ingold, Tim (2007) *Lines: A Brief History*. London: Routledge.

Iweala, Uzodinma (2016) I dream of a utopian Lagos – but here's what African cities really need to prosper, *The Guardian*, October 13.

Jacobs, Jane (2012) Urban geographies! Still thinking the city relationally, *Progress in Human Geography*, 36: 412–22.

Jaglin, Sylvy (2014) Regulating service delivery in Southern cities: rethinking urban heterogeneity, in Susan Parnell and Sophie Oldfield (eds) *The Routledge Handbook on Cities of the Global South*. London and New York: Routledge, pp. 434–48.

_____ (2015) Is the network challenged by the pragmatic turn in African cities? Urban transition and hybrid delivery configurations, in Olivier Coutard and Jonathan Rutherford (eds) *Beyond the Networked City: Infrastructure Reconfigurations and Urban Change in the North and South*. London: Routledge.

Jeffery, Patricia, and Jeffery, Roger (2012) South Asia: intimacy and identities, politics and poverty, in Richard Fardon, Olivia Harris, Trevor H. J. Marchand, Mark Nuttall, Cris Shore, Veronica Strang and Richard A. Wilson (eds) *Sage Handbook of Social Anthropology*. London: Sage.

Johnson, Alan (2013) Progress and its ruins: ghosts, migrants, and the uncanny in Thailand, *Cultural Anthropology*, 28: 299–319.

Jones, Gavin (2002) Southeast Asian urbanization and the growth of mega-urban regions, *Journal of Population Research*, 19: 119–36.

Joseph, Peniel (2009) The Black Power movement: a state of the field, *Journal of American History*, 96: 751–76.

Jusionyte, Ieva (2015) States of camouflage, *Cultural Anthropology*, 30: 113–38.

Kamete, Amin (2010) Defending illicit livelihoods: youth resistance in Harare's contested spaces, *International Journal of Urban and Regional Research*, 34: 55–75.

Karaman, Ozan (2013) Urban renewal in Istanbul: reconfigured spaces, robotic lives, *International Journal of Urban and Regional Research*, 37: 313–33.

Kayembe wa Kayembe, Matthieu, De Maeyer, Mathieu, and Wolff, Eléonore (2012) The mapping of the urban growth of Kinshasa (DRC) through high resolution remote sensing between 1995 and 2005, in Boris Escalante-Ramirez (ed.) *Remote Sensing – Applications*. Rijeka, Croatia: InTech; www.intechopen.com/books/remote-sensing-applications/the-mapping-of-the-urban-growth-of-kinshasa.

Kilroy, Austin, Mukim, Megha, and Stefano, Negri (2015) *Competitive Cities for Jobs and Growth: What, Who, and How*. Washington, DC: World Bank.

King, Ross (2008) Bangkok space, and conditions of possibility, *Environment and Planning D: Society and Space*, 26: 315–37.

Kirmani, Nida (2015) Fear and the city: negotiating everyday life as a young Baloch man in Karachi, *Journal of the Economic and Social History of the Orient*, 58: 732–55.

Kitchin, Rob, Lauriault, Tracey P., and McArdle, Gavin (2015) Knowing and governing cities through urban indicators, city benchmarking and real-time dashboards, *Regional Studies, Regional Science*, 2: 1–28.

Kornberger, Martin (2012) Governing the city: from planning to urban strategy, *Theory, Culture & Society*, 29: 84–106.

Kusno, Abidin (2013) Housing the margin: *Perumahan Rakyat* and the future urban form of Jakarta, *Indonesia*, 94: 23–56.

Labbé, Danielle (2014) *Land Politics and Livelihoods on the Margins of Hanoi, 1920–2010*. Vancouver: University of British Columbia Press.

Lancione, Michele, and McFarlane, Colin (2016) Life at the urban margins: sanitation infra-making and the potential of experimental comparison, *Environment and Planning A*, 48: 2402–21.

Larkin, Brian (2013) The politics and poetics of infrastructure, *Annual Review of Anthropology*, 42: 327–43.

Lavalle, Adrián Gurza, Acharya, Arnab, and Houtzager, Peter (2005) Beyond comparative anecdotalism: lessons on civil society and participation from São Paulo, Brazil, *World Development*, 31: 951–64.

Law, John (2004) *After Method: Mess in Social Science Research*. London: Routledge.

_____ (2011) Collateral realities, in Fernando Domínguez Rubio and Patrick Baert (eds) *The Politics of Knowledge*. London: Routledge, pp. 156–78.

Lawhon, Mary, and Patel, Zarina (2013) Scalar politics and local sustainability: rethinking governance and justice in the era of political and environmental change, *Environment and Planning C: Government and Policy*, 31: 1048–62.

Lazzarato, Mauricio (2014) *Signs and Machines: Capitalism and Subjectivity*. Cambridge, MA: Semiotext(e) and MIT Press.

Lepawsky, Josh, Akese, Grace, Billah, Mostaem, Conolly, Creighton, and McNabb, Chris (2015) Composing urban orders from rubbish electronics: cityness and the site multiple, *International Journal of Urban and Regional Research*, 39: 185–99.

Lerner, Jaime (2014) *Urban Acupuncture: Celebrating Pinpricks of Change that Enrich City Life*. Washington, DC: Island Press.

Ley, Astrid (2012) Juggling with formality and informality in housing: some lessons from the new South Africa, in Michael Waibel and Colin McFarlane (eds) *Urban Informalities: Reflections on the Formal and Informal*. Farnham, and Burlington, VT: Ashgate.

Lin, George (2014) China's landed urbanization: neoliberalizing politics, land commodification, and municipal finance in the growth of metropolises, *Environment and Planning A*, 46: 1814–35.

Lindell, Ilda (2008) The multiple sites of urban governance: insights from an African city, *Urban Studies*, 45: 1879–901.

Lindell, Ilda, and Ampaire, Christine (2016) The untamed politics of urban informality: "gray space" and struggles for recognition in an African city, *Theoretical Inquiries in Law*, 17: 257–82.

Lingis, Alphonse (2000) *Dangerous Emotions*. Berkeley: University of California Press.

Lorimer, Jamie (2012) Multinatural geographies for the Anthropocene, *Progress in Human Geography*, 36: 593–612.

Lund, Christian (2006) Twilight institutions: public authority and local politics in Africa, *Development and Change*, 37: 685–705.

Lund, Christian, and Boone, Catherine (2013) Introduction: land politics in Africa: constituting authority over territory, property, and persons, *Africa*, 83: 1–13.

Luque-Ayala, Andrés, and Marvin, Simon (2016) The maintenance of urban circulation: an operational logic of infrastructural control, *Environment and Planning D: Society and Space*, 34: 191–208.

Lury, Celia (2012) Going live: towards an amphibious sociology, *Sociological Review*, 60: 184–97.

Lury, Celia, and Wakeford, Nina (eds) (2012) *Inventive Methods: The Happening of the Social*. London and New York: Routledge.

MacKinnon, Danny, and Derickson, Kate Driscoll (2012) From resilience to resourcefulness: a critique of resilience policy and activism, *Progress in Human Geography*, 37: 253–70.

MacLeod, Gavin, and McFarlane, Colin (2014) Introduction: grammars of urban injustice, *Antipode*, 46: 857–73.

Maloutas, Thomas (2004) The glass menagerie of urban governance and social cohesion: concepts and stakes, *International Journal of Urban and Regional Research*, 28: 449–65.

Mansuri, Ghazala, and Rao, Vijayendra (2014) *Localizing Development: Does Participation Work?* Washington, DC: World Bank.

Manyika, James, Chui, Michael, Bughin, Jacques, Dobbs, Richard, Bisson, Peter, and Marrs, Alex (2013) *Disruptive Technologies: Advances that Will Transform Life, Business, and the Global Economy*. New York: McKinsey Global Institute.

Marazzi, Christian (2010) *The Violence of Financial Capitalism*. New York: Semiotext(e).

Marcuse, Peter, Connolly, James, Novy, Johannes, Olivo, Ingrid, Potter, Cuz, and Steil, Justin (eds) (2009) *Searching for the Just City: Debates in Urban Theory and Practice*. London and New York: Routledge.

Mariani, Manuela, and Barron, Patrick (eds) (2014) *Terrain Vague: Interstices at the Edge of the Pale*. London and New York: Routledge.

Marshall, Richard (2003) *Emerging Urbanity: Global Urban Projects in the Asia Pacific Rim*. London and New York: Routledge.

Martin, Randy (2014) What difference do derivatives make? From the technical to the political conjuncture, *Culture Unbound*, 6: 189–210.

Mason, Paul (2012) *Why It's Kicking Off Everywhere: The New Global Revolutions*. London: Verso.

_____ (2015) *Postcapitalism: A Guide to our Future*. London: Penguin.

Massey, Doreen, and Rustin, Michael (2014) Whose economy? Reframing the debate, *Soundings*, 57: 170–91.

Massumi, Brian (2015) *Ontopower: War, Powers, and the State of Perception*. Durham, NC: Duke University Press.

Mathews, Gordon (2011) *Ghetto at the Center of the World: Chungking Mansions, Hong Kong*. Hong Kong: Hong Kong University Press.

Mauro, Sebastián, and Rossi, Federico (2015) The movement of popular and neighborhood assemblies in the city of Buenos Aires, 2002–2011, *Latin American Perspectives*, 42: 107–24.

Mazzucato, Mariana (2015) The green entrepreneurial state, in Ian Scoones, Melissa Leach and Peter Newell (eds) *The Politics of Green Transformations*. London: Routledge.

McCann, Eugene, and Ward, Kevin (eds) (2011) *Mobile Urbanism: Cities and Policymaking in the Global Age*. Minneapolis: University of Minnesota Press.

McFarlane, Colin (2011) *Learning the City: Knowledge and Translocal Assemblage*. Oxford: Wiley-Blackwell.

McFarlane, Colin, and Desai, Renu (2015) Sites of entitlement: claim, negotiation and struggle in Mumbai, *Environment and Urbanization*, 27: 441–54.

McQuade, Brendan (2015) Cognitive capitalism and contemporary politics: a world historical perspective, *Science & Society*, 79: 363–87.

McQuarrie, Michael, Fernandes, Naresh, and Shepard, Cassim (2013) The field of struggle, the office, and the flat: protest and aspiration in a Mumbai slum, *Public Culture*, 25: 315–348.

Mbembe, Achille (2015) Africa in the new century, *Cityscapes*, no. 7, www.cityscapesdigital.net/2015/12/09/africa-new-century/.

Menzies, Nick, Ketya, Sou, and Adler, Daniel (2008) *Land, Development and Conflict: Urban and Peri-Urban Phnom Penh*. Phnom Penh: Center for Advanced Study; www.academia.edu/3758683/Land_Development_and_Conflict_Urban_and_Peri-Urban_Phnom_Penh.

Mezzadra, Sandro, and Neilson, Brett (2012) Between inclusion and exclusion: on the topology of global space and borders, *Theory, Culture & Society*, 29: 58–75.

Mikkelsen, Flemming (2005) Working-class formation in Europe and forms of integration: history and theory, *Labor History*, 46: 277–306.

Mitchell, Don (2003) *The Right to the City: Social Justice and the Fight for Public Space*. New York: Guilford Press.

Mitchell, Timothy (2002) *Rule of Experts: Egypt, Techno-Politics, Modernity*. Berkeley: University of California Press.

_____ (2008) Rethinking economy, *Geoforum*, 39: 1116–21.

Mo Ibrahim Foundation (2015) *Facts and Figures: African Urban Dynamics*. London: Mo Ibrahim Foundation.

Monstadt, Jochen (2009) Conceptualizing the political ecology of urban infrastructures: insights from technology and urban studies, *Environment and Planning A*, 41: 1924 –42.

Moore, Jason (2015) *Capitalism in the Web of Life: Ecology and the Accumulation of Capital*. London: Verso.

Mörtenböck, Peter, Mooshammer, Helge, Cruz, Teddy, and Forman, Fonna (eds) (2015) *Informal Market Worlds Reader: The Architecture of Economic Pressure*. Rotterdam: NAI010.

Moss, Timothy (2001) Flow management in urban regions: introducing a concept, in Simon Guy, Simon Marvin and Timothy Moss (eds) *Urban Infrastructure in Transition: Networks, Buildings, Plans*. London: Earthscan.

Mota, Nelson (2015) From the Kebele to the condominium: accommodating social and spatial practices in Ethiopia's politics of affordable housing, paper given at the interdisciplinary conference "Housing: A Critical Perspective," Liverpool, 8–9 April; http://repository.tudelft.nl/view/ir/uuid:f9465975-e569-417 1-a4e5-2d2a9ce2726e/.

Moten, Fred (2003) *In the Break: The Aesthetics of the Black Radical Tradition*. Minneapolis: University of Minnesota Press.

Mouffe, Chantal (2000) *The Democratic Paradox*. London: Verso.

_____ (2009) The importance of engaging the state, in Jonathan Pugh (ed.) *What is Radical Politics Today?* Basingstoke: Palgrave Macmillan.

Moulaert, Frank, and Ailenei, Oana (2005) Social economy, third sector and solidarity relations: a conceptual synthesis from history to present, *Urban Studies*, 42: 2037–53.

Mulgan, Geoff (2005) Government, knowledge and the business of policy making: the potential and limits of evidence-based policy, *Evidence and Policy*, 1: 215–26.

Muniesa, Fabian (2014) *The Provoked Economy: Economic Reality and the Performative Turn*. London and New York: Routledge.

Naím, Moisés (2005) *Illicit: How Smugglers, Traffickers, and Copycats are Hijacking the Global Economy*. New York: Anchor Books.

Narayan, Deepa, and Kapoor, Soumya (2008) Beyond sectoral traps: creating wealth for the poor, in Caroline Moser and Anis A. Dani (eds) *Assets, Livelihoods and Social Policy*. Washington, DC: World Bank, pp. 299–321.

Nayar, Reema, Gottret, Pablo, Mitra, Pradeep, Betcherman, Gordon, Lee, Yue Man, Santos, Indhira, Dahal, Mahesh, and Shrestha, Maheshwor (2012) *More and Better Jobs in South Asia*. Washington, DC: World Bank.

Ndifuna Ukwazi (Dare to Know) (2016) *Safety, Justice & People's Power: A Companion to the O'Regan–Pikoli Commission of Inquiry into Policing in Khayelitsha*. Cape Town: Ndifuna Ukwazi.

Nederveen Pieterse, Jan (2010) *Development Theory*. 2nd edn, London: Sage.

Negarestani, Reza (2011) Drafting the inhuman: conjectures on capitalism and organic necessity, in Levi R. Bryant, Nick Srnicek and Graham Harman (eds) *The Speculative Turn: Continental Materialism and Realism*. Melbourne: Re.press.

224   References

_____ (2014) The labor of the inhuman, *e-flux* no. *52*, www.e-flux.com/ journal/the-labor-of-the-inhuman-part-i-human/.

Neilson, Brett, and Rossiter, Neil (2006) Towards a political anthropology of new institutional forms, *Ephemera: Theory and Politics in Organization*, 6: 393–410.

Neiva, Julia Mella, Serafim, Lizandra, and Manoela Miklos (eds) (2012) *Citizen Participation in Challenging Contexts*. São Paulo: Polis.

Neuwirth, Robert (2011) *Stealth of Nations: The Global Rise of the Informal Economy*. New York: Anchor.

Nielsen, Morten (2014) The negativity of times: collapsed futures in Maputo, Mozambique, *Social Anthropology*, 22: 213–26.

Nixon, Rob (2012) *Slow Violence and the Environmentalism of the Poor*. Cambridge, MA: Harvard University Press.

Nuijten, Monique (2013) The perversity of the "citizenship game": slum-upgrading in the urban periphery of Recife, Brazil, *Critique of Anthropology*, 33: 8–25.

Nyamnjoh, Francis B., and Brudvig, Ingrid (2014) Conviviality and negotiations with belonging in urban Africa, in Engin F. Isin and Peter Nyers (eds) *Routledge Handbook of Global Citizenship Studies*. London and New York: Routledge.

Obeng-Odoom, Franklin (2015) Africa: on the rise, but to where? *Forum for Social Economics*, 44: 234–50.

Okri, Ben (1986) *Dangerous Love*. London: Weidenfeld & Nicolson.

Ortega, Arnisson Andre C. (2012) *Desakota* and beyond: neoliberal production of suburban space in Manila's fringe, *Urban Geography*, 33: 1118–43.

Painter, Joe (2012) Regional biopolitics, *Regional Studies*, 47: 1235–48.

Parenti, Chris (2011) *Tropic of Chaos: Climate Change and the New Geography of Violence*. New York: Nation Books.

Parikka, Jussi (2010) *Insect Media: An Archaeology of Animals and Technology*. Minneapolis: University of Minnesota Press.

Parisi, Luciana (2012) Digital design and topological control, *Theory, Culture & Society*, 29: 165–92.

_____ (2013) *Contagious Architecture: Computation, Aesthetics and Space*. Cambridge, MA: MIT Press.

Parker, Simon (2004) *Urban Theory and Experience: Encountering the City*. London and New York: Routledge.

Parr, John (2008) Cities and regions: problems and potentials, *Environment and Planning A*, 40: 309–26.

Peck, Jamie (2005) Struggling with the creative class, *International Journal of Urban and Regional Research*, 29: 740–70.

Peck, Jamie, Theodore, Nik, and Brenner, Neil (2009) Neoliberal urbanism: models, moments, mutations, *SAIS Review*, 29: 49–66.

Perera, Nihal (2015) *People's Spaces: Coping, Familiarizing, Creating.* New York and London: Routledge.

Perez, Carlota (2009) *Technological Revolutions and Techno-Economic Paradigms*, Working Papers in Technology Governance and Economic Dynamics no. 20. Tallinn: University of Technology.

_____ (2013) Unleashing a golden age after the financial collapse: drawing lessons from history, *Environmental Innovation and Societal Transitions*, 6: 9–23.

_____ (2014a) *A Green and Socially Equitable Direction for the ICT Paradigm*, Globelics Working Paper series, www.globelics.org/wp-content/uploads/2016/05/GWP2014-01.pdf.

_____ (2014b) A new age of technological progress, in Chuka Umunna (ed.) *Owning the Future: How Britain Can Make it in a Fast-Changing World.* London: Rowman & Littlefield International.

Perlman, Janice (2010) *Favela: Four Decades of Living on the Edge in Rio de Janeiro.* Oxford: Oxford University Press.

Perry, Imani (2004) *Prophets of the Hood: Politics and Poetics in Hip Hop.* Durham, NC: Duke University Press.

Pettit, Jethro (2013) *Power Analysis: A Practical Guide.* Stockholm: SIDA.

Pieterse, Edgar (2008) *City Futures: Confronting the Crisis of Urban Development.* London: Zed Books.

_____ (2011) Grasping the unknowable: coming to grips with African urbanisms, *Social Dynamics*, 38: 5–23.

_____ (2013) City/university interplays amidst complexity, *Territorio*, 66: 26–32.

_____ (2015a) Epistemological practices of Southern urbanism, in Wowo Ding, Arie Graafland and Andong Lu (eds) *Cities in Transition II: Power, Environment, Society.* Rotterdam: NAI010.

_____ (2015b) Reaching for adaptive urbanism, in Michael Holm and Mette Kallehauge (eds) *Africa: Architective, Culture, Identity.* Humlebaek, Denmark: Louisiana Museum of Modern Art.

Pieterse, Edgar, and Cirolia, Liza (2016) South Africa's emerging national urban policy and upgrading agenda, in Liza Cirolia, Tristan Görgens, Mirjam van Donk, Warren Smit, and Drimie, Scott (eds) *Upgrading Informal Settlements in South Africa: A Participatory Approach.* Johannesburg: Juta.

Pieterse, Edgar, and Hyman, Katherine (2014) Disjunctures between urban infrastructure, finance and affordability, in Susan Parnell and Sophie Oldfield (eds) *The Routledge Handbook on Cities of the Global South.* London: Routledge.

Polk, Merrit (ed.) (2015) *Co-producing Knowledge for Sustainable Cities: Joining Forces for Change.* New York: Routledge.

Pollalis, Spiro, Georgoulias, Andreas, Ramos, Stephen, and Schodek, Danie (eds) (2012) *Infrastructure Sustainability and Design*. London and New York: Routledge.

Prashad, Vijay (2013) *The Poorer Nations: A Possible History of the Global South*. London: Verso.

Protevi, John (2009) *Political Affect: Connecting the Social and Somatic*. Minneapolis: University of Minnesota Press.

Provoost, Michelle (2015) *Cape Town: Densification as a Cure for a Segregated City*. Rotterdam: NAI010.

Purcell, Mark (2013) To inhabit well: counter-hegemonic movements and the right to the city, *Urban Geography*, 34: 560–74.

Raco, Mike, Imrie, Rob, and Lin, Wen I. (2011) Community governance, critical cosmopolitanism and urban change: observations from Taipei, Taiwan, *International Journal of Urban and Regional Research*, 35: 274–94.

Rakodi, Carole (2002) Order and disorder in African cities: governance, politics, and urban land development processes, in Okwui Enwezor, Ute Meta Bauer, Susanne Ghez, Sarat Maharaj, Mark Nash and Octavio Zaya (eds) *Under Siege: Four African Cities. Freetown, Johannesburg, Kinshasa, Lagos*. Berlin: Hatje Cantz.

Ratti, Carlo, and Claudel, Matthew (2016) *The City of Tomorrow: Sensors, Networks, Hackers and the Future of Urban Life*. New Haven, CT: Yale University Press.

Read, Stephen, de Laat-Lukkassen, Martine, and Jonauskis, Tadas (2013) Revisiting "complexification," technology, and urban form in Lefebvre, *Space and Culture*, 16: 381–96.

Ren, Xufei (2015) City power and urban fiscal crises: the USA, China, and India, *International Journal of Urban Science*, 19: 73–81.

Rifkin, Jeremy (2014) *The Zero Marginal Cost Society: The Internet of Things, the Collaborative Commons, and the Eclipse of Capitalism*. New York: Palgrave Macmillan.

Robinson, Jennifer (2016) Thinking cities through elsewhere: comparative tactics for a more global urban studies, *Progress in Human Geography*, 40: 3–29.

Rojas, Eduardo (ed.) (2010) *Building Cities: Neighbourhood Upgrading and Urban Quality of Life*. Washington, DC: Inter-American Development Bank.

Romaya, Sam, and Rakodi, Carole (eds) (2002) *Building Sustainable Settlements: Approaches and Case Studies in the Developing World*. London: ITDG.

Rose, Nikolas (1999) *Powers of Freedom: Reframing Political Thought*. Cambridge: Cambridge University Press.

Rossi, Ugo (2013) On life as a fictitious commodity: cities and the biopolitics of late neoliberalism, *International Journal of Urban and Regional Research*, 37: 1067–74.

Roy, Ananya (2009) Civic governmentality: the politics of inclusion in Beirut and Mumbai, *Antipode*, 41: 159–79.

_____ (2011) Urbanisms, worlding practices and the theory of planning, *Planning Theory*, 10: 6–15.

Rydge, James, Jacobs, Michael, and Granoff, Ilmi (2015) *Ensuring New Infrastructure is Climate-Smart*. London and Washington, DC: New Climate Economy; http://newclimateeconomy.report/2015/wp-content/uploads/sites/3/2015/10/Ensuring-infrastructure-is-climate-smart.pdf.

Sánchez, Rafael (2008) Seized by the spirit: the mystical foundation of squatting among Pentecostals in Caracas (Venezuela) today, *Public Culture*, 20: 267–305.

Sandercock, Leonie (2003) *Mongrel Cities of the Twenty-First Century*. 2nd edn, New York: Bloomsbury.

Sassen, Saskia (2010) The repositioning of cities and urban regions in a global economy, in Peter Karl Kresl (ed.) *Economic Strategies for Mature Industrial Economies*. Cheltenham: Edward Elgar.

Satterthwaite David (2007) *The Transition to a Predominantly Urban World and its Underpinnings*. London: International Institute for Environment and Development; http://pubs.iied.org/pdfs/10550IIED.pdf.

Schwenkel, Christina (2013) Post/socialist affect: ruination and reconstruction of the nation in urban Vietnam, *Cultural Anthropology*, 28: 252–77.

Scoones, Ian, Leach, Melissa, and Newell, Peter (eds) (2015) *The Politics of Green Transformations*. London: Routledge.

Scott, James C. (2012) *Two Cheers for Anarchism: Six Easy Pieces on Autonomy, Dignity, and Meaningful Work and Play*. Princeton, NJ: Princeton University Press.

Sen, Atreyee (2012) "Exist, endure, erase the city" (*sheher mein jiye, is ko sahe, ya ise mitaye?*): child vigilantes and micro-cultures of urban violence in a riot-affected Hyderabad slum, *Ethnography*, 13: 71–86.

Sevilla-Buitrago, Alvaro (2015) Capitalist formations of enclosure: space and the extinction of the commons, *Antipode*, 47: 999–1020.

Shapiro, Michael (2010) *The Time of the City: Philosophy, Politics, and Genre*. London and New York: Routledge.

Sheller, Mimi (2012) *Citizenship from Below: Erotic Agency and Caribbean Freedom*. Durham, NC: Duke University Press.

Sheppard, Eric, Gidwani, Vinay, Goldman, Michael, Leitner, Helga, Roy, Ananya, and Maringanti, Anant (2015) Introduction: urban revolutions in the age of global urbanism, *Urban Studies*, 52: 1947–61.

Shin, Hyun Bang (2016) Economic transition and speculative urbanisation in China: gentrification versus dispossession, *Urban Studies*, 53: 471–87.

Silver, John (2014) Incremental infrastructures: material improvisation and social collaboration across post-colonial Accra, *Urban Geography*, 35: 788–804.

Simondon, Gilbert (2009a) The position of the problem of ontogenesis, *Parrhesia*, 7: 4–16.

_____ (2009b) Technical mentality, *Parrhesia*, 7: 17–27.

Simone, AbdouMaliq (1998) Urban social fields in Africa, *Social Text*, 56: 71–89.

_____ (2004) *For the City yet to Come: Changing African Life in Four Cities*. Durham, NC: Duke University Press.

_____ (2010) *City Life from Jakarta to Dakar: Movements at the Crossroads*. London and New York: Routledge.

_____ (2014) *Jakarta: Drawing the City Near*. Minneapolis: University of Minnesota Press.

Simone, AbdouMaliq, and Pieterse, Edgar (1993) Civil societies in an internationalized Africa, *Social Dynamics*, 19: 41–69.

Singerman, Diane (2009) *Cairo Contested: Governance, Urban Space, and Global Modernity*. Cairo: American University in Cairo Press.

Sinha, Sumita (2012) *Architecture for Rapid Change and Scarce Resources*. London and New York: Routledge.

Slater, David (2004) *Geopolitics and the Post-Colonial: Rethinking North–South Relations*. Oxford: Wiley-Blackwell.

Smith, Nick R. (2014) Change and continuity: Chinese villages in transition (III) – Hailong Village, *China City Planning Review*, 23: 1–8.

Söderström, Ola (2014) *Cities in Relations: Trajectories of Urban Development in Hanoi and Ouagadougou*. Oxford: Wiley-Blackwell.

Sørensen, Eva, and Torfing, Jacob (eds) (2007) *Theories of Democratic Network Governance*. New York: Palgrave.

Srnicek, Nick, and Williams, Alex (2015) *Inventing the Future: Postcapitalism and a World without Work*. London: Verso.

Stiegler, Bernard (2013) *What Makes Life Worth Living: A Pharmacology*. Cambridge: Polity.

Stillerman, Joel (2006) The politics of space and culture in Santiago, Chile's street markets, *Qualitative Sociology*, 29: 507–30.

Stirling, Andy (2015) Emancipating transformations: from controlling "the transition" to culturing plural radical progress, in Ian Scoones, Melissa Leach and Peter Newell (eds) *The Politics of Green Transformations*. London: Routledge.

Suhail, Adeem (2015) *The Clothes Have No Emperor! Reflections on the Crisis of Violence in Lyari Town, Pakistan*, Working Paper presented to the Center for Muslim and Non-Muslim Understanding at the University of South Australia, www.unisa.edu.au/Documents/EASS/MnM/working-papers/The_Clothes_Have_No_Emperor_2015.pdf.

Sundaram, Ravi (2009) *Pirate Modernity: Delhi's Media Urbanism*. New Delhi: Routledge.

_____ (2015) Publicity, transparency, and the circulation engine, *Current Anthropology*, 56: S297–S305.

Swilling, Mark (2006) Sustainability and infrastructure planning in South Africa: a Cape Town case study, *Environment & Urbanization*, 18: 23–50.

_____ (2011) Reconceptualising urbanism, ecology and networked infrastructures, *Social Dynamics*, 38: 78–95.

_____ (2013) Economic crisis, long waves and the sustainability transition: an African perspective, *Environmental Innovations and Societal Transitions*, 6: 95–115.

_____ (2016) Towards sustainable urban infrastructures for the urban Anthropocene, in Adriana Allen, Andrea Lampis and Mark Swilling (eds) *Untamed Urbanisms*. New York: Routledge.

Swilling, Mark, and Annecke, Eve (2012) *Just Transitions: Explorations of Sustainability in an Unfair World*. Cape Town and Tokyo: UCT Press and United Nations University Press.

Swyngedouw, Erik (2009) The antinomies of the postpolitical city: in search of a democratic politics of environmental production, *International Journal of Urban and Regional Research*, 33: 601–20.

Szeman, Imre (2014) Conclusion: on energopolitics, *Anthropological Quarterly*, 87: 453–64.

Tadiar, Neferti X. M. (2012) Life-times in fate playing, *South Atlantic Quarterly*, 111: 783–802.

Taussig, Michael (1999) *Defacement: Public Secrecy and the Labor of the Negative*. Stanford, CA: Stanford University Press.

Telles, Vera da Silva, and Hirata, Daniel Veloso (2007) The city and urban practices: in the uncertain frontiers between the illegal, the informal and the illicit, *Estudos Avançados*, 21: 173–91.

Terranova, Tiziana (2004) *Network Culture: Politics for the Information Age*. London: Pluto Press.

Thieme, Tatiana A. (2013) The "hustle" amongst youth entrepreneurs in Mathare's informal waste economy, *Journal of Eastern African Studies*, 7: 389–412.

Thrift, Nigel (2008) *Non-Representational Theory: Space, Politics, Affect*. London: Routledge.

Thurow, James (2014) Youth employment prospects, in Danielle Resnick and James Thurow (eds) *African Youth and the Persistence of Marginalization: Employment, Politics, and Prospects for Change*. London and New York: Routledge.

Tonkiss, Fran (2014) *Cities by Design: The Social Life of Urban Form*. Cambridge: Polity.

Touraine, Alain (2001) *Beyond Neoliberalism*. Cambridge: Polity.

Turok, Ivan, and McGranahan, Gordon (2013) Urbanisation and economic growth: the arguments and evidence for Africa and Asia, *Environment and Urbanization*, 25: 465–82.

UCLG (United Cities and Local Government) (2016) *Co-Creating the Urban Future: The Agenda of Metropolises, Cities and Territories*, Fourth Global Report on Decentralization and Local Democracy. Barcelona: UCLG.

UN-DESA (United Nations, Department of Economic and Social Affairs) (2013) *World Economic and Social Survey 2013: Sustainable Development Challenges*. New York: United Nations.

_____ (2015a) *World Population Prospects: the 2015 Revision*. New York: United Nations.

_____ (2015b) *World Urbanization Prospects: The 2014 Revision* (ST/ESA/SER.A/366). New York: United Nations.

UNEP (United Nations Environment Programme) (2011) *Towards a Green Economy: Pathways to Sustainable Development and Poverty Eradication*. Paris: UNEP; www.unep.org/greeneconomy.

_____ (2013) *City Level Decoupling: Urban Resource Flows and the Governance of Infrastructure Transitions*. New York: UNEP.

UN-Habitat (United Nations Human Settlements Programme) (2010) *State of the World's Cities Report 2010/11: Bridging the Urban Divide*. London: Earthscan.

_____ (2012) *Urban Patterns for a Green Economy: Optimizing Infrastructure*. Nairobi: UN-Habitat.

_____ (2013) *Streets as Public Spaces and Drivers of Urban Prosperity*. Nairobi: UN-Habitat.

_____ (2015) *E-Governance and Urban Policy Design*. Nairobi: UN-Habitat.

_____ (2016) *World Cities Report 2016: Urbanization and Development: Emerging Futures*. Nairobi: UN-Habitat.

UNRISD (United Nations Research Institute for Social Development) (2010) *Combating Poverty and Inequality: Structural Change, Social Policy and Politics*. Geneva: UNRISD.

Vasudevan, Alexander (2015) The makeshift city: toward a global geography of squatting, *Progress in Human Geography*, 39: 338–59.

Verver, Michiel (2012) Templates of "Chineseness" and trajectories of Cambodian Chinese entrepreneurship in Phnom Penh,

Cross-Currents: East Asian History and Culture Review, no. 4; http://cross-currents.berkeley.edu/e-journal/issue-4.

Vigar, Sarwat (2014) Constructing Lyari: place, governance, and identity in a Karachi neighbourhood, *South Asia History and Culture*, 5: 365–83.

Virno, Paolo (2004) *Grammar of the Multitude: For an Analysis of Contemporary Forms of Life*. New York: Semiotext(e).

_____ (2009) Natural-historical diagrams: the "new global" movement and the biological invariant, *Cosmos and History: The Journal of Natural and Social Philosophy*, 5: 92–104.

Vlassenroot, Koen, and Büscher, Karen (2009) *The City as Frontier: Urban Development and Identity Processes in Goma*. London: London School of Economics and Political Science, Crisis States Research Centre.

von Schnitzler, Antina (2013) Travelling technologies: infrastructure, ethical regimes, and the materiality of politics in South Africa, *Cultural Anthropology*, 28: 670–93.

Walker, Jeremy, and Cooper, Melinda (2011) Genealogies of resilience from systems ecology to the political economy of crisis adaptation, *Security Dialogue*, 42: 143–60.

Watson, Vanessa (2009) Seeing from the South: refocusing urban planning on the globe's central urban issues, *Urban Studies*, 46: 2259–75.

_____ (2013) African urban fantasies: dreams or nightmares?, *Environment and Urbanization*, 26: 215–31.

Watts, Michael (2015) Now and then: the origins of political ecology and the rebirth of adaptation as a form of thought, in Tom Perrault, Gavin Bridge and James McCarthy (eds) *The Handbook of Political Ecology*. London and New York: Routledge.

Weinstein, Liza (2013) Demolition and dispossession: toward understanding of state violence in millennial Mumbai, *Studies in Comparative International Development*, 48: 285–307.

Williams, Rhonda (2005) *The Politics of Public Housing: Black Women's Struggles against Urban Inequality*. Oxford: Oxford University Press.

World Bank (2012) *Transformation through Infrastructure*. Washington, DC: World Bank.

Wu, Fulong, Zhang, Fangzhu, and Webster, Chris (2013) Informality and the development and demolition of urban villages in the Chinese peri-urban area, *Urban Studies*, 50: 1919–34.

Wyly, Elvyn (2015) Gentrification on the planetary urban frontier: the evolution of Turner's noösphere, *Urban Studies*, 52: 2515–50.

Yepes, Tito, Pierce, Justin R., and Foster, Vivien (2009) *Making Sense of Africa's Infrastructure Endowment: A Benchmarking*

Approach, World Bank Policy Research Working Paper no. 4912. Washington, DC: World Bank.

Yiftachel, Oren (2015) Epilogue – from "gray space" to equal "metrozenship"? Reflections on urban citizenship, *International Journal of Urban and Regional Research*, 39: 726–37.

Yu, Shuenn-Der (2004) Hot and noisy: Taiwan's night market culture, in David K. Jordan, Andrew D. Morris and Marc L. Moskowitz (eds) *The Minor Arts of Daily Life: Popular culture in Taiwan*. Honolulu: University of Hawai'i Press.

Zeiderman, Austin (2016) *Endangered City: The Politics of Security and Risk in Bogota*. Durham, NC: Duke University Press.

Zeiderman, Austin, Kaker, Sobia Ahmad, Silver, Jonathan, and Wood, Astrid (2015) Uncertainty and urban life, *Public Culture*, 27: 281–304.

Zhang, Charlie Yi (2014) Untangling the intersectional biopolitics of neoliberal globalization: Asia, Asian, and the Asia-Pacific rim, *Feminist Formations*, 26: 167–96.

Index

Page numbers in **bold** refer to a table; page numbers in *italic* refer to a figure in the text.

234 *Index*

China 24–5
choices 95–6, 140, 165
Chongqing, China 25
Chungking Mansions, Hong
    Kong 113
circulation 96, 98–9, 100–1,
    104, 105, 190
cities, Northern 36, 37
    see also global North
cities, Southern 190
    see also global South
citizen-led transitions 56, 58
citizenship 13, 126, 128, 134,
    155, 166
"City Desired" exhibition
    174–7
City of Cape Town
    metropolitan
    government 168
CityLabs 175, 177
Cityscapes magazine 171–2,
    206n3
civil society organizations xvii,
    56, 127, 154
claim-making 13, 67, 134–40,
    162
claim-staking 73–4
Clean and Safe Sanitation
    Campaign 166, 168
clientelism 154, 157, 171
climate change xvii–xviii, 9,
    133–4, 140, 175, 176
    carbon emissions 124,
    133–4, 135–6, 151
Clos, Joan 48
"cloudy strivings" 27, 28
coalition building xviii
coercion 108–9, 132
cohesion 119, 123, 199n2
Cold War 53
collaboration, social 17, 66,
    92, 101–4, 147, 157,
    161, 181, 194
    "village councillors" 169,
    170–1

colonialization 50, 53, 164
    post-colonialism 52–3, 191
Coltrane, John 196
commoditization 130
communities 46, 48, 66, 93–4,
    108–9, 126–9, 141–4,
    147
    see also neighborhoods
communities, gated 43, 45,
    190
community institutions 26
community involvement 8–9,
    128–9, 151, 166, 167–8
    and finance 169, 171
    and residents xv–xvii, 66,
    75–6, 170, 188–9
    see also activism
competition 83, 129, 130, 151
complicities 15, 107–8, 179
components 79–80, 81, 82, 83,
    195–6
Conference of the Parties
    (COP), Paris 33, 133
Connolly, William 27, 65–6
consolidation 8, 23, 30, 92,
    102, 117, 158, 195
construction 47, 79, 81, 83
    autoconstruction 160, 194,
    206n1
    self-construction 78, 186–7
consumption 69, 101–2, 126
    and middle classes 43, 184
    and operating systems
    133–4, 136
    and technological change 57,
    58
contemporary urbanism xii, 9,
    45, 47, 85, 127, 128
contiguity 7, 197
control 190–1, 195
    control systems 82, 87–8
    government control xiv,
    129–30, 184
    and secretion 113–14,
    116–17, 119–20

Sartre, Jean-Paul 67
Sassen, Saskia 2
Satterthwaite, David 50
Schmid, Christian 2, 14
scholarship 171–6
Scoones, Ian 56
secretion 4, 14–16, 29, 59, 94,
    95–121, 179, 200n9
security 4, 50, 71, 96, 126,
    167–8
  securitization 130, 193
  of tenure 105, 144, 177
self-aggrandizement 181
self-construction 68, 75, 78,
    186–7
self-improvement 68, 69
self-management 89
self-reliance 68
self-worth 77, 162
Seoul, South Korea 37
service delivery 38–9, 139,
    144–7, 150, 161
services, basic 125, 141–50,
    166
sex 3–4
shareholder corporations 25
sharing 7
shelter *142*, 144
"showcase" projects 9
Simone, AbdouMaliq 169
simulation technologies 81
Singapore 43
slavery 53
slums 36–8, 75, 166
  and experimentation 177,
    178
  and infrastructure 45, 49, 146
  and urban transition 50,
    53–4
"smart buildings" 79
smart cities 45, 47–9, 81, 83,
    86–7, 125
social action *see* action,
    collective; community
    involvement

social class 60, 177
  see also elites; middle
    classes; working classes
social-cultural infrastructure
    128
Social Justice Coalition 166–8
social media 55, 89, 99–100,
    137
social movements xviii, 70,
    122, 126–7, 160,
    166–71
social policy 57
sociality 3, 39, 181
solar energy 137, **148**
Souk Libya, Khartoum 112
South African Police Service
    167
space, inhabitable and
    uninhabitable 61, 77–8
space, parametric 77–82
space, private 130, 146, 156
space, public 43, 48, 130, 156,
    162, 192
space, social 143
spaces, boundaries and
    intersections 10–13,
    111, 122, 123, 141
spaces, consolidation of 7–8,
    195
spaces, n-dimension 11
spatial form 2, 130, *131*
speculation 74, 82–8
speed 181
Srnicek, Nick 55
stability 18, 22, 165
  and re-description 80–1,
    84–5
  and secretion 96, 100–1
state institutions xvii, 30, 97,
    158
state-led transitions 57
state ownership 117–18
states 9, 92, 97, 146, 179–80
status quo 45–6, 47, 58, 123,
    127, 144–6